ᴛʜᴇ**new** biology

Aging

Revised Edition

THE new biology

Aging

Modern Theories and Therapies
Revised Edition

JOSEPH PANNO, PH.D.

An imprint of Infobase Publishing

AGING: Modern Theories and Therapies, Revised Edition

Copyright © 2011, 2005 by Joseph Panno, Ph.D.

Facts On File, Inc.
An imprint of Infobase Publishing
132 West 31st Street
New York NY 10001

Library of Congress Cataloging-in-Publication Data

Panno, Joseph.
    Aging: modern theories and therapies / Joseph Panno.—Rev. ed.
        p. cm.—(The new biology)
    Includes bibliographical references and index.
    ISBN 978-0-8160-6846-3
    1. Aging. 2. Longevity. I. Title.
    QP86.P33 2001
    612.6'7—dc22   2009047717

Facts On File books are available at special discounts when purchased in bulk quantities for businesses, associations, institutions, or sales promotions. Please call our Special Sales Department in New York at (212) 967-8800 or (800) 322-8755.

You can find Facts On File on the World Wide Web at http://www.factsonfile.com

Excerpts included herewith have been reprinted by permission of the copyright holders; the author has made every effort to contact copyright holders. The publishers will be glad to rectify, in future editions, any errors or omissions brought to their notice.

Text design by Erik Lindstrom
Composition by Hermitage Publishing Services
Illustrations by the author
Photo research by Diane K. French
Cover printed by Bang Printing, Brainerd, Minn.
Book printed and bound by Bang Printing, Brainerd, Minn.
Date printed: October 2010
Printed in the United States of America

10 9 8 7 6 5 4 3 2 1

This book is printed on acid-free paper.

 # Contents

Preface

When the first edition of this set was being written, the new biology was just beginning to come into its potential and to experience some of its first failures. Dolly the sheep was alive and well and had just celebrated her fifth birthday. Stem cell researchers, working 12-hour days, were giddy with the prospect of curing every disease known to humankind, but were frustrated by inconsistent results and the limited availability of human embryonic stem cells. Gene therapists, still reeling from the disastrous Gelsinger trial of 1998, were busy trying to figure out what had gone wrong and how to improve the safety of a procedure that many believed would revolutionize medical science. And cancer researchers, while experiencing many successes, hit their own speed bump when a major survey showed only modest improvements in the prognosis for all of the deadliest cancers.

During the 1970s, when the new biology was born, recombinant technology served to reenergize the sagging discipline that biology had become. This same level of excitement reappeared in the 1990s with the emergence of gene therapy, the cloning of Dolly the sheep, and the successful cultivation of stem cells. Recently, great excitement has come with the completion of the human genome project and the genome sequencing of more than 100 animal and plant species. Careful analysis of these genomes has spawned a new branch of biological research known as comparative genomics. The information that scientists can now extract from animal genomes is expected to improve all other branches of biological science. Not to be outdone, stem cell researchers have found a way to produce embryo-like stem cells from ordinary skin cells. This achievement not only marks the end of the great stem cell debate, but it also provides an immensely powerful procedure, known as cellular dedifferentiation, for studying and manipulating the very essence of a cell. This procedure will become a crucial weapon in the fight against cancer and many other diseases.

The new biology, like our expanding universe, has been growing and spreading at an astonishing rate. The amount of information that is now available on these topics is of astronomical proportions. Thus, the problem of deciding what to leave out has become as difficult as the decision of what to include. The guiding principle in writing this set has always been to provide a thorough overview of the topics without overwhelming the reader with a mountain of facts and figures. To be sure, this set contains many facts and figures, but these have been carefully chosen to illustrate only the essential principles.

This edition, in keeping with the expansion of the biological disciplines, has grown to accommodate new material and new areas of research. Four new books have been added that focus on areas of biological research that are reaping the benefits of genome science and modern research technologies. Thus, the New Biology set now consists of the following 10 volumes:

1. *Aging, Revised Edition*
2. *Animal Cloning, Revised Edition*
3. *Cancer, Revised Edition*
4. *The Cell, Revised Edition*
5. *Gene Therapy, Revised Edition*
6. *Stem Cell Research, Revised Edition*
7. *Genome Research*
8. *The Immune System*
9. *Modern Medicine*
10. *Viruses*

Many new chapters have been added to each of the original six volumes, and the remaining chapters have been extensively revised and updated. The number of figures and photos in each book has increased significantly, and all are now rendered in full color. The new volumes, following the same format as the originals, greatly expand the scope of the New Biology set and serve to emphasize the fact that these technologies are not just about finding cures for diseases but are helping scientists understand a wide range of biological processes. Even a partial list of these revelations is impressive: detailed information on every gene and every protein that is needed to build a human being; eventual identification of all cancer genes, stem cell–specific genes, and longevity genes; mapping of safe chromosomal insertion sites for gene therapy; and the identification of genes that control the growth of the human brain, the development of speech, and the maintenance of mental stability. In a stunning achievement, genome researchers have been able to trace the exact route our human ancestors used to emigrate from Africa nearly 65,000 years ago and even to estimate the number of individuals who made up the original group.

In addition to the accelerating pace of discovery, the new biology has made great strides in resolving past mistakes and failures. The Gelsinger trial was a dismal failure that killed a young man in the prime of his life, but gene therapy trials in the next 10 years will be astonishing, both for their success and for their safety. For the past 50 years, cancer researchers have been caught in a desperate struggle as they tried to control the growth and spread of deadly tumors, but many scientists are now confident that cancer will be eliminated by 2020. Viruses, such as HIV or the flu, are resourceful and often deadly adversaries, but genome researchers are about to put the fight on more rational grounds as detailed information is obtained about viral genes, viral life cycles, and viruses' uncanny ability to evade or cripple the human immune system.

These struggles and more are covered in this edition of the New Biology set. I hope the discourse will serve to illustrate both the power of science and the near superhuman effort that has gone into the creation and validation of these technologies.

Acknowledgments

I would first like to thank the legions of science graduate students and postdoctoral fellows who have made the new biology a practical reality. They are the unsung heroes of this discipline. The clarity and accuracy of the initial manuscript for this book was much improved by reviews and comments from Diana Dowsley, Michael Panno, Rebecca Lapres, and later by Frank K. Darmstadt, executive editor, and the rest of the Facts On File staff. I am also indebted to Diane K. French and Elizabeth Oakes for their help in securing photographs for the New Biology set. Finally, as always, I would like to thank my wife and daughter for keeping the ship on an even keel.

Introduction

I wasted time, and now doth time waste me.
—William Shakespeare

It is a fact of life that with the slow progression of time we all lose the health and vigor we enjoyed as children and young adults. Statisticians, in a long version of Shakespeare's eloquent statement, sum it up by saying our chance of dying on any given day increases the older we get. Biologists call this the aging process or, more specifically, cellular senescence.

Aging is a common phenomenon, but it is not universal. It does not occur among prokaryotes, protozoans, and simple multicellular creatures such as sponges and corals. Indeed, if we think of prokaryotes or protozoans as being a single lineage, it is a life-form that has been alive for 3 billion years (sponges can, in theory, live a very long time, but because of predation few survive beyond 100 years).

There are those who think a human life span of 85 years is long enough, but compared to 3 billion years it truly is the short end of the stick. There are, to be sure, many animals that have a shorter life span than we do: A horse has an average of 20 years, a dog is lucky to see 15 summers, and the common housefly is born and dead of old age in 30 days. On the other hand, some animals, such as the Galápagos tortoise and the sturgeon, live for more than 200 years.

On a cosmic scale, however, the difference in life span between a housefly and a sturgeon is of no consequence. Moreover, the comparison begs the question of why we age in the first place. After all, we have a reasonably good immune system; we heal well after being hurt; we have a group of enzymes that monitor and repair our DNA; and, as long as we eat well, our cells have plenty of energy to take care of themselves from day to day. Yet, despite all that, we get old with monotonous regularity. There appears to be neither rhyme nor reason to it. Some scientists think aging is due to evolutionary neglect: Natural selection was so busy finding ways to make us successful in the short term that it forgot to cover us in our old age. It is almost as though Mother Nature is saying, "I will do what I can to get you up to your reproductive years, so you can have offspring, but after that you are on your own."

Being on our own has meant that our bodies begin to break down soon after our peak reproductive years have past. The elderly cannot run as far, think as fast, or fight off infectious diseases nearly as well as they did when they were young. Moreover, one's physical appearance changes dramatically with age: The hair turns gray, muscle mass declines, the ears get bigger, and the skin becomes thin and wrinkled. On a deeper level, men and women approaching their 80s converge on a common phenotype; men become more feminine, and women become more masculine. In men this trend becomes apparent as the shoulders get narrower, the hips broader, the beard thinner, and the voice develops a higher pitch. In women the shoulders become broader, the voice huskier, and hair begins to grow on the chin and upper lip. Gerontologists (scientists who study gerontology, or the mechanisms involved in the aging process), in noting these changes, have pondered one of the most difficult questions pertaining to the aging process: Is aging caused by the degenerative changes in a single organ, which then acts like an aging-clock for the rest of the body, or are all organs breaking down simultaneously?

Answering this question has proven to be extremely difficult. Researchers have studied age-related changes in virtually all tissues, organs, and organ systems of the body (the endocrine system, consisting of many hormone-producing glands, is an example of an organ system). Some evidence suggest that the brain may be an aging-clock that determines the rate at which the whole body ages, but the results of many other studies suggest that the rate at which an animal ages may be the sum of age-related changes occurring simultaneously in all parts of the body.

Consequently, the attempts to understand the aging process, involving such a complex system, have generated a great number of theories but few practical therapies. Traditional therapies are available that treat age-related diseases such as cancer and arthritis, but do not reverse the aging process itself. A common trend in gerontology, particularly since the completion of the human genome project, is to search for genes that have a demonstrable effect on life span, the so-called longevity genes. Many such genes have been identified, and although the manipulation of these genes does not stop the aging process, they are providing many valuable insights into the cellular mechanisms of aging. More recently interest has turned to the use of cloning technology, stem cell analysis, and genetic manipulation in order to produce an effective rejuvenation therapy for cells and the body as a whole.

Aging, Revised Edition, one volume in the multivolume the New Biology set, describes the field of gerontology and the many theories that scientists have developed over the years to explain the age-related changes that occur in nearly all animals. This edition, now with color photographs and line drawings, has been extensively revised and expanded.

Three new chapters (3, 8, and 9) have been added. Chapter 3 discusses the way in which humans age, and how the aging process has changed over the past thousand years. Chapter 8 discusses the theoretical aspects of rejuvenation: how it could be accomplished and what the consequences will be. Rejuvenation is usually discussed in very general terms, but this chapter gives a detailed account of how current technologies could be used to produce an effective rejuvenation therapy. More practical therapies, based on clinical trials, are discussed in chapter 9. This chapter describes some exciting studies that may provide effective treatments for Alzheimer's disease, cardiovascular disease, and osteoporosis. The final chapter, as before, provides background material on cell biology, biotechnology, and other topics that are relevant to gerontology. The cell biology and biotechnology primers presented in this chapter have been revised and condensed in the hope that the reader will be able to obtain the necessary background information as quickly as possible.

The Quest
for Immortality

Concerns about human mortality date back at least 20,000 years when Cro-Magnons, the first *Homo sapiens,* prepared one of their own for burial. Evidence for the existence of these people and their burial practices was discovered simultaneously at Les Eyzies, France, in 1868 (Les Eyzies is a village located in the Dordognes region of southwest France). One day some hikers were exploring a rock shelter, or cave, just south of the village when they came across a number of flint tools and weapons. Archaeologists called to the scene uncovered what was clearly a burial site containing at least four individuals: a middle-aged man, two younger men, a young woman and an infant two to three weeks old. They were buried with flint tools, weapons, and seashells and animal teeth pierced with holes. The teeth and seashells were probably part of necklaces and bracelets that the adults wore, but the strings holding them together had long since disintegrated. The artifacts were about 20,000 years

1

old, and scientists have since determined that people inhabited the site for at least 25,000 years. That rock shelter was known to the Les Eyzies villagers as Cro-Magnon. It was named after a local hermit named Magnou who had lived there for many years. The name of that cave is now synonymous with the name of our earliest human ancestors.

Cro-Magnon funerals are taken as evidence by anthropologists that those people thought about life and death the same way that modern humans do. This is suggested by their habit of adorning the corpse with prized possessions, possibly thinking they would be of

Cro-Magnon fossil. Fossilized skeleton of a Cro-Magnon human from the caves at Abri de Villabruna, Italy. Cro-Magnons were anatomically modern humans that lived in Europe from about 50,000 years ago. They are renowned for their cave paintings and the tools and ornaments that they made. It is thought that they were the direct ancestors of modern humans. Many of the bodies that have been found show signs of ceremonial burial. This specimen has been dated at around 12,000 years old. *(Pascal Goetgheluck/Photo Researchers, Inc.)*

use in a spiritual afterlife. In grieving for their lost loved ones, Cro-Magnons were drawn to a quest for immortality, but one that dealt with the soul rather than the body.

Distant relatives of the Cro-Magnons, living 4,000 years ago in Egypt, carried on the same tradition, but on a colossal scale. Egyptian pharaohs were buried with all of their worldly possessions and even a little food to see them on their way. Karnak, a village on the Nile River at the northern extremity of Luxor, is the site of the greatest assembly of ancient temples in Egypt. They occupy an area of about 120 acres and are extremely old. By far the largest and most important is the temple of Amun (Amon-Re) that was built more than 4,000 years ago. Amun, called king of the gods, was the supreme state god in the New Kingdom (1570 to 1085 B.C.E.). During this period the Egyptians were ruled by such famous kings as Amenhotep, Ramses, and Tutankhamun. The tombs of these kings and the famous Egyptian queen Nefertari, wife of Ramses II, were decorated with scenes carved in relief depicting religious ceremonies and historical events. Hieroglyphic inscriptions usually accompanied these scenes. Egyptian tombs also contained many prized possessions, such as a beautiful sculpture of Nefertari and a gold funeral mask of King Tutankhamun. Indeed, 3,500 items were recovered from King Tut's tomb, including 143 precious jewels and amulets. Interestingly, Tut's tomb is generally considered to be of modest size and wealth. Ramses and Amenhotep had much grander tombs, but most of the artifacts were pillaged by grave robbers long before the archeologists found them.

Although some of the objects placed within the tombs were simply favored possessions, many of them were intended to help the deceased in the afterlife. King Tut's funeral mask, for example, was carved in his likeness so that the gods would recognize him after he was dead. Many of the inscriptions on the walls and on papyrus scrolls were a collection of magic spells intended to help the deceased survive the afterlife. A large number of hymns praising

Gold death mask of King Tutankhamun. Egyptian Museum: Cairo, Egypt *(Brian Brake/Photo Researchers, Inc.)*

various gods were also included for the same purpose. This collection of spells and hymns has come to be known as *The Book of the Dead.* According to the mythology of the ancient Egyptians, the dead, if recognized and accepted, could pass to the spirit world of the Sun god, Amun-Re, and his sister, Amunet, where they would live for eternity. The practice of burying the dead with all of their belongings disappeared down through the millennia, but many people still believe in the eternal life of chosen spirits.

With the rise of science, and the appearance of powerful medical therapies, the quest for immortality has shifted from the spiritual to the physical. The accomplishments of Louis Pasteur and other microbiologists at the turn of the last century, and the explosive growth in biological research since then have provided cures for many terrible diseases: diphtheria, polio, and smallpox, to name but a few. These triumphs have given us reason to hope that someday scientists will be able to reverse the effects of age. If protozoans can live millions of years, why not the human body? But so far, all attempts at physical rejuvenation have failed. Many such attempts date back to the turn of the early 1900s and involved the use of concoctions, potions, and even radioactive cocktails, often with disastrous results. One such concoction, popular in the 1920s, was Tho-Radia, a skin cream containing thorium and radium, two radioisotopes discovered by the great French physicist Marie Curie. The radioactive material was supposed to have an anti-aging effect on the skin, but their use was abandoned when Curie and other scientists working with radioisotopes began having serious medical problems. Madame Curie developed cataracts, kidney failure, and a fatal leukemia, all from overexposure to radioactive materials.

More recently a new wave of anti-aging therapies have been developed, employing everything from a shift in lifestyle to specific hormone supplements. Anti-aging creams are still with us, only now the active ingredient is retinoic acid (vitamin A), instead of radium. Whether any of these treatments will be successful is in doubt, but the failures so far are like the first tentative steps of a toddler. Scientists are only beginning to understand the tremendous complexities of the cell and the way an organism changes with time. As the science matures, it may be possible to reverse some affects of age, but whether this leads to physical immortality is a hotly debated topic.

ONE HOUR UPON THE STAGE

When William Shakespeare's Macbeth compared the human life span to one hour on the stage, he was being very generous. If humankind's life span were indeed 1/24 of the 3 billion years that microbes have been alive, humans would live 125 million years. As it is, humankind's life span, on a 24-hour timescale, is but a wink of an eye.

Life spans vary considerably among the animal kingdom. In general, tiny animals bearing many offspring have short life spans, while large animals bearing few offspring live much longer. The fruit fly, *Drosophila melanogaster,* is an example of a small animal with a short life span. *Drosophila* has a maximum life span of 40 days, but most of them are dead in two weeks. These animals are called holometabolous insects because the eggs hatch into worm-like larvae that feed for a time before pupating, during which time the larvae metamorphose into the adult form. The newly emerged males and females waste no time in producing the next generation. The females mate within 24 hours, and throughout their short lives, produce tens of thousands of offspring. In a survival strategy such as this, all of the biological adaptations have focused on preservation of the species at the expense of the individual. Flies have many predators, and adaptations that could lengthen their life span would be useless since the flies would be eaten long before their biological time was up.

Elephants, on the other hand, are large animals with few predators, and they produce a single offspring every five years. Elephants are mammals and, like all mammals, spend a great deal of time rearing and caring for their young. In this case adaptations to increase the life span make a lot of sense. With reduced

Scanning electron micrograph (SEM) of the fruit fly *(Drosophila melanogaster)*. This little insect is about 3mm long, is commonly found around spoiled fruit, and is an example of a very short-lived animal. It is also much studied by gerontologists and geneticists around the world. Mutant flies, with defects in any of several thousand genes are available, and the entire genome has been sequenced. *(David M. Phillips/ Photo Researchers, Inc.)*

pressure from predators, the young can afford a leisurely developmental period, during which time the adults teach them how best to deal with their environment. The longer the adults live, the more they learn, and the more they can pass on to their offspring. Consequently, these animals have a relatively long life span of 75 to 100 years, similar to that of humans. In general, long-lived animals tend to be rather intelligent, but there are some exceptions, the most notable of which are the sturgeon and the Galápagos tortoise.

The sturgeon is an extremely ancient fish that has existed for more than 200,000 years, predating the rise of the dinosaurs during the Jurassic period. Twenty species have been identified, all of which live in the oceans, seas, and rivers of North America, Europe, and Asia; none are found in the Tropics or the Southern Hemisphere. Sturgeons often grow to a length of 30 feet and weigh a ton or more. The adults can take up to 20 years to mature, after which the females spawn every four to six years. Sturgeon eggs, called caviar, are considered to be a great delicacy in many parts of the

African elephants *(Loxodonta africana)* in the Amboseli National Park, Kenya. These large intelligent animals have a maximum life span of about 100 years, very similar to that of humans. *(Martin Harvey/Photo Researchers, Inc.)*

world, a fact that has led to the near extinction of several species in North America and Europe. The Caspian Sea beluga sturgeon, for example, lost 90 percent of its population in just 20 years, due entirely to overfishing for the caviar. The situation has become so serious that in 2006 the United Nations instituted an international trading ban on sturgeon caviar for the entire year. The ban was lifted in 2007, but the beluga sturgeon is still in danger of going extinct in the wild.

The sturgeon is possibly the longest-lived animal, sometimes reaching 200 years or more, and yet they are no more intelligent than any other fish. Moreover, sturgeons like most fish, have thousands of offspring each year and spend no time taking care of them. The sturgeon's strategy for longevity is simply to keep growing. They have hit upon a rule of nature that states that happy cells are dividing cells. As long as a sturgeon keeps growing, its longevity is regulated by external forces, such as accidents and predators, not by cellular senescence. Being a poikilotherm (cold-blooded animal) reinforces the sturgeon's continuous-growth strategy since it minimizes the growth rate and activity level of the animal. Continuous growth is a strategy that also explains the longevity of certain plants, such as the California redwood or the oak tree, which can live a thousand years or more.

Another long-lived animal, the Galápagos tortoise, owes its discovery to a fluke of nature. In winter 1535 a Spanish galleon on its way to Peru was blown off course by a fierce storm that raged for more than a week. When it passed, the exhausted crew spotted an island on which they hoped to restock their depleted stores. When

Giant tortoise from the Galápagos Islands (Santa Cruz Island). These animals have very long life spans that may exceed 200 years. *(Jeffrey Greenburg/Photo Researchers, Inc.)*

they reached shore, they discovered many strange animals, the most remarkable of which was an enormous land tortoise. So impressed were they with this animal that they decided to name the island Galápagos (Spanish for tortoise). Subsequent surveys by the Spanish and the English showed that Galápagos Island was part of an archipelago (island chain) located 600 miles (965.6 km) west of Ecuador, off the coast of South America. The Galápagos Islands figured prominently in the travels of Charles Darwin on the HMS *Beagle* (1826 to 1830) and the development of his theory of evolution.

The Galápagos tortoise, as observed by the Spanish sailors, is indeed a very large animal; it grows to a length of five feet (1.5 m) and can weigh more than 500 pounds (226.9 kg). The adults reach sexual maturity when they are 20 to 25 years old and can live for 250 years. These animals grow very slowly, so that even at two years of age they are still no larger than a baseball. At this rate it takes them more than 40 years to reach an adult size. They are not highly intelligent animals, at least not as mammals understand intelligence; nor do they spend any time taking care of their young. Indeed, the adults never see their young. The female lays a dozen spherical eggs in the sand, covers them over, and the rest is left to Mother Nature and a bit of luck. When the young hatch, they dig their way to the surface, a feat that can take a month to accomplish, and make straight for the water, which is usually 10 to 20 yards (9.1 to 18.2 m) away. The dash for the water is made through a predator gauntlet, and many of the young tortoises are caught by seagulls along the way. Those that make it to the water are preyed upon by fish in the sea, and the few that survive to adulthood return to the beaches of their birth, where they live out the rest of their lives. The tortoise, unlike the sturgeon, reaches a standard adult size, so that most of the cells in the adult's body stop dividing, as occurs in mammals. The unusual longevity of this animal is believed to be due to its very low growth rate and, as it is a poikilotherm like the sturgeon, to its low metabolic rate and activity level.

Jeanne Calment, believed to be the world's oldest person, died August 4, 1997, at the age of 122 in her nursing home in Arles, southern France. *(Associated Press)*

Humans have a maximum life span of more than 100 years. The longest-lived human on record was Jeanne Calment, a woman from Arles, France, who died in 1997 at the age of 122. Although the oldest old are rare (people 85 years or older), their numbers have increased from 3 million in 1994 (just more than 1 percent of the population) to more than 6 million in 2009 (2 percent of the population), and are expected to reach 19 million in 2050 (5 percent of the population). The number of American centenarians (those aged 100 years or older) is expected to increase from the current 96,548 to more than 600,000 by 2050. As impressive as these life spans are, they pale in comparison to the record holder from the plant kingdom. This goes to Methuselah, a 4,600-year-old pine that lives on a mountainside in Arizona.

A sculpture of an elderly couple in their 80s showing the general effects of age and the age-related convergence of physical characteristics described in the introduction. *(the author)*

GROWING YOUNGER

Many gerontologists have claimed that it is impossible for humans to grow younger because it would be too difficult to rejuvenate all the cells and organs of the body. Such claims need to be taken with a large grain of salt; it should be remembered that just five years before the first sheep was cloned, most scientists thought that cloning a mammal was biologically impossible. In addition, what scientists have learned about animal cloning and stem cells since 1996 suggests that it may indeed be possible to produce a therapy that will allow an individual to grow younger.

Growing younger, at the cellular level, is analogous to the reprogramming of a cloned cell nucleus: Both are a matter of converting a cell from an aged phenotype (the physical expression of an organism's genes) to a youthful phenotype. In a sense the cloning of a cell nucleus is the most successful attempt at rejuvenation that has yet been accomplished. In a cloning experiment the cytoplasm of the recipient oocyte converts the donor nucleus from an aged phenotype to one that is capable of supporting full embryonic development. At the organismic level this is equivalent to converting an adult to an embryo. If it can be done in one cell, it could be done in many. And if all the nuclei in an old person's body could be reprogrammed to a youthful phenotype, it would lead to the complete rejuvenation of all the cells in the body. If that happened, the individual would grow younger. This possibility will be discussed in chapter 8.

THE ROAD AHEAD

In 1900 life expectancy for the average North American was only 45 years. This has increased to the current expectancy of 80 years primarily because of a dramatic reduction in infant mortality, cures for various diseases, better hygiene, and better living conditions. This increase occurred despite the enormous number of deaths per year from cigarette smoking. A further increase of 20 to 30 years is expected if cures are found for cancer and cardiovascular disease. Beyond that, advances in life expectancy will have to wait for an improvement in our understanding of the basic mechanisms of cellular senescence.

Developing therapies that will reverse the aging process, allowing individuals to grow younger, is theoretically possible, but the realization of that goal will likely turn out to be the most difficult challenge that biologists have ever faced. The development of aging therapies will require a fusion of animal cloning, gene therapy, and stem cell technologies. But even these technologies, as powerful as they are, will not be enough. Gaining a deep understanding of the basic mechanisms of aging will require detailed information about every gene in our bodies and about what those genes are doing as humans grow old. This information is only now being made available, but over the next 10 years researchers expect to see real gains being made in the field of gerontology.

2

The History
of Gerontology

Gerontology is a branch of the biological sciences devoted to
the study of the aging process and its effects on cells and organisms. Philosophers and scientists have been interested in this
subject for thousands of years, but this history will be confined to
the modern era, extending back no further than the late 1800s. The
history of gerontology, like many other branches of biological research, may be divided into four epochs. The first, covering the early
years, began around 1870, with the invention of the compound microscope and ended in the 1950s. The second epoch began with the
discovery of the DNA double helix in 1952 and extended to the early
1970s. The third epoch began with the introduction of recombinant
DNA technology in 1973, ending in the early 1990s. The current
epoch, known as the post-genomic era, began with the formation
of a genome-sequencing consortium in 1990 and continues to the
present day.

Gerontological research has always been driven by the same questions: Why do people grow old? Why do they change with time? Can the effects of age be reversed? Gerontologists have tried to answer these questions using a variety of techniques, but with the approach of the third and fourth epochs, the questions became more numerous, more specific, and much more complex.

THE EARLY YEARS

In 1868 the German physicist Ernst Abbe perfected the design of the compound microscope and in so doing made it possible for scientists to study the structure and function of individual cells in a way that was never before possible. While many microbiologists of the time concentrated on studying the link between disease and microbes, many others began studying the life cycle of bacteria and protozoa in the hope that it would shed some light on the aging process. These studies were descriptive in nature; that is, the researcher observed the behavior of the cells and recorded it without subjecting the system to experimental procedures that would modulate the rate of the aging process.

During this period scientists realized that senescence is not universal; it occurs in multicellular creatures only. Bacteria and protozoans do not grow old and die, but rejuvenate themselves every hour or so by dividing into two new cells. A lifestyle such as this can hardly serve as a model system for gerontological research. Consequently, scientists all but abandoned the use of these cells to gain insights into the cellular mechanisms of the aging process (see the error catastrophe theory below for two exceptions).

In 1882 August Weismann, a German embryologist, proposed the first theory of senescence that tried to link life span to natural selection. Weismann argued that the termination of life may have a selective advantage, and that there is a connection between a species' life span and its ecological niche, body size, and intelligence. During this same period German chemists were developing the first biochemical techniques that allowed Hans Krebs to work out the cyclic details of energy metabolism that now bear his name (Krebs cycle, also known as the citric acid cycle). The new biochemical techniques were used by chemists to begin cataloging the many molecules of the cell, and by the time the citric acid cycle had been worked out in 1937, DNA had been identified and localized to the cell nucleus. During the last three decades of the 1800s, European scientists, most notably Anton Schneider, Paul Ehrlich, Santiago Ramón y Cajal, and Camillo Golgi, were developing special dyes and procedures that could be used to stain cells in order to better study the nucleus, cell division, and cytoplasmic organelles, giving birth to histochemistry and histology.

Thus it was that light microscopy, biochemistry, histochemistry, and histology became the basic tool kit for gerontologists during the early years of scientific research in this field. Scientists at that time believed they had all the techniques that were needed to fully understand the structure and the function of cells and animals. They were only partly right. The techniques of that day made it possible for scientists to gain a basic understanding of cell structure and, to some extent, how that structure changes with time, but they learned very little about the functional significance of those changes or how their knowledge could be used to form a physiological theory of the aging process. Much of this was due to the limited resolution of the techniques available at the time. Camillo Golgi, the Italian microbiologist, had discovered an unusual cellular structure that now bears his name (the Golgi apparatus), but no one had a clue as to the functional significance of this organelle nor were they able to explore the question with the methods at hand. Elie Metchnikoff, winner of the 1908 Nobel Prize for physiology or medicine for his work on the human immune system, attempted to form a physiological theory of the aging process by suggesting that lactic-acid bacteria (such as *Bacillus acidophilus*) in the digestive tract could prolong life by preventing putrefaction (decay). He noted that Bulgarian villagers, who eat large quantities of curded milk and yogurt, were known for their longevity. Other scientists of the time believed the secret of long life depended on hormones and, in particular, claimed that an extract of dog endocrine glands could reverse the signs of age. Studies such as these make it clear that the early gerontologists had only vague notions about the mechanisms of cellular senescence.

Metchnikoff's theory and the interest in hormone extracts was part of a tendency among scientists of the era to believe in magic potions that could cure many maladies at once or even reverse all signs of the aging process. This is an ancient idea that can be found in the medical practices of Egyptian physicians 4,000 years ago, and the witchcraft of the Middle Ages. The ancient Egyptians had magical spells and potions that were reputed to be powerful rejuvenators. Ancient Chinese physicians had a similar potion in the form of a broth produced from the ginseng root. The favorite elixir of the Middle Ages was the philosopher's stone, popularized by J. K. Rowling in the Harry Potter book series. The "stone" was a mineral, or mineral concoction, of mythical powers that was discovered by Nicholas Flamel, a French alchemist who lived in the 14th century. Flamel and his followers claimed that in addition to transmuting mercury and silver to gold, the philosopher's stone could also reverse the aging process. Potions and elixirs of this kind have never been authenticated, but the allure of a quick fix is always tempting, even to scientists.

DNA STRUCTURE INSPIRES NEW THEORIES

On April 25, 1953, James Watson and Francis Crick published a classic paper on DNA in the journal *Nature:* "A Structure for Deoxyribose Nuclei Acid" not only proposed a structural model for the DNA molecule but also showed how DNA could store a genetic code, specifying a unique protein, and how that code could be duplicated, in a process now known as DNA replication. Watson and Crick were also the first to propose the existence of a molecular intermediary (messenger RNA) between DNA and protein synthesis,

The discoverers of the structure of DNA. James Watson (b. 1928) at left and Francis Crick (1916–2004), seen with their model of part of a DNA molecule in 1953. Crick and Watson met at the Cavendish Laboratory, Cambridge, in 1951. Their work on the structure of DNA was performed with a knowledge of Chargaff's ratios of the bases in DNA and some access to the X-ray crystallography of Maurice Wilkins and Rosalind Franklin at King's College London. Combining all of this work led to the deduction that DNA exists as a double helix, thus to its structure. Crick, Watson, and Wilkins shared the 1962 Nobel Prize in physiology or medicine, Franklin having died of cancer in 1958. *(A. Barrington Brown/Photo Researchers, Inc.)*

and special adaptor molecules (transfer RNA) that were part of the protein synthesis machinery. By 1966, using synthetic messenger RNAs, other scientists had worked out the complete genetic code thereby establishing the one-gene-one-protein hypothesis and describing the functional relationships between replication, tran-scription, and translation.

Gerontologists of the second epoch quickly realized that the genetic code and the events of protein synthesis gave them, for the first time, testable theories of the aging process. The first, proposed by Denham Harman in 1956, was the free radical theory, and the second, proposed by Leslie Orgel in 1963, was the error catastrophe theory. Both of these theories (discussed in chapter 4) suggest that aging is due to errors in biosynthesis, due either to free radicals or to inherent error frequencies associated with transcription and transla-tion. In either case, according to the theories, the result is a buildup of dysfunctional proteins that damage normal cellular functions, thus reducing cell viability with time. The error catastrophe theory was first tested on bacteria, experimental organisms introduced to ger-ontology during the early years. To further test this theory and the free radical theory, gerontologists of the second epoch began using baker's yeast *(Saccharomyces cerevisiae),* the housefly *(Musca domes-tica),* the fruit fly *(Drosophila melanogaster),* the rat, and the mouse *(mus musculus).* Experiments on all of these organisms, though of-fering some support for the free radical theory, failed to substantiate the original formulation of the error catastrophe theory.

Many investigators, however, realized that even though in-duced errors in protein synthesis had no effect on the rate of ag-ing, other errors, involving replication or the repair of the DNA molecule, could still be an important, if not primary, cause of the aging process. Testing the revised catastrophe theory required detailed information about the gene, but at the time there was no way to sequence DNA or to infer the sequence of messenger RNA. Throughout the 1960s physicists were busy perfecting the electron microscope, which offered unparalleled resolution of cellular organ-elles and tissue ultrastructure. Consequently, many gerontologists turned their attention to refining the structural and biochemical analysis of age-related changes that was begun by scientists of the first epoch. These studies, carried out on the housefly, *Drosophila,* and mouse, introduced methods for modulating the life span of the organism. The life span of houseflies, for example, was tripled when they were reared in tiny cages that minimized flight activity. Caloric restriction was also introduced, which could extend the life span of a mouse by 30 to 40 percent. Finally, with extensive genetic data available for *Drosophila,* many researchers conducted studies on long-lived or short-lived mutants in an attempt to correlate their life span with changes at the cellular or biochemical level. Although the research in the second epoch used more powerful techniques than were available during the first epoch, the results were still largely descriptive in nature and generally fell far short of achieving a deeper understanding of the aging process.

BIOTECHNOLOGY REVOLUTIONIZES THE FIELD

In 1973 Paul Berg, a professor of biochemistry at Stanford University, produced the first recombinant DNA molecule, consisting of a piece of mammalian DNA joined to a bacterial plasmid (a bacterial mini-chromosome). Bacteria have a natural tendency to take up plasmids from the medium they are growing in; once they do, the plasmid DNA, with any insert it may contain, is replicated along with the bacterial chromosome each time the cell divides. This proliferation of a segment of DNA is called amplification.

To amplify a mammalian gene, bacteria are coaxed to take up a recombinant plasmid in a small test tube containing a special medium, after which they are transferred to a large flask containing nutrient broth and allowed to grow for 24 hours. By the end of the culturing period, the amount of cloned insert has increased more than a million fold. In 1977 Fred Sanger, a professor at Cambridge University, and Walter Gilbert, a professor at Harvard, developed methods for sequencing DNA. The production of recombinant clones, combined with the new sequencing technology, made it possible to isolate any gene and to produce enough of it for sequencing and expression studies (see chapter 10 for more information).

Expression studies observe the transcription of a gene to produce messenger RNA (mRNA), and the resulting translation of mRNA into protein. Because most mRNA is automatically translated into protein, conducting an expression study involves determining the amount of mRNA being produced by a specific gene. The information gained by doing so is extremely important because all cellular processes are ultimately controlled by the differential expression of various genes. Some genes in some cells always stay off, whereas some are always on (constitutive expression), and some turn on or off, as conditions demand (regulative expression). One theory of aging suggests that the aging process is caused by subtle disruptions in the normal control of gene expression. At first gerontologists tried to test this assumption by examining the protein products of translation with protein electrophoresis, a technology introduced in the 1960s and refined in 1977. In this procedure proteins are isolated from the tissue of interest and then separated on a small gel slab subjected to an electric field (see Gel Electrophoresis in chapter 10). After separation the gel is stained, dried, and photographed. Proteins of different sizes appear as blue bands in the photograph.

But protein electrophoresis can detect only a few hundred proteins; a typical cell is capable of producing thousands of different proteins. Despite its limitations, many studies were conducted with this procedure throughout the 1980s on wild-type (normal) or mutant *Drosophila*. The hope was that electrophoresis would show that old animals were completely missing a protein present in young animals or that a new protein would appear in old animals that might be responsible for the age-related changes. But no such results were ever obtained, at least not on a consistent basis. The studies failed to show a consistent change in any of the proteins that could be visualized with this technique. The animals were clearly aging, but they seemed to be making the same proteins when they were old as when they were young.

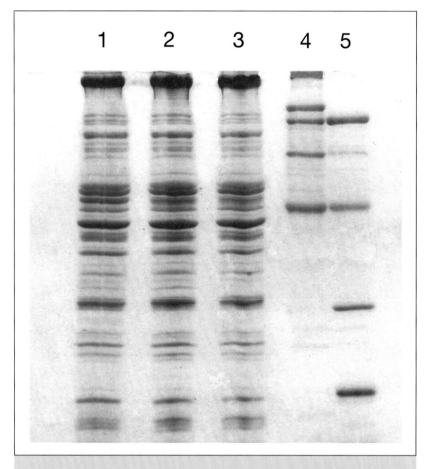

Protein electrophoresis. In this procedure, proteins are extracted from cells of interest and then fractionated by electrophoresis on a polyacrylamide gel. After the gel is stained, or exposed to X-ray film, the proteins appear as bands. In the example shown, approximately 30 different proteins (bands) have been identified. Lanes 1 to 3 are proteins extracted from housefly flight muscle at one, four, and eight days of age. Lanes 4 and 5 are size markers, which decrease in size from top to bottom. In a different form of this procedure, called two-dimensional protein electrophoresis, the proteins appear as spots over the face of the gel. Two-dimensional protein gels have a higher resolution and can detect about 1,000 different proteins, but this is still much less than the more than 20,000 proteins a typical animal cell can produce. (the author)

To address the question of whether the absence or presence of a given protein influenced aging, scientists abandoned protein electrophoresis in favor of recombinant technology. With this technology it is possible to study the mRNA expression of every gene in the cell. Consequently, gerontologists of the third epoch conducted a large number of expression studies involving genes coding for globin, actin, liver enzymes, microtubules, apolipoprotein (a protein that carries lipids in the blood), brain- and kidney-specific proteins, and several oncogenes. In most cases, the choice of which gene to study was an equal mix of educated guess and common practicality. If an investigator had a hunch that a particular liver enzyme was responsible for some aspect of cellular aging, the expression of the gene could be studied, but only if it had already been cloned (the clone, as explained in chapter 10, serves as probe to localize and quantify the mRNA). Since no one at the time had a clear idea of which genes were responsible for the aging process, virtually any gene for which a probe was available made a good candidate for an expression study.

It was during this epoch that Daniel Rudman and his colleagues at Emory University Hospital in Atlanta, Georgia, demonstrated the striking age-related decline in the expression of growth hormone (GH) in humans. Soon after, many other investigators demonstrated an age-related decline in a number of other hormones, such as thyroid hormone, dehyroepiandrosterone (DHEA), estrogen, and insulin-like growth factor (IGF). These studies, conducted on humans, rats, and mice, all showed a similar trend. Other expression studies, however, carried out on rat, *Drosophila,* and housefly tissues did not produce the striking results that most scientists were expecting. The expression of some genes was shown to increase with age while others decreased, but there was no obvious connection to cellular senescence. Even worse, the expression of some genes was shown to decrease with age in the rat, but not in *Drosophila* or the mouse. Since the aging process should be similar for all animals, those genes could not be the cause of a universal aging mechanism. When all expression studies were taken together, there appeared to be a general decline in the rate of gene expression with age, with the hormones mentioned above (GH, thyroid hormone, DHEA, estrogen, and IGF) showing the most consistent trend.

Scientists interested in chromatin structure and the role it plays in regulating gene expression adopted a different approach to the study of the aging process. Eukaryote chromosomes are a complex of DNA and proteins, called histones, that are arranged on the DNA like beads on a string. Each bead, consisting of several different kinds of histone, is called a nucleosome. This complex of DNA and histones is known as chromatin. The histones are essential for packing up the chromosomes in preparation for cell division. Phosphorylating the nucleosomes (adding phosphate groups to the proteins) is like releasing a stretched rubber band: The chromosome contracts to form a compact structure that is 10,000 times shorter than the bare piece of DNA. Just as a suitcase makes it possible for us to take our clothes on a trip, histones and the chromatin structure they produce make it possible for the cell to package its genes in preparation for cell division (see Cell Biology in chapter 10 for additional information).

Chromatin compaction, or condensation, is also used during interphase (the period between cell divisions) to help manage the chromosomes. It is also one mechanism for controlling gene expression. The packing ratio of interphase chromatin (condensed length divided by relaxed length) is about 1:1,000 overall, but there are highly condensed regions where it can be as low as 1:10,000. This variation in the density of the chromatin accounts for the blotchy appearance that most interphase nuclei have. Areas of the nucleus that are very dark represent highly compacted chromatin, whereas the lighter regions contain chromatin in a more relaxed state. At the molecular level, chromatin condensation is an extremely dynamic process that is used to close down single genes or whole neighborhoods consisting

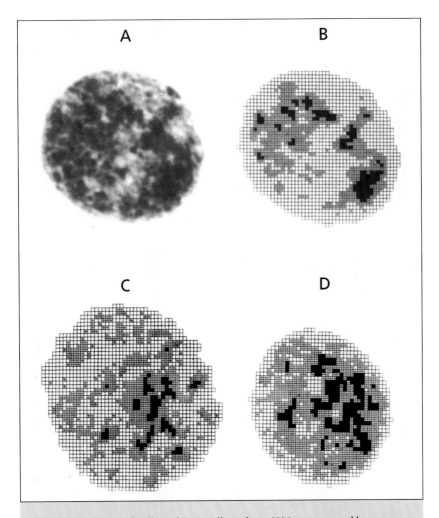

Pattern analysis of cell nuclei. A cell nucleus (A) is processed by a computer to show low- (LDC), medium- (MDC), and high- (HDC) density chromatin components. (B) Each component is analyzed for quantity and spatial distribution. This type of analysis was used to characterize nuclei from young and old houseflies. The computer then selected images from the data files that best represented young (C) and old (D) flies. These images show a dramatic decrease in total nuclear area, an increase in the amount of HDC, a change in the HDC spatial distribution, and a decrease in the number of MDC clusters. LDC (pale blue), MDC (blue), HDC (black). *(the author)*

of hundreds of genes. The mechanism by which this occurs is fairly straightforward: Highly condensed chromatin blocks the transcription machinery so it cannot get access to the gene.

Many gerontologists of the third epoch studied chromatin condensation as a function of age. These studies were either biochemical or they relied on computerized histochemistry. The biochemical analysis depended on the fact that uncondensed chromatin is easy to dissociate (i.e., it is easy to separate the histones from the DNA) in certain buffers, whereas highly condensed chromatin is either very difficult to dissociate or does not dissociate at all. Studies such as these invariably showed that chromatin became more condensed with age. Consequently, condensed chromatin was believed to be responsible for the age-related reduction in transcriptional activity. Computerized histochemical analysis of intact nuclei supported the biochemical results and in addition, provided a way to visualize the progressive condensation of cell nuclei. Scientists produced a model of this event by analyzing the condensation pattern over the surface of the nucleus, and then, with the aid of computer algorithms, selecting nuclei that best represent the young and old groups.

The third epoch was a productive period for gerontological research that provided many insights into the mechanisms controlling the aging process. But many scientists came to realize that the available DNA sequence data was inadequate. They needed more in order to expand the expression profiles for the organisms being studied. Indeed, they needed the complete genomic sequence for humans and for all organisms for which age-related studies were under way.

THE POST-GENOMIC ERA

An international genome-sequencing consortium was formed in 1990 to sequence the human, bacteria, yeast, nematode *(Caenorhabditis elegans,* or simply *C. elegans), Drosophila,* and mouse genomes. This project was initiated by the U.S. Department of Energy and the National Research Council and is coordinated by the Human Genome Organization (HUGO). The principal consortium members include the United States, United Kingdom, France, Germany, Japan, and China. Sequencing of the human genome was completed in early 2003, and work on the other organisms was completed in 2008.

In 1993 the American National Institute of Aging (NIA) started a program to identify longevity genes in yeast, nematode, *Drosophila,* and mice. This program provided research funding for scientists at NIA, as well as other scientists working in university laboratories around the country. The main interest of this program is single-gene mutants that may be used to identify genes and physiological factors that favor longevity in all animal species. These include the insulinlike signaling pathway, stress resistance, and most recently, chromosome and nuclear architecture. The ultimate goal is to use information gathered from lower animals (i.e., invertebrates and insects) to identify longevity genes in humans.

In addition to financial support, the NIA program and the genome-sequencing consortium provided encouragement and focus to the gerontological community. Research focus came in two forms. First, by settling on just four research organisms, different research groups could easily compare results. Gerontology of previous epochs was carried out to a great extent on houseflies and rats, neither of which are genetically defined (i.e., mutants have not been identified or characterized). The four organisms chosen by NIA are well characterized genetically, and there are many long- and short-lived mutants available that greatly expedite aging research. Second, aging research shifted from projects aimed at testing one of the many theories of the aging process to a narrower, thus more practical approach involving the search for longevity genes. This was done by selecting for long-lived individuals or by searching for naturally occurring short-lived mutants. In some cases exposing the animals to chemical mutagens generated short-lived mutants.

There is also a great deal of interest in Werner's syndrome, a human disease that is characterized by a greatly accelerated rate of aging. Individuals suffering from this disease age so rapidly that they appear to be in their 70s or 80s by the time they are 10 years old.

The great value of the sequencing consortium in the effort to identify aging genes lies in the fact that all of the organisms under study, including humans, share a common cellular and genetic heritage. Thus, if a longevity gene is discovered in *Drosophila*, its homolog (a gene having a similar or identical sequence) can be identified in humans simply by searching the human database for a gene that matches the *Drosophila* sequence. Research of this kind (discussed in chapter 5) is bringing us closer to identifying the physiological processes and molecular mechanisms that are important for longevity. Reversal of the aging process and treatment of its clinical symptoms will become a practical reality after all of the genes controlling these processes have been identified and their functions clearly defined.

3

Aging Characteristics

All animals pass through three stages of development: embryogenesis, growth and development, and senescence. The final stage is commonly recognized as the aging process. That is, it represents those events that add up to a gradual deterioration of the body and mind. A major problem associated with the study of senescence is distinguishing between those traits that are caused by the aging process and those that are caused by disease and illness. Senility used to be thought of as a normal part of the aging process, but scientists now know that it is caused by Alzheimer's disease and does not affect a large portion of the aging human population. Humans become frail with age, but severe frailty is due to the modern, sedentary lifestyle and not the aging process.

In the absence of disease, the body still ages, but the extent and magnitude of the eventual disabilities are greatly reduced. This gentle form of aging would have been common a thousand years ago when humans were more active and had a leaner diet. Many scientists refer to this as healthy or successful aging, whereas aging that is associated with disease is called normal aging. Unfortunately, this convention is confusing since "normal" often implies healthy. In the discussion that follows, aging in the absence of disease will be referred to as classical aging, and aging that is associated with disease will be called modern aging.

CLASSICAL AGING

Classical aging may be characterized as a gradual reduction in the functional capacity of the individual without the onset of severe disabilities. People who age in this way remain physically active well into their 80s and 90s. One such person was Jeanne Calment, mentioned earlier on page 11, who rode her bike on daily errands until she was 100 years old. Such people seem rare now, but they represent the condition of the elderly that was likely common hundreds of years ago. This is obscured by the fact that the mean human life span during the Middle Ages was only about 30 years as compared to the current average of more than 70 years. This difference implies that people aged more rapidly during the Middle Ages than they do now, but this is not the case. The short human life span during that period was due primarily to infectious diseases, which killed young and old alike and had nothing to do with the rate at which those people aged.

MODERN AGING

The modern lifestyle, characterized by lack of exercise, smoking, and the consumption of high-fat foods, has seriously distorted the way humans age. Individuals who age by the classical route remain hearty well into their 80s and 90s, whereas those who take the modern route are frail and racked with multiple disorders by the time they reach their 70th year. The difference between these two modes of aging is profound. Jeanne Calment, who typifies classical aging, lived 47 years beyond the typical North American life span of 75 years.

Critics point out that while Calment lived 122 years, many others who apparently followed the classical route did not. This discrepancy is due to a genetic component that modulates the aging process; long-lived individuals often come from long-lived families. But the full extent of gene penetrance, or the influence of an individual's genes, has yet to be determined. Are genes responsible for long-lived families, or are such families long-lived because they have a long cultural tradition of eating healthy foods and of getting regular exercise?

In 1987, to clarify the interpretation of aging rates, NIA launched the Biomarkers of Aging Project to identify biological signs, or biomarkers, in human subjects that best characterize the classical aging process. Biomarkers, which include the performance of the cardiovascular system, blood insulin levels, blood pressure, and several other factors, provide a way of estimating an individual's physiological age (see the table on page 32). The same biomarkers for modern aging are shown in the table on page 33. These markers provide a simple way of distinguishing between classical aging and modern aging. If the biomarkers indicate a physiological age of 85 years, but the individual's chronological age is only 65, then that individual's rate of aging has been accelerated and is an example of modern aging. On the other hand, if the physiological age is less than or equal to the chronological, then that individual is aging by the classical route.

Note that individuals aging by the classical or modern route share some characteristics: Both may develop osteoporosis, but it is generally much milder with classical aging. Classical and modern aging are both associated with a decline in the levels of certain hormones, but the change in the hormonal environment is believed to be more extreme with modern aging. When it comes to the skin, vision, and hearing, the two modes of aging appear to be very similar.

Some gerontologists, in the hope of further characterizing human aging, have focused their attention on centenarians, individuals who invariably follow the classical pattern of aging. The New England Centenarian Study has observed the following:

1. Centenarians are rarely obese. This is particularly true for men, who are nearly always lean.

BIOMARKERS OF CLASSICAL AGING[1]

BIOMARKER	CHANGE WITH AGE
Arteries	Increased rigidity without atherosclerosis
Blood pressure	Increases
Body fat	Slight increase
Bones	Mild osteoporosis
Brain	Some neurons lost; basic functions remain intact
Cancer	Some benign tumors
Cholesterol	Slight Increase
Eyes	Decreased accommodation, acuity, and color sensitivity
Hearing	Detection of high frequencies is lost
Heart	Thickness of ventricular wall increases
Hormones	Growth hormone, testosterone, estrogen, thyroid hormone, and dehyroepiandrosterone (DHEA)[2] decrease; insulin, adrenalin, parathyroid hormone, and vasopressin increase
Immune system	Slight decrease in T cell activity
Joints	Mild arthritis
Kidneys	Mild reduction in urine output
Lungs	Vital capacity[3] declines by about 20 percent
Skin	Increased wrinkling, and atrophy of sweat glands
Vision	Ability to focus close up is lost, night vision becomes poor, and the ability to detect moving objects is impaired

Notes
[1]Classical aging occurs in the absence of diseases, such as Alzheimer's or Parkinson's disease.
[2]DHEA is a precursor of the sex hormones, estrogen and testosterone.
[3]Vital capacity is the maximum amount of air inspired with each breath.

2. A history of smoking is rare.
3. Centenarians are invariably better able to handle stress than the majority of the population.
4. Many centenarians are mentally alert and show no signs of senility or the presence of Alzheimer's disease.

BIOMARKERS OF MODERN AGING[1]

BIOMARKER	CHANGE WITH AGE
Arteries	Increased rigidity with atherosclerosis
Blood pressure	Large Increase
Body fat	Large increase
Bones	Severe osteoporosis
Brain	Many neurons lost; basic functions may be lost
Cancer	Benign and malignant tumors
Cholesterol	Increases greatly
Eyes	Decreased accommodation, acuity, and color sensitivity
Hearing	Detection of high frequencies is lost
Heart	Thickness of ventricular wall increases
Hormones	Growth hormone, testosterone, estrogen, thyroid hormone, and dehyroepiandrosterone (DHEA)[2] decrease; insulin, adrenalin, parathyroid hormone, and vasopressin increase
Immune system	A decrease in T cell activity
Joints	Severe, crippling arthritis
Kidneys	Reduction in urine output
Lungs	Vital capacity[3] declines by about 40 percent
Skin	Increased wrinkling, and atrophy of sweat glands
Vision	Ability to focus close up is lost, night vision becomes poor, and the ability to detect moving objects is impaired

Notes
[1]Modern aging is associated with several diseases, such as cancer, Alzheimer's, or Parkinson's disease.
[2]DHEA is a precursor of the sex hormones, estrogen and testosterone.
[3]Vital capacity is the maximum amount of air inspired with each breath.

5. Many centenarian women have a history of bearing children later in life (ages 35 to 40), suggesting that their reproductive system is aging at a lower rate than the general population.
6. Metastatic cancer is relatively rare among this group of people.
7. About 88 percent of centenarians delay or escape the development of cardiac disease, stroke, and diabetes.
8. More than 90 percent of centenarians are functionally independent.
9. Exceptional longevity runs in families.

AGING MOSAICS

The difference between modern and classical aging suggests that the human population is an aging mosaic, consisting of individuals that age at different rates. Aging mosaics can also be found at the level of the cells and tissues and were implied by the neuroendocrine theory of the aging process, first proposed in the 1970s. This theory, described at length in the next chapter, suggests that the rate at which an individual ages is governed by the hypothalamus. The hypothalamus is assumed to be aging at its own rate, which would be higher than other tissues in the body.

The existence of an aging mosaic, involving cells and tissues, was tested experimentally in the 1980s. A computerized histochemical analysis of intact nuclei was used to determine the rate at which chromatin changes with age in various tissues of the housefly. This analysis indicated that certain neurons in the housefly brain (type II) were aging at the highest rate, followed by muscle, and Malpighian tubule (insect kidney). Interestingly, not all of the neurons were aging at the type II rate. Most of the neurons examined were aging at the more leisurely pace observed in the Malpighian tubule.

The existence of aging mosaics is extremely important. At the population level, long-lived individuals can be compared to their short-lived brethren in the hope of identifying the factors that are responsible for the difference, and at the same time shed some light on the nature of the aging process itself. A similar strategy may also be applied at the cellular and tissue levels. Some cells or tissues may age more rapidly than others simply because the body places a greater demand on their time; as a consequence, they are forced to be extremely active and thus burn out more quickly. A common example is the human heart, which has to beat nonstop for the life of the individual. It is not surprising, therefore, that this organ is often the first to go. A second example is the pancreatic β-cell. These cells synthesize insulin, which stimulates the uptake of glucose by all of the cells in the body. This is a very demanding job; so much so, that β-cells often suffer metabolic burnout, resulting in the age-related disease known as type II diabetes.

By studying aging mosaics, gerontologists hope to gain a deeper insight into the process of cellular and tissue senescence. This information will be crucial for the development of therapies designed to slow or reverse the aging process.

Aging Theories

A ging theories cover the genetic, biochemical, and physiological properties of a typical organism, as well as the way these properties change with time. Genetic theories deal with speculations regarding the identity of aging genes, accumulation of errors in the genetic machinery, programmed senescence, and telomeres. Biochemical theories are concerned with energy metabolism, generation of free radicals, the rate of living, and the health of mitochondria. Physiological theories deal almost entirely with the endocrine system and the role of hormones in regulating the rate of cellular senescence.

ERROR CATASTROPHE THEORY

Running a cell is a complex affair. RNA and proteins have to be synthesized on a regular basis to maintain and run the cell's machinery (see chapter 10 for more information). Production of proteins, either for enzymes or structural materials, occurs in a two-step process: transcription of the gene to produce mRNA, followed by translation of the message to produce the protein. For cells that are actively dividing, a third step, replication of the DNA, precedes the other two. Errors can occur all along the way; when they do, defective genes, mRNA, and proteins are produced. The error catastrophe theory, first proposed in the 1960s, suggests that over time, the number of errors build up to a catastrophic level leading to the death of the cell and, possibly, the entire organism.

Soon after this theory was proposed, many scientists conducted experiments that attempted to force a buildup of errors to see how the cells would cope with it. Bacteria were grown on medium containing defective amino acids to maximize the error frequency of protein synthesis. Similar experiments were conducted on fruit flies (*Drosophila melanogaster*) and mice, both of which were given food containing defective amino acids. To everyone's surprise, these experiments had no effect on the bacteria's or animal's health, vigor, or life span. Somehow the cells were able to avoid an error catastrophe. Today scientists understand why those experiments failed: Cells have elaborate repair systems and strategies that detect and destroy defective molecules. If a defective protein is synthesized, it is quickly broken down and replaced with a normal copy. Only in cases where the repair systems have been damaged would an error catastrophe occur (e.g., Werner's syndrome).

In its original formulation, the error catastrophe theory focused on protein synthesis, which apparently can tolerate a high error frequency. Consequently, many scientists began to wonder if errors in the genome, or possibly a defective regulation of the genes, might be responsible for the aging process. After all, cells avoid an error catastrophe at the translational level because they can always try again with a fresh mRNA from a good gene. But if the genes themselves are damaged, or programmed for senescence, the outcome would be a gradual decline in cell vigor and the eventual death of the organism.

GENES AND PROGRAMMED AGING

Are humans programmed to get old? If so, is it like the program that guides our development from a single fertilized egg to a multicellular organism? Or is aging the unfortunate side effect of adaptations that make it possible for us to have and protect our offspring? Many gerontologists believe that aging is a matter of evolutionary neglect, rather than design.

However life spans evolved, it is clear that our genes have the final say in how long an individual will be on the stage. Even though flies and humans are constructed from the same kinds of cells (eukaryotes), one animal lives two weeks, the other 80 years. If those eukaryotes had remained free-living, as their protozoan ancestors have done, they would live for millions of years.

The genes in a multicellular organism appear to be regulating life span for the good of the cell community as a whole. The size of the community, the animal's intelligence, the number of offspring, and the pressure the animal experiences from its predators, are all taken into account. The final life span seems to be a balance of all these forces, and given these forces may be the best deal the organism can hope for. There would be no point to nature's producing a fruit fly that could live a thousand years since their predators eat them all in a matter of days. Scientists might try producing a fly that could live that long, but what in the world would an animal with that level of intelligence do for all that time? This is not just a whimsical point. There is a very strong correlation between longevity and the weight of the brain: "Smart" animals usually live longer than "dumb" animals.

The goal of gerontologists is to try to get a better understanding of the covenant between the genes, the organism, and the environment. Whether intended by evolution or not, many genes are directly responsible for an animal's life span. These genes may be exerting their effects through inappropriate behavior (that is, they are turning on or off at the wrong time) or through a mutation that eventually damages the protein product.

Damage at the gene level reinvokes the error catastrophe theory, but many experiments have failed to establish a role for genetic (or somatic) mutations in cell senescence. This is because the cell can detect and repair DNA damage as easily as it deals with errors in translation, and those repair systems remain intact long after the animal shows visible signs of age.

The inappropriate expression of certain genes as a major cause of aging is only now being addressed in a comprehensive way. With the sequence of the human genome now at hand, it will soon be possible to screen for the expression of all human genes, in every tissue and organ of the body. When this job is complete (and it will be as big a job as the genome project itself) researchers will finally have an idea of which genes are responsible for the human life span.

TELOMERES

Although scientists have not identified the genes controlling our life span, there is a genetic element called a telomere that clearly regulates the replicative life span of human cells in culture. A telomere is a simple DNA sequence that is repeated many times, located at the tips of each chromosome. Telomeres are not genes, but they are needed for the proper duplication of the chromosomes in dividing cells. Each time the chromosomes are duplicated, the telomeres shrink a bit, until they get so short the DNA replication machinery can no longer work. This occurs because the enzyme that duplicates the DNA (DNA polymerase) has to have some portion of the chromosome out ahead of it. Much like a train backing up on a track, DNA polymerase preserves a safe distance from the end of the DNA, so it does not slip off the end. Telomeres also provide a guarantee that genes close to the ends of the chromosomes have been replicated. DNA polymerase stalls automatically whenever it gets too close to the end of the chromosome, permanently blocking the ability of the cell to divide. When this happens, the cell is said to have reached replicative senescence.

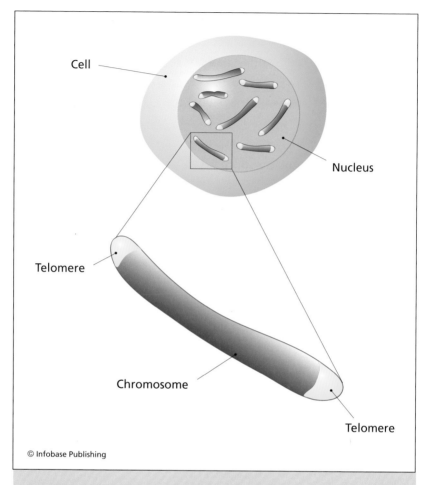

Telomeres. A telomere is a simple DNA sequence, located at the tips of each chromosome, that is repeated many times. Telomeres are not genes, but they are needed for the proper duplication of the chromosomes in dividing cells.

The telomeres in human fibroblasts are long enough to permit about 50 rounds of DNA replication. That is, the cell can divide about 50 times in culture. This is often referred to as the Hayflick limit, after Leonard Hayflick, the scientist who was the first to notice that normal cells cannot divide indefinitely in culture. Cancer cells, on the other hand, can divide indefinitely, and from them scientists isolated an enzyme called telomerase that restores the telomeres after each cell division. If the telomerase gene is added to normal fibroblasts, they are no longer bound by the Hayflick limit and can divide indefinitely, like an immortal cancer cell. The transformation of normal fibroblasts with the telomerase gene was conducted for the first time in 1998 at the Geron Corporation, a biotechnology company. The results generated a tremendous amount of excitement, for they seemed to imply that reversal of replicative senescence would be followed very quickly by the reversal of the aging process. Scientists at Geron began talking about human life spans of several hundred years.

Experiments since have shown, however, that while telomerase can block replicative senescence in cultured cells, it has little to do with the life span of the animal as a whole. Indeed, some animals with long life spans have short telomeres and negligible telomerase activity, while other animals with short life spans have long telomeres and active telomerase. This is not surprising if one remembers that most cells in an animal's body are post-mitotic; they stop dividing soon after the individual is born. So the life span of the individual made from those cells cannot be regulated by the length of the telomeres.

RATE-OF-LIVING THEORY

This theory takes a pragmatic approach to the regulation of life span. Simply put, it claims that if you are going to live fast and hard, your life will be short. The engine in a race car, run at full throttle, is lucky to last a full day. On the other hand, engines that are driven carefully, at modest RPMs, can last for 10 to 20 years and may even log 200,000 miles (321,868 km). Of course, if you buy a new car, park it in a garage, and rarely drive it, it will last even longer. This theory is not concerned with the underlying mechanism of aging, but simply advocates repair or replacement of body parts as they wear out, much in the way one deals with a broken-down car.

Of course, some body parts, such as our brain and muscles, cannot be replaced, and if anything serious happens to them, it would likely be fatal. The rate-of-living theory tries to deal with senescence by adopting a preventive strategy, involving a reduction in activity level and caloric intake. These strategies have been tested in houseflies, mice, and rats with some success.

Houseflies normally live one month in laboratory conditions, that is, in a large cage where they are fed and protected from their predators. If they are kept in tiny cages, no bigger than a teacup, their flight activity is severely restricted, and as a consequence, their life span is more than doubled. Caloric restriction has the same effect, but is most likely due to the forced reduction in flight activity, due to a lack of energy. Raising mice or rats in confined quarters to lower their activity level has no effect and may even reduce the life span because of the stress that it causes in these animals. Caloric restriction, however, can increase a rat's life span by 50 to 60 percent.

Researchers at the University of Wisconsin, led by Drs. Ricki Colman and Richard Weindruch, have recently completed a 20-year experiment in which rhesus monkeys were raised on a low-calorie diet (30 percent fewer calories per day). Compared to a control group that received a standard diet, the experimental group has shown a dramatic reduction in the incidence of diabetes, heart disease, neurological disorders, and cancer. Moreover, the low-calorie group looks younger and healthier than the control group, with slim physiques and smooth glossy coats. In terms of survival, Weindruch estimates that the life span of the experimental group will be extended by 10 to 20 percent. This is not as dramatic as the results for mice and rats, but it does suggest that a calorie-restricted diet could extend the human life span as well.

FREE RADICALS

The role of free radicals is closely related to the rate-of-living theory and was originally proposed in the 1950s. Free radicals are molecules that have an unpaired electron, which makes them very reactive. One of the most important, the oxygen free radical, is a toxic exhaust produced by mitochondria during the very important metabolic process of oxidative phosphorylation. This process produces the ATP that cells need to survive. The oxygen free radical can remove an electron from virtually any molecule in the cell, including DNA, RNA, proteins, and the lipids in the cell membrane. When it does so, it triggers a chain reaction of destabilized molecules reacting with other molecules to form new free radicals and a variety of potentially dangerous compounds. Many gerontologists believe free radicals are directly responsible for cellular senescence and the aging of the animal as a whole.

But cells do not give free radicals a free rein. A special enzyme, called superoxide dismutase (SOD), neutralizes oxygen free radicals as they are produced. Gerontologists in favor of the free radical theory maintain that SOD does not neutralize all of the free radicals, and that the damage is done by those that escape. Alternatively, aging may reduce the efficiency of SOD, such that the amount of free radicals increases gradually with age. An anti-aging remedy, consisting of a regular diet of antioxidants (chemicals that inactivate free radicals) such as vitamin E or vitamin C, has been proposed. Many experiments have been conducted on mice and rats to test this remedy, but with limited success. The most recent study, conducted in 2008 at the University College London, used the nematode *C. elegans* to test the free radical theory. The UCL team, led by Drs. Ryan Doonan and David Gems, genetically modified a group of nematodes to permanently reduce their levels of free radicals. According to the theory, the experimental group should have had a much longer life span than the controls, but the results failed to show such a difference. The researchers concluded that oxidative damage is not a major driver of the aging process.

NEUROENDOCRINE THEORY
The neuroendocrine system, which consists of several endocrine glands under the control of the central nervous system, coordinates

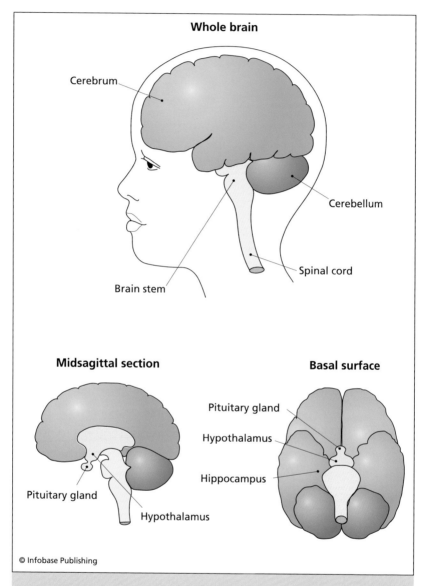

Whole brain

Cerebrum

Cerebellum

Spinal cord

Brain stem

Midsagittal section

Basal surface

Pituitary gland

Hypothalamus

Hippocampus

Pituitary gland

Hypothalamus

© Infobase Publishing

The human central nervous system. The human brain consists of the cerebrum, the cerebellum, and the brain stem, which is continuous with the spinal cord. The brain and spinal cord are called the central nervous system (CNS). The pituitary gland, a crucial part of the neuroendocrine system, is connected to the hypothalamus at the base of the brain (mid-sagittal section). The hippocampus, located on the basal surface of the brain, coordinates memory functions.

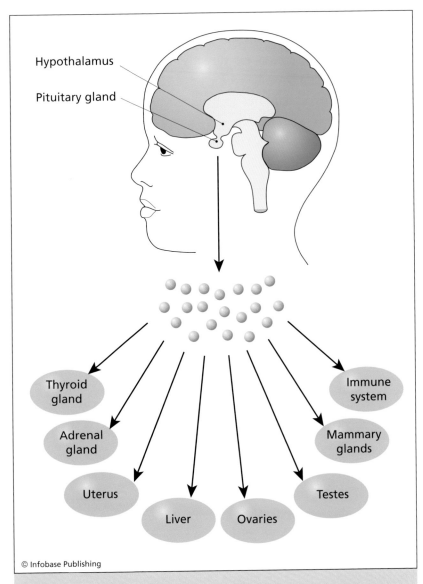

Hypothalamus

Pituitary gland

Thyroid gland

Immune system

Adrenal gland

Mammary glands

Uterus

Testes

Liver

Ovaries

© Infobase Publishing

The human endocrine system is controlled by the hypothalamus, which regulates the production and release of various hormones from the pituitary gland. The pituitary hormones, in turn, regulate other glands, tissues, and organs of the body.

an animal's physiology. This system consists of a command center located in the hypothalamus; a master endocrine gland called the pituitary, which is connected directly to the hypothalamus; and a variety of secondary endocrine glands located in various parts of the body. The hypothalamus controls the pituitary by releasing hormone messengers that pass directly to the gland, where they stimulate or inhibit the release of pituitary hormones.

The pituitary gland, also known as the master gland of the vertebrate body, is located at the base of the brain and is about the size of a cashew nut. Despite its small size, this gland is in charge of producing all of the hormones that coordinate the many physiological processes occurring in animals and humans. There are 10 different kinds of pituitary cells, all constructed of cuboidal epithelium. Each cell type specializes in the synthesis and release of a different hormone, and is named after the hormone it produces. Thus, growth hormone-producing cells are known as GH cells or somatotrophs, and thyroid hormone-producing cells are known as thyrotrophs.

The cells that produce hormones that stimulate the gonads (ovaries and testes) to develop are known as gonadotrophs. Other pituitary cells produce hormones that stimulate the adrenal glands (adrenocorticotrophs) and lactation (lactotrophs). The three remaining cell types are involved in the production of oxytocin, vassopressin, and melanocyte-stimulating hormone (MSH). Oxytocin is a hormone that causes milk ejection from the breasts and contraction of the uterus during birth. Vassopressin is a hormone that regulates salt and water balance by stimulating the kidneys to retain water. MSH stimulates melanin synthesis in human melanocytes and is very important in lower vertebrates, such as lizards and amphibians, where its release can stimulate a rapid change in skin color. The pituitary hormones, released into the blood, control the activity of other glands, such as the adrenal and thyroid glands, as well as organs such as the ovaries, testes and liver. All of the hypothalamic messengers and the pituitary hormones are small proteins. Overall, the system is responsible for regulating reproductive cycles, growth,

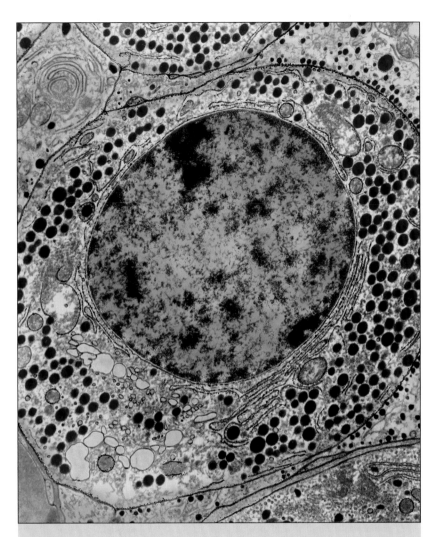

Hormone-producing cell (Somatotrope). Colored transmission electron micrograph of a growth hormone-producing cell from the pituitary gland. The pituitary gland is located at the base of the brain. Here a growth hormone-secreting endocrine cell, known as a somatotroph, is shown (large round). The hormone is in the numerous granules (brown) within the cell cytoplasm (yellow). Visible cell organelles include mitochondria (round, green) and the nucleus (purple, center) with its chromatin (pink). There are large amounts of rough endoplasmic reticulum (thin green) with the protein-synthesizing ribosomes (black dots). Magnification 1,000×. (Quest/Photo Researchers, Inc.)

energy metabolism, storage and mobilization of food molecules, and the fight-or-flight response (see the table on page 51).

The endocrine system is self-regulating, as illustrated by the control of the thyroid gland. The hypothalamus releases a messenger molecule called thyrotropin-releasing hormone, which stimulates the release of thyrotropin (also known as thyroid-stimulating hormone) from the pituitary. Thyrotropin, in turn, stimulates the thyroid gland to release thyroid hormones, the most important of which is thyroxin, a hormone that stimulates cell metabolism and growth. The self-regulating feature of this system is the ability of the hypothalamus to monitor the level of thyroxine in the blood. When it gets too high, the hypothalamus signals the pituitary to cut back on the release of thyrotropin, or to stop releasing it altogether.

The regulation of the human female reproductive, or ovarian, cycle involves the same general scheme. In this case, the hypothalamus releases a molecule called gonadotropin-releasing factor, which stimulates the pituitary to release follicle-stimulating hormone (FSH). FSH stimulates growth and development of ovarian follicles, each of which contain an oocyte. As the follicle cells mature, they synthesize and release the female hormone estrogen into the blood. The hypothalamus monitors the level of estrogen in the blood. Low levels of estrogen result in continuous release of FSH from the pituitary gland, but high levels, achieved when the follicle is mature, cause the hypothalamus to block release of FSH from the pituitary and, at the same time, to stimulate release of luteinizing hormone (LH) to trigger ovulation. If the mature oocyte is fertilized and successfully implants in the uterus, cells surrounding the embryo produce large amounts of estrogen to prepare the mother's body for the pregnancy and to block further release of FSH. If the egg is not fertilized, estrogen levels drop, signaling the hypothalamus to stimulate renewed synthesis and release of FSH to complete the cycle. FSH also promotes development of sperm in the male (see the table on page 51).

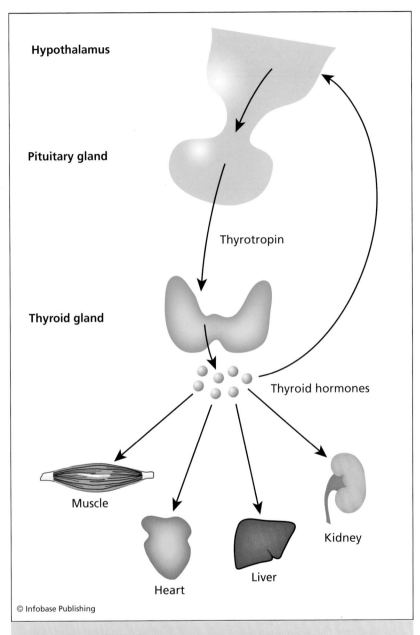

Hypothalamus

Pituitary gland

Thyrotropin

Thyroid gland

Thyroid hormones

Muscle

Kidney

Heart

Liver

© Infobase Publishing

Regulation of the thyroid gland. The hypothalamus instructs the pituitary gland to release thyrotropin, leading to secretion of thyroid hormones, which stimulate the activity of several organs. Thyroid hormone levels are monitored by the hypothalamus. When they get too high, thyrotropin release is reduced or stopped.

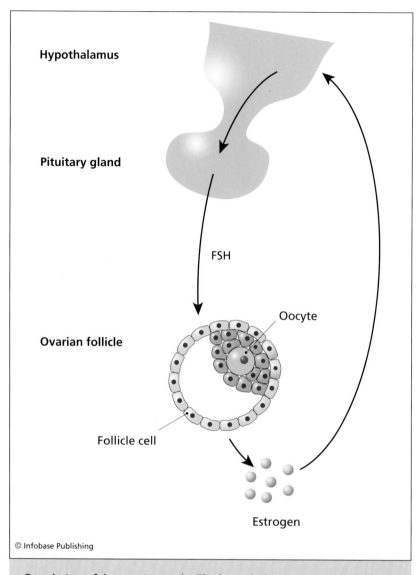

Hypothalamus

Pituitary gland

FSH

Oocyte

Ovarian follicle

Follicle cell

Estrogen

© Infobase Publishing

Regulation of the ovarian cycle. The hypothalamus instructs the pituitary gland to release follicle-stimulating hormone (FSH), promoting maturation of ovarian follicle cells, which in turn begin synthesizing and releasing estrogen. Low estrogen levels stimulate FSH release. High levels of estrogen inhibit the release of FSH but stimulate the release of a pituitary hormone (not shown) that initiates ovulation.

HORMONES OF THE PITUITARY GLAND

HORMONE	DESCRIPTION
Adrenocortico-tropin (ACTH)	This hormone stimulates release of adrenalin and other steroids from the adrenal cortex. Adrenalin is involved in the "flight-or-fight" response. ACTH is controlled by a hypothalamic messenger called corticotropin-releasing hormone.
Antidiuretic hormone (ADH)	ADH promotes water conservation by the kidneys. It is controlled by sensors that monitor the degree of body dehydration.
Follicle stimulating hormone (FSH)	This hormone promotes development of sperm in the male and oocyte follicles in the female. Its release is controlled by a hypothalamic messenger called FSH-releasing hormone.
Growth hormone (GH)	GH stimulates the uptake of glucose and amino acids by all tissues (except neurons). Its release is blocked by a hypothalamic messenger called GH-inhibiting hormone.
Luteinizing hormone (LH)	LH Stimulates synthesis of testosterone by the testes and ovulation in females. Its release is controlled by a hypothalamic messenger called LH-releasing hormone.
Oxytocin	Oxytocin stimulates uterine contractions during childbirth and the release of milk from mammary glands. Its release is stimulated by cervical distension and suckling.
Prolactin	Prolactin stimulates the growth of mammary glands and milk production. Its release is blocked by a hypothalamic messenger called prolactin-inhibiting hormone.
Thyrotropin	This hormone initiates the release of thyroid hormones from the thyroid gland. Thyroid hormones are growth factors that stimulate cellular activity and growth. The release of thyrotropin is controlled by a hypothalamic messenger called thyrotropin-releasing hormone (TRH).

Given its breadth of influence, it is no wonder the endocrine system has captured the attention of gerontologists, many of whom believe that aging of the organism as a whole begins with the senescence of the hypothalamus. In this sense, the hypothalamus is like a clock that regulates the rate at which the individual grows older. With the age-related failure of the command center, hormonal levels of the body begin to change, and this in turn produces the physical symptoms of age.

One of the most dramatic age-related changes in humans is the loss of the ovarian cycle in females, generally referred to as the onset of menopause. Menopause usually occurs as women reach 50 years of age and is marked by a cessation in development of ovarian follicles, and as a consequence, a dramatic drop in estrogen levels. Estrogen, aside from its role in reproduction, is important to female physiology for the maintenance of secondary sexual characteristics, skin tone, and bone development. Female mice and rats also go through menopause, although in these animals it is called diestrus, or the cessation of the estrous cycle.

For gerontologists, the onset of menopause in mice and rats provides an experimental system that can be used to test the idea that the hypothalamus is an aging clock; that is, menopause or diestrus occurs because the hypothalamus stops releasing the necessary messenger molecules. When this happens, the reproductive system grinds to a halt. Many experiments were conducted in which pituitary glands or ovaries from old female rats were transplanted into young rats. In general, they showed that old pituitary glands functioned well in young bodies, and that old ovaries regained their estrus cycle. When prepubertal ovaries were transplanted to old female rats the majority of them fail to regain their cycles. Similarly, when young pituitaries are transplanted into old rats, they are usually unable to support a normal estrous cycle.

Additional evidence in support of the role of the hypothalamus in the aging process comes from the observation that the levels of several hormones gradually decrease with age. The overall effect of this change is believed to be the loss of vigor, physical strength, and endurance that is typical in an aging human. Accordingly, many attempts have been made to reverse these effects with hormone therapies that include GH, estrogen, or testosterone supplements. While these therapies have alleviated some of the symptoms of old age, they have not been able to reverse the aging process. With our limited knowledge of the cell and the complexities of human physiology and endocrinology, there are real dangers associated with hormone therapies. Estrogen supplements can minimize bone thinning in menopausal women, but constant exposure to this hormone can lead to breast cancer. Similarly, androgen supplements in men can increase vigor and physical strength, but constant exposure to testosterone is known to be a leading cause of prostate cancer. Growth hormone supplements suffer from similar problems in that they can induce cancers; they can also lead to the development of bone deformations.

Despite its great promise and the fact that it has generated some useful geriatric therapies, the hormonal disregulation or imbalance theory has failed to produce a definitive model of the aging process; nor have any of the hormonal therapies inspired by this theory been able to reverse the effects of age. Instead, the application of this theory, as with the other theories already discussed, merely allows a somewhat healthier old age, an effect that can also be obtained simply by eating well and getting lots of fresh air and exercise.

CONCLUDING REMARKS

With the exception of the age-related role of telomeres, all of the theories just described have been with us for more than 40 years, and during that time scientists have subjected those theories to thousands of experiments. The results have shown clearly that a disregulation of the endocrine system is a central feature of human aging, and that caloric restriction can increase the life span of several mammalian species, including the rhesus monkey. Molecular and genetic models of cellular senescence have been more difficult to pin down, but with the sequence of the human genome now available, the search for longevity genes is well under way, the results of which are expected to revolutionize our understanding of the aging process.

5

Longevity Genes

Aging research throughout the first three epochs of gerontology was primarily concerned with describing general aspects of the process covering all levels of biological organization, from the molecular to the organismal. The data collected spawned a large number of theories touching on all aspects of cellular structure and function, as well as changes that may occur at the physiological level. Although these theories were crucial for producing advances in the discipline, they failed to produce a clear picture of fundamental mechanisms responsible for the aging process. Gerontology was placed on firmer ground with an NIA program to isolate genes that influence longevity, an effort that has greatly improved the genetic analysis of the aging process.

Thus, with the beginning of the current epoch and the launching of comprehensive genome sequencing projects, the goal of gerontology shifted to the identification and characterization of genes that promote longevity. Despite their name, longevity genes were not always selected by evolutionary forces to give an organism a long life span. Quite the contrary, since some of these genes, when functioning normally, limit the life span; only after being mutated and made dysfunctional do they increase the organism's life span. This type of longevity gene is said to be a negative regulator of life span because their normal function is to limit an organism's life span. Other longevity genes are said to be positive regulators because expression (or overexpression) of these genes increases the life span.

The normal life span of an organism is produced by a complex mix of positive and negative regulator genes that seem to produce the optimum—not necessarily the longest—life span that best fits the organism's size, metabolic rate, and activity level, as well as its position in the grander theater of predator-prey relationships. The search for longevity genes in yeast, nematode, *Drosophila*, mice, and humans has led to a much clearer picture of the mechanisms controlling the aging process. It has also shed light on how those mechanisms can be modulated to fine-tune an organism's life span to maximize the survival, not of the individual, but of the species to which it belongs. But gerontologists expect that a clear understanding of all longevity genes will provide a way of reversing or forestalling human aging.

YEAST

Yeast are unicellular organisms that divide at regular intervals and, as a population, are nearly immortal. Each cell begins as a mother cell that produces a daughter cell each time it divides, but the mother cell ages with each cell division; thus its life span is limited to a finite number of cell divisions, after which it dies, while the daughter cells continue on for the same finite number cell divisions. The measure of the yeast life span is thus the number of divisions of the mother cell before it dies, not the amount time that it has lived. The identification of longevity genes in yeast provided the first

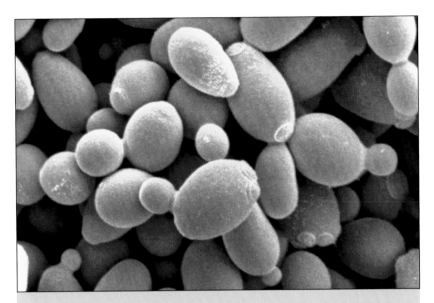

Yeasts, such as *Saccharomyces cerevisiae,* have been used by researchers in the search for longevity genes. This image shows several of the cells in the process of cell division by budding, which produces a daughter cell that is initially smaller than the mother cell. *(SciMAT/ Photo Researchers, Inc.)*

comprehensive list consisting of four processes that are believed to control the aging process. These processes are metabolic control, resistance to stress, gene disregulation, and the maintenance of genetic stability.

The first longevity gene, called *Lag-1* (longevity assurance gene number 1), was isolated from yeast by Dr. S. Michel Jazwinski and his team at Louisiana State University in 1994. Since that time, 14 additional longevity genes have been identified in yeast. The *Lag-1* protein (Lag-1) is located in the membrane of the endoplasmic reticulum and is involved in the production of glycolipids (gene and protein nomenclature is discussed in chapter 10). Glycolipids are an important component of the glycocalyx, a molecular "forest" that covers the surface of all cells. The glycocalyx is essential for cell-to-cell communication and contains many receptors that regulate a host of cellular functions. Many glycolipids are involved in signaling pathways that regulate growth, stress resistance, and apoptosis. Lag-1 is a positive regulator of life span, and while the mechanism by which it influences life span is unclear, a mutation in this gene could reduce the cell's ability to cope with stress, to block proliferation, or to induce apoptosis (see the table on page 59).

All eukaryotes have an intracellular signaling pathway, known as the retrograde response, that serves to coordinate mitochondrial function with the expression of mitochondrial genes in the cell nucleus. Although mitochondria have their own genome, most of the Krebs cycle enzymes (all of which function inside the mitochondrion) are coded for by the cellular genome. The rate at which these genes are transcribed depends on how badly the mitochondria need the enzymes. During periods of stress, caused by high temperatures or an unfavorable environment, mitochondria are extremely active. Enzymes usually have a short life span, and during periods of extreme activity they must be replaced more frequently. The main function of the retrograde response is to ensure that the mitochondria always have enough Krebs cycle enzymes. Two other longevity genes, called *Ras-1* and *Ras-2* (rhymes with "gas"), regulate this pathway. Mutations in either or both of these genes eliminate the retrograde response, thus abolishing the cell's ability to deal with stress of the kind described. Consequently, the cell does not receive sufficient amounts of ATP, the main energy source, at a time when it needs it the most, resulting in cellular damage and early death. Overexpression of *Ras-2* can completely abolish the negative effect on life span of chronic heat stress. Yeast demonstrating natural thermotolerance early in life invariably have longer life spans than is normal.

Gene disregulation has been observed in yeast that lose transcriptional silencing of genes in heterochromatic regions of the genome

YEAST LONGEVITY GENES

GENE	KNOWN OR PROPOSED FUNCTION
Lag-1	The *Lag-1* protein product (Lag-1) regulates traffic between the endoplasmic reticulum and Golgi complex and is required for the construction of a normal glycocalyx. The aging mechanism is unclear but may involve cell-surface signaling (mediated by the glycocalyx) that influences growth, stress resistance, and apoptosis.
Ras-1	The *Ras-1* product (Ras-1) is responsible for regulating the stress response.
Ras-2	Its product regulates the mitochondrial retrograde response, participates in the regulation of the stress response, and is necessary for genetic stability.
Rpd-3	Its product is a histone deacetylase that is needed for proper gene silencing and regulation.
Hda-1	Its product is another histone deacetylase that regulates silencing of ribosomal RNA genes.
Sir-2	*Sir-2* regulates ribosomal RNA genes.
Sgs-1	The *Sgs-1* protein product (Sgs-1) codes for a DNA helicase that is required for DNA replication. This gene is homologous to the human *wrn* gene, which, when mutated, greatly accelerates the rate of aging.

Note: Gene and protein naming conventions are explained in chapter 10.

(i.e., genes in highly condensed regions are supposed to be turned off). Active regions of the genome are associated with chromatin that is acetylated; that is, the histones are modified with the addition of acetyl groups, thus marking the region as being transcriptionally active. Two yeast longevity genes, *Rpd-3* and *Hda-1,* code for enzymes called deacetylases that remove the acetyl groups, thus converting chromatin from an active to an inactive configuration. A third gene, called *Sir-2,* is also responsible for gene silencing, but its mechanism of action is not clear. Damage to any of these silencing genes can shorten the life span of a yeast cell. Ribosomal RNA (rRNA) gene expression is one system that is affected by these longevity genes. Without appropriate gene silencing, production of rRNA is excessive and is not balanced by the synthesis of ribosomal proteins. The consequence is the assembly of defective ribosomes and a reduction in the efficiency of protein synthesis.

The maintenance of genetic stability, the fourth major process affected by the aging process, is provided by a host of nuclear proteins and enzymes that repair DNA damage and by many other proteins that are needed for accurate replication. One such enzyme, called a helicase, is encoded by the *Sgs-1* gene. The function of a helicase is to unwind the DNA helix in preparation for replication. Mutation of this gene leads to the corruption of many genes during replication and is associated with accelerated aging.

NEMATODE

A nematode is a very small round worm that inhabits the soil and sometimes the digestive tracts of mammals. Mammalian parasite nematodes are known as pinworms. The nematode *Caenorhabditis elegans* is a popular research organism among developmental biologists and gerontologists. Several longevity genes have been identified in *C. elegans,* most of which are involved in an insulin-like signaling pathway. At the head of this pathway is the insulin-like receptor, encoded by the gene *Daf-2* (see the table on page 62).

The Daf-2 pathway mediates growth and proliferation signals necessary for the active lifestyle of an adult nematode. Mutation of *Daf-2* shifts the entire physiology of the animal from active behavior to something resembling hibernation in mammals. Hibernation behavior in nematodes is known as a diapause state. Nematode diapause is characterized by a shift from active glucose metabolism (i.e., burning calories) to storage functions, such as the deposit of fat. The animal's activity level drops, and the life span is increased by nearly 80 percent. Thus, *Daf-2* is a negative regulator of life span; it is an example of the kind of gene that limits life span as a result of maximizing activity level and metabolic performance. The effects observed in *Daf-2* mutants are very similar to the response of mammals to hibernation or caloric restriction. The products of other nematode longevity genes, such as *Age-1, Daf-18, Akt-1,* and *Daf-16,* transduce the signal received by the Daf-2 receptor protein (e.g., the *Age-1* protein conveys the signal from the Daf-2 receptor to the interior of the cell). Consequently, a mutation in any of these genes will lead to the diapause state and extended life span.

A second pathway has been identified that affects nematode longevity. The *Daf-12* gene codes for a steroid hormone receptor that is linked to a pathway that appears to regulate the stress response. Indeed, this pathway specifies resistance to heat, ultraviolet radiation, and oxidative stress. Accordingly, *Daf-12* is a positive regulator of life span. A mutation in *Daf-12* or in *Ctl-1,* a component of the pathway, shortens life span.

FRUIT FLY

The fruit fly *Drosophila melanogaster* is a popular research organism. During the 1980s researchers managed to isolate long-lived *Drosophila* through selective breeding. These flies showed a greater metabolic capacity and enhanced resistance to stress initiated by heat, desiccation, and ethanol vapors. In addition, they have higher activities of antioxidative enzymes, they are more efficient at utilizing nutrients, and they have enhanced stores of lipid and glycogen. Many of these features are held in common with long-lived nematodes and yeast.

Direct support for the free radical theory of the aging process came with the isolation and characterization of *Sod-1,* the gene coding for superoxide dismutase. Transgenic fruit flies overexpressing *Sod-1* live longer than normal and suffer much less oxidative damage induced by free radicals. Interestingly, overexpression of *Sod-1* in motorneurons alone is sufficient to nearly double the mean life span of these animals. Overexpression of another gene, *Mth*, also increases life span. The *Mth* protein product, called methuselah, is a cell surface receptor that is linked to a pathway that regulates the stress response (see the table on page 63).

The retrograde response (described above) involving traffic between the cell nucleus, cytoplasm, and the mitochondria, is also involved in *Drosophila* aging. The *Indy* (*I'm not dead yet*) gene

CAENORHABDITIS ELEGANS LONGEVITY GENES

GENE	KNOWN OR PROPOSED FUNCTION
Daf-2	The product of this gene is an insulin-like cell membrane receptor (Daf-2). Disrupting this pathway extends life span.
Age-1 / Daf-23	These genes code for two kinases, directly linked to the Daf-2 signaling pathway.
Daf-18	The protein product is on the Daf-2 pathway, downstream from the *Age-1/Daf-23* products.
Akt-1 / Aakt-2	The products of these genes are on the Daf-2 pathway downstream from *Daf-18*.
Daf-16	*Daf-16* is a multifunction factor that is activated by the Daf-2, and Daf-12 pathways. Loss of function promotes a "hibernation" response, involving the storage of fat and glycogen that extends life span.
Daf-12	*Daf-12* is a steroid hormone receptor that is linked to a pathway important in stress resistance. A mutation in this gene shortens life span.
Ctl-1	The protein product is a cytoplasmic enzyme (catalase) on the Daf-12 stress-resistance pathway.

Note: Gene and protein naming conventions are explained in chapter 10.

DROSOPHILA LONGEVITY GENES

GENE	KNOWN OR PROPOSED FUNCTION
Indy	This gene codes for a mitochondrial membrane protein involved in transport of Krebs cycle intermediates. The loss of function increases life span by reducing the availability of nutrients (caloric restriction).
Sod-1	The protein product is superoxide dismutase (Sod). Overexpression increases life span by enhanced inactivation of free radicals.
Mth	Its product codes for a cell membrane receptor called methuselah, which enhances the stress response, thus increasing life span.
Chico	The protein product, Chico, is a hormone similar to mammalian insulin. Loss of function increases life span through caloric restriction.
Inr	This gene codes for the Chico receptor. Lose of function has the same effect as a *Chico* mutation. This receptor is very similar to the nematode DAF-2 receptor.
Sugar baby	The protein product is a maltose permease. Overexpression increases life span by shifting metabolism away from glucose, thus invoking partial caloric restriction.

Note: Gene and protein naming conventions are explained in chapter 10.

codes for a mitochondrial membrane protein involved in transport of Krebs cycle intermediates. A mutation in the *Indy* gene blocks import of these compounds, with an effect similar to caloric restriction—a near doubling of life span. Insulin and insulin receptors modulate life span in *Drosophila* much as they do in nematodes. The *Drosophila* genes *Chico* and *Inr* (*In*sulin *r*eceptor) encode an insulin protein and insulin receptor that are very similar to those found in nematodes and mammals. Mutations in *Chico* or *Inr* have the same physiological effects as described for the *Daf-2* gene in nematodes. The *Sugar baby* gene achieves a similar though muted effect on life span. This gene codes for a maltose permease, an enzyme that enhances the uptake of maltose into cells. Overexpression of this gene shifts the animal's physiology away from glucose utilization, thus mimicking the effects of caloric restriction. In this case, the increase in life span is about 20 percent, compared with the more than 80 percent increase observed in *Inr* mutants.

MOUSE

The most consistent way to extend the life span of a mammal is by caloric restriction. Such experiments (described in chapter 4) have extended the life spans of mice and rats by up to 50 percent. Moreover, these calorie-restricted animals show similar metabolic responses observed in yeast, nematodes, and fruit flies, including resistance to stress. In addition, calorie-restricted rodents show a postponement of age-related diseases, such as cancer, and have an increased lifetime metabolic capacity. These changes, like the hibernation response in nematodes and flies, are due to more efficient utilization of glucose and a shift toward deposit of fat and glycogen.

Three mouse genes have been identified that, when mutated, extend life span in a manner similar to caloric restriction. The gene *Prop-1* ("Prophet of *pit-1*") codes for a protein that regulates another gene, *Pit-1,* that codes for a pituitary-specific transcription factor. Mutation of *Prop-1* or *Pit-1* leads to developmental arrest of the pituitary gland, thus drastically reducing the normal levels of growth-inducing hormones such as growth hormone (GH) and thyroid hormone (TH). In the absence of these hormones, cells cannot utilize glucose or amino acids to promote growth and maturation. Consequently, *Prop-1* mutants are dwarfs, but they have an extended life span. This mutation mimics a calorie-restricted diet that begins in the womb.

Lab mouse *(Alix/Photo Researchers, Inc.)*

A second type of longevity gene has been identified in mice. This is the $P66^{shc}$ gene, which codes for a component of a signaling pathway that regulates the stress response and apoptosis. As with the other positive longevity genes already described, overexpression of this gene increases life span, while animals possessing a normally expressed $P66^{shc}$ have shorter life spans (see the table on page 66).

HUMAN

Identification of longevity genes in lower organisms has stimulated a search for similar genes in the human genome. The human homolog of yeast *Lag-1* has already been cloned and is located on chromosome 19. Although the sequence homology is low, it can replace the yeast gene where it performs a longevity function. Consequently, human *Lag-1* may be thought of as a human longevity gene, although much work is needed to confirm its function in humans.

MOUSE LONGEVITY GENES

GENE	KNOWN OR PROPOSED FUNCTION
Prop-1	The protein product is a regulator of a pituitary-specific transcription factor (Pit-1). Inactivation leads to poor development of the pituitary and production of pituitary hormones, particularly growth hormone. Mutated Prop-1 increases life span by about 50 percent.
Pit-1	This gene codes for Pit-1, a protein transcription factor. The inactivation of Pit-1 has the same effect as a Prop-1 mutation.
$P66^{shc}$	The protein product is a component of a signal transduction pathway that makes cells resistant to apoptosis and oxidative stress.

Note: Gene and protein naming conventions are explained in chapter 10.

Perhaps the most striking similarity between longevity genes in humans and lower organisms is the yeast *Sgs-1* gene and the human *Wrn* gene. The *Sgs-1* gene codes for a helicase, and when mutated, can accelerate the aging process. Werner's syndrome is a disease in humans that is also associated with accelerated aging. The gene responsible for this disease, called *Wrn* (for Werner's syndrome), has been identified. The protein product of the *Wrn* gene is a helicase, not the same helicase encoded by the *Sgs-1* gene, but a member of the same family, possessing a similar function. Mutations in these two genes provide dramatic evidence in support of the connection between life span and the maintenance of genetic stability.

SUMMARY

The search for longevity genes has identified four processes that influence life span. They are metabolic control, resistance to stress, gene disregulation, and genetic stability. Evidence supporting the involvement of metabolic control comes from the roles of *Lag-1* in yeast, *Daf-2* in nematodes, *Indy* and *Sod-1* in *Drosophila,* and *Prop-1* in mice. Resistance to stress is a function of several longevity genes, such as *Ras-2, Daf-12, Mth,* and *P66^{shc}*. Gene disregulation, as a mechanism of aging, has been clearly demonstrated in yeast with the isolation of three histone deacetylase genes, *Rpd-3, Hda-1,* and *Sir-2.* Finally, the relationship between genetic stability and life span is indicated by the effects of *Sgs-1* mutants in yeast and the human disease known as Werner's syndrome, which is associated with accelerated aging and is caused by the gene *Wrn,* a homolog of *Sgs-1.*

This collection of genes, small though it is, has given a powerful boost to aging research and provides an important conceptual framework that future research may follow. The goal is to isolate even more longevity genes from lower animals, and then to find their counterparts in the human genome. This work has already begun with the isolation of human *Lag-1.* The characterization of all longevity genes will improve our understanding of cellular senescence. Manipulation of these genes might also provide a way to reverse some of the effects of the aging process.

6

Age-Related Diseases

Growing old holds many pleasures, but for someone with Alzheimer's disease (AD), it can be a confusing and frightening experience. The image of an absentminded elderly man or woman has been with us for a long time. People today are in the habit of thinking that this is the natural consequence of growing old, but gerontologists have taught us to be cautious of this stereotype. Old people may be slower at certain tasks, but they are not necessarily senile or any more absentminded than a 20-year-old. Aging makes us more susceptible to certain diseases, but those diseases are not an inevitable consequence of growing old. Several other age-related diseases are described in this chapter, but there are none so devastating as Alzheimer's disease.

ALZHEIMER'S DISEASE

Alzheimer's disease (AD) is a neurological disorder affecting the central nervous system (CNS) that leads to a progressive loss of memory, language, and the ability to recognize friends and family. The average course of the disease, from early symptoms to complete loss of cognitive ability, is 10 years. Alois Alzheimer, a German neurologist, first described AD in 1907, and it has since become the fifth-leading cause of death among the elderly. The incidence of this disease increases with age and is twice as common in women as in men. The reason for this difference is unclear, but may be due to the sharp decline in the amount of estrogen that occurs during menopause. In 2009 more than 5 million men and women were living with AD in the United States alone, and this number is expected to increase to 16 million by 2050. Worldwide, there are more than 20 million recorded cases, but because poor medical facilities and diagnostic procedures in many parts of the world result in underreporting of the disease, the real number is likely to be much higher. In the United States, the annual cost of treating AD and other dementias is 148 billion dollars.

Understanding AD, and finding ways to treat it, has proved to be extremely challenging. It affects the brain, the most complex organ ever to evolve. Indeed, for most of the past 100 years scientists have thought that this disease would prove be too difficult to resolve. The brain, after all, consists of 100 billion neurons linked into a three-dimensional network consisting of 100 trillion connections. Nevertheless, over the past 10 years scientists have gained a much better understanding of AD and are now using their discoveries to develop therapies for this terrible disease. These discoveries are the subject of this chapter. AD therapies will be described more fully in chapter 9.

The Central Nervous System, which is affected by AD, consists of the brain and the spinal cord. The main part of the brain is called the cerebrum, which is the home of human intellect and the source of individual personality. It also processes and analyzes information from all the sensory nerves of the body. The cerebrum consists of two morphologically identical cerebral hemispheres, connected by a thick bundle of nerves called the corpus callosum. All of the nerve cell bodies are located in the outer layer of the cerebrum called the cerebral cortex. A special area of the cerebrum called the hippocampus is important for processing memories for long-term storage in other parts of the brain. The cerebellum regulates fine motor control over our muscles, making it possible for a person to learn how to play the piano, knit a sweater, and perform other activities that require intricate coordination. The brain stem is in control of our automatic functions, such as the rate at which the heart beats, the contraction of muscles of the digestive tract, and respiratory rate. It also controls our ability to sleep and to stay awake (see the figure on page 44).

AD begins in the basal cerebral cortex, quickly spreading to the hippocampus. During the early stages, known as preclinical AD, some damage occurs to the brain, but not enough to produce outward signs of the disease. Over a period of years, AD spreads to many areas of the cerebrum, but it does not affect the cerebellum or the brain stem.

The CNS is constructed of neurons, remarkable cells that are designed for communication. These cells have special structures, known as dendrites and axons, that receive and transmit signals. A signal in the form of an electrochemical jolt enters a neuron at its dendrites and is passed along to another neuron through the axon, a process that takes less than a microsecond. Neural circuits are constructed when axons make contact with the dendrites of other neurons. The connection between an axon and a dendrite is called a synapse. Circuits in the human brain consist of billions of neurons, each forming thousands of synaptic junctions with other neurons. These circuits give us our intellect, emotions, senses, and the ability to recognize our friends and loved ones.

Although neurons communicate through the synapse, they do not actually touch one another. Close inspection of a synapse shows a small gap separating the axon from the dendrite. A signal

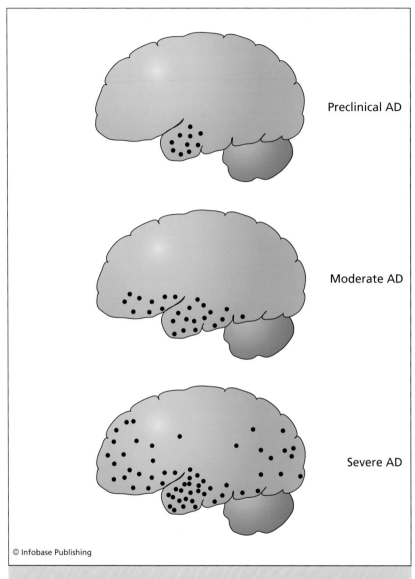

Preclinical AD

Moderate AD

Severe AD

© Infobase Publishing

Progression of AD. Alzheimer's disease (black circles) begins in the hippocampus, spreading over a period of years to affect several regions of the cerebrum.

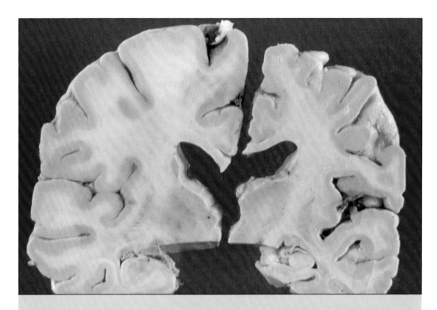

Alzheimer's disease. Sliced sections from two brains. On the left is a normal brain of a 70-year-old. On the right is the brain of a 70-year-old with Alzheimer's disease. The right brain is atrophied with a loss of cortex and white matter. Alzheimer's disease is not a normal part of aging. It is a dementing disorder that leads to the loss of mental and physical functions. The chance of developing this disease increases with age. *(Biophoto Associates/Photo Researchers, Inc.)*

is transmitted across the gap by the release of small proteins called neurotransmitters, which are stored at the axon terminus in Golgi vesicles. The vesicles travel to the axon terminus on a "railroad" constructed of microtubules. When a neuron receives a signal, the Golgi vesicles at the terminus are released from the microtubules and fuse with the axonal membrane, dumping their cargo into the synaptic gap. The neurotransmitters quickly diffuse across the gap and bind to receptors on the dendrite membrane, triggering an electrochemical impulse in the target neuron, thus completing transmission of the signal. This may seem like an awkward way for neurons to signal one another, but the synaptic gap and the use of

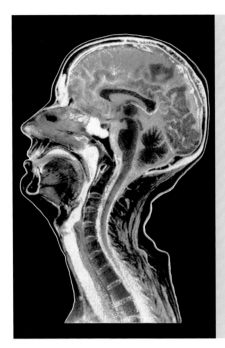

Colored magnetic resonance imaging (MRI) scan of a sagittal section through the brain of a 51-year-old male, showing cerebral atrophy. Atrophy of parts of the cerebrum of the brain occurs in various disorders, including stroke, Alzheimer's disease, and AIDS dementia. Here the area of the upper cerebrum affected by atrophy is colored dark red. Atrophy is shrinkage and wasting away of tissue. In stroke, brain cells die due to deprived blood supply to the brain; in Alzheimer's disease, the brain shrinks leading to senile dementia. *(Simon Fraser/Photo Researchers, Inc.)*

neurotransmitters are crucial for maintaining the strength of the signal over a network that consists of billions of cells.

Four genes have been identified as associated with the onset of AD. The first of these is *Tau*, which codes for a protein (Tau) needed for the construction of microtubules. The second gene, *APP*, codes for amyloid precursor protein, APP, a glycoprotein that is embedded in the cell membrane and may function as a cell-signaling receptor. The third gene, *Sen* (senilin, also known as presenilin and secretase), codes for a protease (an enzyme that can cut a protein into two or more pieces) that is involved in processing APP. The fourth gene, *ApoE*, codes for a protein called apolipoprotein E. Defects in any of these genes can lead to the death of neurons that is characteristic of AD.

The *Tau* gene and its product have a crucial role in the maintenance of neuronal signal transmission. The Tau protein is an important component of the microtubule railroad the Golgi vesicles

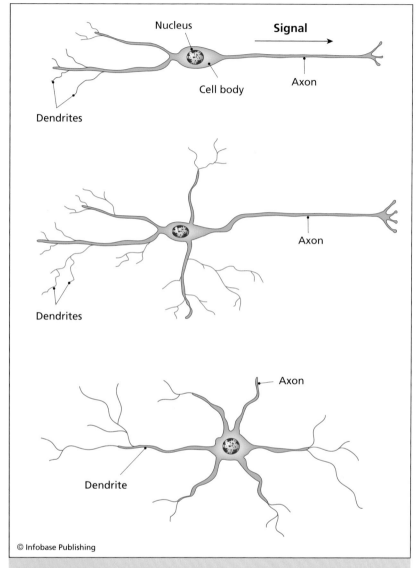

Nucleus

Signal

Cell body

Axon

Dendrites

Axon

Dendrites

Axon

Dendrite

© Infobase Publishing

A neuron receives signals at its dendrites and passes them on to other neurons through its axon. Simple bipolar neurons (top) have the dendrites and the axon at opposite ends of the cell. Multipolar neurons (middle and bottom) have a complex dendritic structure that often surrounds the cell body (bottom). In such cases, the identity of the axon is not always obvious.

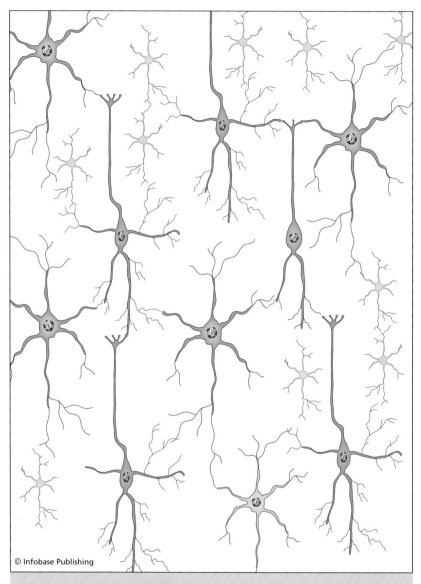

Neural circuits. These circuits are constructed with axon terminals making connections with the dendrites of other neurons. The connection between an axon and a dendrite is called a synapse. Circuits in the brain consist of billions of neurons, each forming thousands of synaptic junctions with other neurons. These circuits give humans intellect, emotions, ability to see the world, and much more.

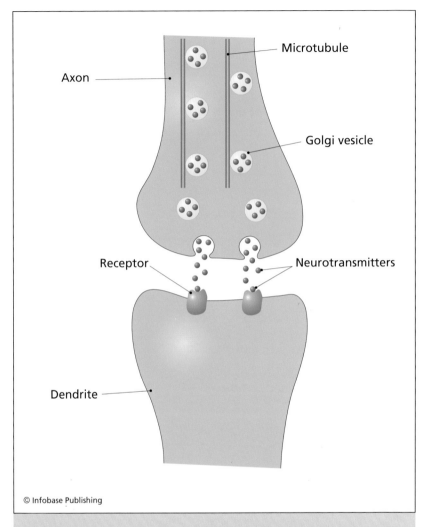

Microtubule

Axon

Golgi vesicle

Receptor

Neurotransmitters

Dendrite

© Infobase Publishing

Synaptic junction. Axons and dendrites do not touch each other but are separated by a small gap called the synapse or synaptic junction. A signal is transmitted by the release of small molecules called neurotransmitters that are stored at the axon terminus in Golgi vesicles. Binding of the neurotransmitter to the receptor on the dendrite membrane completes the transmission. The Golgi vesicles travel to the axon terminus on a transportation network constructed from microtubules.

use to reach the axon terminus. A mutation in this gene produces a defective protein, leading to the breakdown of microtubules and a virtual collapse of the cell's ability to pass on incoming signals. The abnormal Tau and the disintegrating microtubules collect within the cell as neurofibrillary tangles (NFTs). When a neuron loses its ability to communicate, it is as though it loses its will to live. This phenomenon has been observed in patients suffering from a damaged or severed spinal cord. Peripheral nerves starved for signals from the CNS degenerate and die. Similarly, neurons in the brain of an AD patient degenerate and die when signals stop coming in. In this case, however, the loss is more than the movement of an arm or a leg; it results in the destruction of the persona, the core of a person's being.

A second route to the development of AD involves the *APP* and *Sen* genes. Neurons, like all cells, are covered in a molecular forest called the glycocalyx. This forest consists of a wide variety of glycoproteins, resembling trees, that have many functions: Some are hormone or glucose receptors; others are involved in processing the electrochemical signals generated by neurotransmitters. An important member of a CNS neuron's glycocalyx is the APP protein, which is believed to be involved in hormonal signal transduction. APP is processed through the Golgi complex and planted on the cell surface by fusion of the Golgi vesicles with the cell membrane.

Neurons suffering from AD fail to process App properly. Scientists believe that senilin is activated as part of a normal signal transduction pathway. Activation of the pathway begins when a signaling molecule (as yet unidentified) binds to APP, which in turn activates senilin in order to produce a secondary messenger, truncated App (tAPP), as well as two other fragments: beta-amyloid and the glycosylated portion of the protein. According to this hypothesis, tAPP translocates into the nucleus, where it activates the appropriate gene or genes. AD develops when a mutation in *Sen* results in the production of a permanently activated senilin with a subsequent

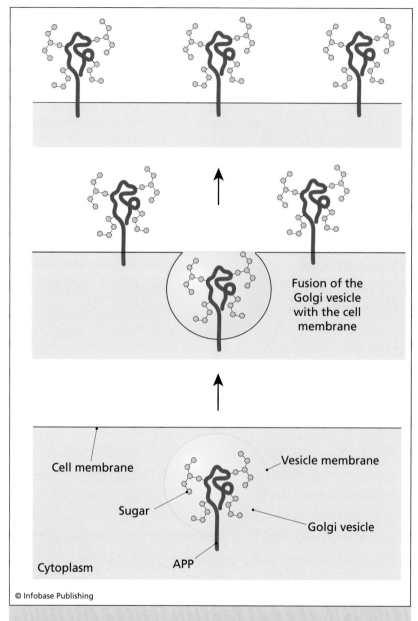

Cell membrane

Vesicle membrane

Sugar

Golgi vesicle

Cytoplasm

APP

Fusion of the Golgi vesicle with the cell membrane

© Infobase Publishing

Planting an APP forest. Amyloid precursor protein (APP) is a glyco-protein with a treelike structure that is an important member of the cell's glycocalyx. The "trunk" (brown) is protein, and the "leaves" are sugar molecules (blue). Vesicles from the cell's Golgi apparatus carry APP to the cell surface. Fusion of the vesicle membrane with the cell membrane automatically plants APP in the cell membrane.

buildup of tAPP and beta-amyloid. Scientists have long assumed that the accumulation of beta-amyloid plaques was toxic to neurons and was directly responsible for the extensive neuronal death that is typical of AD. In addition, the fourth AD gene, *ApoE,* was thought to code for a product that helped clear beta-amyloid from the brain. Loss of this function was the result of mutation being then responsible for excessive plaque formation. Some research suggests that neural damage is caused by an excess of tAPP, which somehow orchestrates the hyperphosphorylation of the Tau protein, leading to its disintegration and the destruction of the cell's railway.

The chronic and inappropriate destruction of APP by a mutated senilin poses an additional threat to the health of affected neurons. APP is a major component of a neuron's surface "forest." A normal glycocalyx is crucial for a cell's survival in more ways than one. The immune system uses the exact composition of the glycocalyx to distinguish self from nonself. Those cells that are a normal part of the body can be branded nonself, or invaders, if the glycocalyx is abnormal. If this happens, the immune system can order the affected cells to commit suicide, in a process known as apoptosis. Thus, whether the onset of AD is through a defective *Tau* or *Sen* gene, the final outcome—extensive neuronal death—is the same.

At present, there is no way to cure AD, although treatments are being developed to inhibit senilin and to reduce the accumulation of the beta-amyloid, which could be responsible for some of the neural damage. Other treatments being planned involve a combination of gene therapy and stem cell transplants to correct the mutated *Tau* and *Sen* genes and to replace the damaged or dying neuronal population. Experiments show that stem cells injected into damaged rat brains do differentiate into appropriate neurons; whether they make the correct connections, however, is yet to be determined. Given the delicacy of the central nervous system and the complexity of its circuits, it is likely that such therapies will be extremely difficult to develop. These therapies will be discussed in chapter 9.

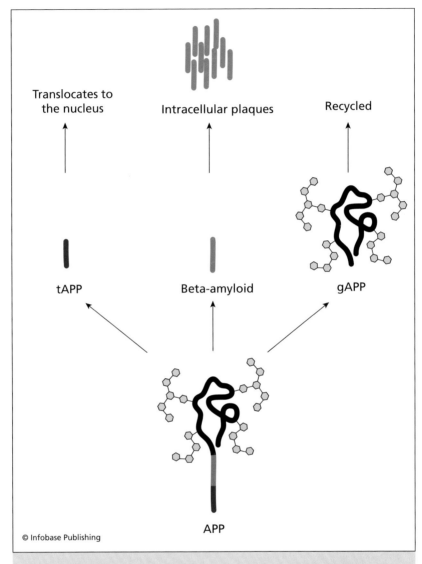

Production of beta-amyloid. In Alzheimer's disease, APP is cut in two places, producing three fragments by a protease called presenilin or secretase: truncated APP (tAPP), beta-amyloid, and glycosylated APP (gAPP). The fate of tAPP is unclear, although it may translocate to the nucleus, where it acts as a transcription factor. Beta-amyloid collects in the intracellular space, where it forms the plaques that are characteristic of AD. The gAPP is recycled and does not contribute to the clinical symptoms of the disease.

Researchers have long been frustrated by the lack of an effective diagnostic procedure validating new AD therapies. Drs. William Klunk and Chester Mathis, at the University of Pittsburgh, were

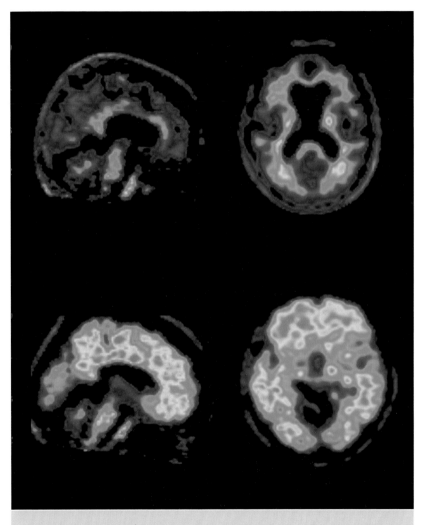

Imaging beta-amyloid. A PET scan of the brain of a healthy volunteer (top pair) and a patient with Alzheimer's disease (bottom pair). Amyloid plaques show up as red, indicating high uptake of florbetapir. *(Dr. Daniel Skovronsky; reproduced with permission of Avid Radiopharmaceuticals, Inc.)*

among the first to develop an effective AD diagnostic procedure. They began by testing various forms of a biological dye called thioflavin, which has a special affinity for beta-amyloid. They then found a way to attach the radioisotope carbon-11 to the molecule without reducing the dye's affinity for beta-amyloid while at the same time ensuring that the labeled dye could enter the brain. This labeled dye is now known as Pittsburgh compound B (PiB). After injecting PiB into a patient, the location of the dye is determined with positron emission tomography (PET). The intensity of the signal is proportional to the amount of beta-amyloid present. While accurate, this procedure is difficult to implement because of the very short half-life of carbon-11, which is only 20 minutes. Thus, PiB can only be used in a few hospitals that have the equipment to produce the dye onsite. Moreover, in many cases the PET scan can take up to 90 minutes to administer, which is nearly five times the half-life of the label.

Dr. Daniel Skovronsky and his team have improved on this procedure by using a dye labeled with fluorine-18, a radioisotope with a half-life of 110 minutes. This labeled dye, called florbetapir, has an affinity for beta-amyloid that is similar to that of PiB and is more convenient to use. Skovronsky's team has also gone to great lengths to validate the procedure by comparing the PET scan results with tissue sections obtained from the same patients after they have died. In most cases, the correspondence is good: Tissue sections testing positive for beta-amyloid were shown to have come from patients testing positive with the PET scan. In some cases, patients diagnosed with AD tested negative with the PET scan, and their tissue sections also tested negative, meaning the diagnosis had been wrong.

ARTHRITIS

Although the term literally means "joint inflammation," *arthritis* really refers to a group of more than 100 rheumatic diseases and

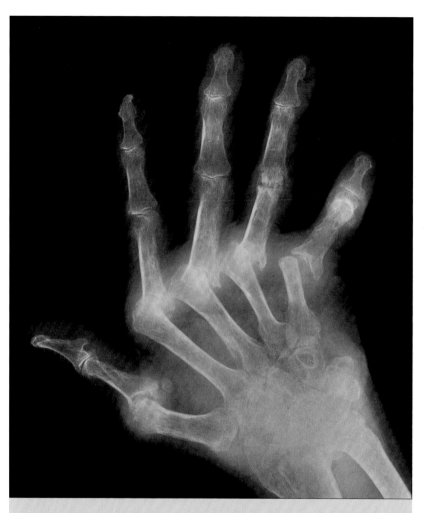

Arthritic hand. Colored X-ray of the deformed hand of a patient suf-fering from rheumatoid arthritis. The patient's fingers are abnormally bent because of damage to the joints (orange). Rheumatoid arthritis is an autoimmune disorder. It occurs when the body's immune sys-tem attacks joint tissue, commonly in the hands and feet. Affected joints become inflamed and painful, limiting movement. There is no cure for the disease, but anti-inflammatory drugs and immunosup-pressants may relieve the symptoms. Physiotherapy can help to keep the joints supple, and special tools may compensate for the lack of mobility. *(CNRI/Photo Researchers, Inc.)*

conditions that can cause pain, stiffness, and swelling in the joints. If left undiagnosed and untreated, arthritis can cause irreversible damage to the joints. There are two forms of this disease: osteoarthritis and rheumatoid arthritis.

Osteoarthritis, previously known as degenerative joint disease, results from the wear and tear of life. The pressure of gravity and extensive use causes physical damage to the joints and surrounding tissues, leading to pain, tenderness, and swelling. Initially, osteoarthritis is noninflammatory, and its onset is subtle and gradual, usually involving one or only a few joints. The joints most often affected are the knee, hip, and hand. Pain is the earliest symptom, usually made worse by repetitive use. Osteoarthritis affects 21 million people in the United States, and the risk of getting it increases with age. Other risk factors include joint trauma, obesity, and repetitive joint use; examples of the latter include pitcher's elbow and the hip joint difficulties that professional dancers develop as they grow old.

Rheumatoid arthritis is an autoimmune disease that occurs when the body's own immune system mistakenly attacks the synovium (thin tissue layer lining the joints). This chronic, potentially disabling disease causes pain, stiffness, swelling, and loss of function in the joints. The cause of this disease is unclear, but could involve a mutation that affects the glycocalyx of the synovium, leading to an immune attack. As described above, autoimmunity may also be responsible for the death of neurons in AD. Rheumatoid arthritis is much rarer than osteoarthritis, affecting about 2 million people in the United States. This disease affects women much more than men (the difference is twofold to threefold) and has led many scientists to suggest it is related to the decline of estrogen levels that occurs in women after menopause. Current treatment involves hormone supplements, but this can place the patient at high risk of developing breast or uterine cancer, as well as cardiovascular disease.

CANCER

Cancer is a genetic disease brought on by the inappropriate expression or mutation of one or more genes. Oncologists (scientists who study cancer) have identified two types of cancer genes: the oncogenes and the tumor suppressor genes (TSGs). Oncogenes code for proteins that stimulate cell growth and cell division, whereas tumor suppressor genes are involved in repairing and maintaining the genome. TSGs also code for proteins that monitor cell division to make sure that all chromosomes are duplicated and aligned properly before the cell divides. Overexpression of an oncogene can force a cell to proliferate (grow and divide), a common characteristic of cancer cells. A mutation in a TSG, which inactivates the gene product, can lead to cancer development because the cell loses the ability to repair its genome and to monitor the cell cycle.

Normal cells become cancerous through a process called transformation, leading to the uncontrolled growth of the cancer cells, which produces a tumor or neoplasm. As long as the tumor remains intact and the cells do not try to invade other parts of the body, the tumor is considered benign and can usually be treated by surgical removal. Tumors become dangerous and potentially deadly when some of the cells develop the ability to leave the main tumor mass and migrate to other parts of the body, where they form new tumors. When this happens, the cancer is malignant and will spread throughout the body by a process known as metastasis. Malignant cancers can be very difficult, if not impossible, to treat. The danger associated with all tumors is that they will switch from benign to malignant before being detected.

Cancers are classified according to the tissue and cell type from which they arise. Cancers that develop from epithelial cells are called carcinomas; those arising from connective tissue or muscles are called sarcomas; and those arising from blood-forming tissue, such as the bone marrow, are known as leukemias. More than 90 percent of all human cancers are carcinomas. Cancer names are derived from their cell type, the specific tissue being affected, and whether the tumor is benign or malignant. An adenoma, for example, is a benign tumor originating in the adenoid gland, or other glandular tissue, which consists of epithelial cells. A malignant tumor from the same source is called an adenocarcinoma. A chondroma is a benign tumor of cartilage, whereas a chondrosarcoma is a malignant cartilage tumor. Some cancer names can be real tongue twisters: A type of leukemia that affects blood-forming cells is called myelocytomatosis.

Cancers generally retain characteristics that reflect their origin. One type of skin cancer called basal-cell carcinoma is derived from keratinocytes and will continue to synthesize keratin, the protein of hair and nails. Another form of skin cancer called melanoma is derived from pigment cells and is associated with overproduction of the skin pigment melanin. It is for this reason that these tumors are usually very dark in color. Cancers of the pituitary gland, which produces growth hormone, can lead to production of excessive amounts of this hormone, the effects of which can be more damaging than the cancer itself.

When oncogenes and TSGs were discovered in the 1980s, many scientists believed that cures for all cancers were just around the corner. Their optimism was grounded in the assumption that these genes were the root cause of cancer. But after two decades of research, oncologists have failed to identify a particular set of oncogenes or TSGs that are typical of the most common forms of cancer. Moreover, the list of oncogenes and TSGs keeps increasing (currently, there are more than 100 known oncogenes and 15 TSGs). This could mean that each cancer is unique and that cellular transformation can occur through many different routes. Recent comparisons between normal human karyotypes and karyotypes from cancer cells suggest that the activation of an oncogene or the mutation of a TSG is the result of a prior event (or events) that corrupts the entire genome.

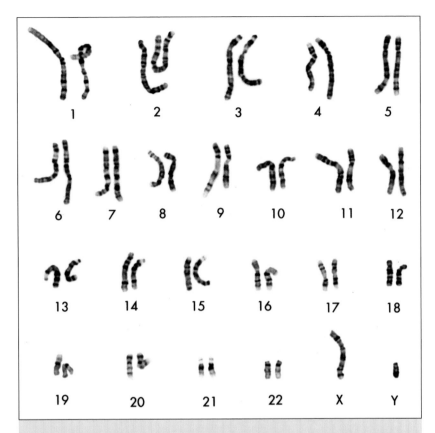

A normal human karyotype. A karyotype represents the full set of chromosomes arranged with respect to size, shape, and number. Human cells contain 23 pairs of chromosomes, 22 autosomes and a pair of sex chromosomes. The sex chromosomes are either "X" or "Y." Females have two "X" chromosomes, whereas males have an "X" and a "Y" chromosome. Karyotypes are used to diagnose genetic illnesses and are also used to characterize different forms of cancer. *(the author)*

Consequently, a typical cancer cell karyotype is radically altered, so much so that the interior of the nucleus sometimes looks shattered. Some of the chromosomes break apart into smaller fragments, some of which fuse with other chromosomes. The fusion process is usually associated with the destruction of genes on the host chromosome, thus amplifying the damage. In addition, whole chromosomes, often containing more than 1,000 genes, are sometimes lost or duplicated during cell division. These abnormalities, known as aneuploidy, alter the normal gene expression profile of the cell with disastrous consequences. The net effect is the destruction of the highly ordered filing system that is typical of a normal genome. Consequently, if the transcription machinery receives an order for a particular protein, it cannot fill the order simply because it is unable to find the gene among the rubble of what was once a functional genome. In the case of a duplication, as mentioned above, the transcription machinery might find the gene, but may end up delivering too much of the required protein, which can be enough to drive the cell even closer to transformation.

A classic example of chromosomal damage that can occur is the Philadelphia chromosome (so named because it was first identified in that city). This chromosomal abnormality involves the partial fragmentation of chromosomes 9 and 22, followed by an exchange or translocation of chromosome fragments between the long arms of each chromosome. This abnormality is associated with chronic myelogenous leukemia and can be found in the leukemic white blood cells of virtually every patient suffering from this form of cancer. The Philadelphia chromosome is but one of many chromosomal abnormalities that are characteristic of aneuploid nuclei.

Many oncologists now believe that aneuploidy is the root cause of all cancers. But what causes the aneuploidy? The fact that most cancers strike when an individual is 50 years of age or older suggests that the most likely cause is the aging process, with environmental toxins, mutagens, and carcinogens holding second place. This does not mean that everyone will develop cancer when they get older. In fact, except for smokers and people who work with known carcinogens, fewer than 30 percent of the population will ever develop

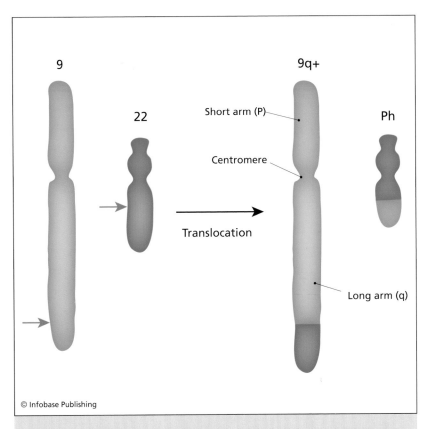

9

9q+

22

Short arm (P)

Centromere

Ph

Translocation

Long arm (q)

© Infobase Publishing

The Philadelphia chromosome (Ph) is produced by a translocation between the long arms of chromosomes 9 and 22. Red arrows mark the fragmentation points. The notation "9q+" indicates an addition to the long arm of chromosome 9. The chromosomes are aligned at the centromeres.

a cancer. This discrepancy may be due to the natural genetic variability within the human population. Everyone ages, but some of us seem to retain the ability to fight cancer well past our 50th year. In addition, there are some exceptions to the relationship between age and the occurrence of cancer. Lung cancer, brought on by cigarette smoke, and childhood leukemias are the most notable examples. The chemicals in cigarette smoke are known to accelerate cancer development, but the factors responsible for cancer acceleration in children are still unclear.

The age of the individual and the time element are important largely because the formation of a tumor is a multistep process that takes many years to complete. Over that time, the aging process weakens the individual's immune system and dramatically alters his or her physiology and endocrinology (hormonal changes) so that the system can no longer deal with aneuploid cells as they appear. Age-related hormonal changes include a shift in the ratio of estrogen to testosterone (ET ratio) in both men and women. Young women naturally have a high estrogen/testosterone ratio (a lot of estrogen, very little testosterone), whereas young men have a low estrogen/testosterone ratio (very little estrogen, a lot of testosterone). Estrogen levels drop dramatically in women after menopause, and men show a similar decline in the level of testosterone at a corresponding age. As a consequence, men and women approach a similar ET ratio throughout their sixth to ninth decades, a condition that is thought to influence the rate at which genetic instability occurs. In addition, many scientists believe the shift in the ET ratio is largely responsible for the weakening of the human immune system, leading to the increased occurrence not only of cancer but of many other diseases as well.

Six steps have been identified that must occur before a normal cell becomes a deadly cancer. At each step the cell acquires new abilities that push it closer to transformation. These abilities include the following: the loss of contact inhibition, or the tendency of cancer cells to keep growing even though neighboring cells are telling them to stop; the ability to divide in the absence of quality control, which tends to perpetuate chromosomal damage; the ability to stimulate angiogenesis (the growth of blood vessels) so that the tumor can receive oxygen and nutrients; the ability to ignore an order to commit suicide from immune system cells that have detected the cancer cell's abnormality; the acquisition of immortality; and finally, the ability to metastasize, to leave the original tumor

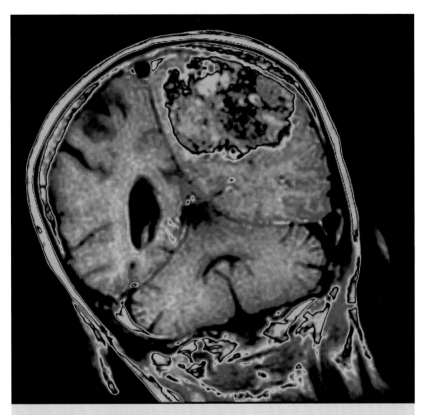

Brain tumor. Colored magnetic resonance imaging (MRI) scan of a coronal section through the brain of a 74-year-old woman, showing a large tumor. At upper center is the tumor (blue) within one cerebral hemisphere (orange) of the brain; the other cerebral hemisphere (at center left) is normal, containing a dark ventricle or cavity. The cerebellum of the brain is seen at lower center. Brain tumors may be primary tumors arising in the brain first, or they may be spread from cancer elsewhere in the body. A large tumor such as this may cause brain compression and nerve damage. *(Simon Fraser/RNC, Newcastle upon Tyne/Photo Researchers, Inc.)*

to colonize other parts of the body. On any given day, thousands of cells in the body acquire one or more of these abilities without causing a problem. Indeed, a cell could acquire the first five abilities without being deadly since the tumor would remain at the original site and could be removed surgically. But eventually, given enough time, one cell will acquire all of the abilities described above, and when it does, a new cancer is born.

CARDIOVASCULAR DISEASE (CVD)

The most common form of cardiovascular disease is called athero-sclerosis, a disease of the arteries that can strike at any age, although it is not a serious threat until our fifth or sixth decades. This disease is caused by an excess of low-density lipoprotein (LDL) in the blood, which leads to the buildup of fatty deposits (plaques) in the arteries. These deposits reduce the flexibility of the arteries, thus increasing blood pressure; they can also impede or block the flow of blood. The most common and deadliest form of atherosclerosis affects the coronary arteries, the vessels that carry blood to the heart. If coronary arteries become blocked or otherwise damaged, the cardiomyocytes (heart muscle cells) die from lack of oxygen. In serious cases, this can lead to a massive heart attack and death of the patient. In milder cases, damage to the heart is minimal, but coronary circulation is insufficient to allow the patient a normal lifestyle.

To fully appreciate the onset and complications of this disease, one needs to take a brief journey back in time, when life first appeared on earth 3.5 billion years ago. The connection between CVD and the origin of life may seem tenuous, but the events of those long-gone days have, in a sense, come back to haunt us. Life on Earth began when single cells appeared in the oceans, very close to shore where the concentration of dissolved nutrients was at its highest level. Among those nutrients was a fatty compound known as phospholipid. The first cells were microscopic phospholipid bubbles that contained a tiny drop of ocean water filled with nutrients and other useful molecules; they wrapped the phospholipid around themselves the way people wrap themselves in warm blankets or raincoats. Phospholipids not only protected the cells from the external world, but they made it possible for the cells to regulate their internal environment. As cells evolved,

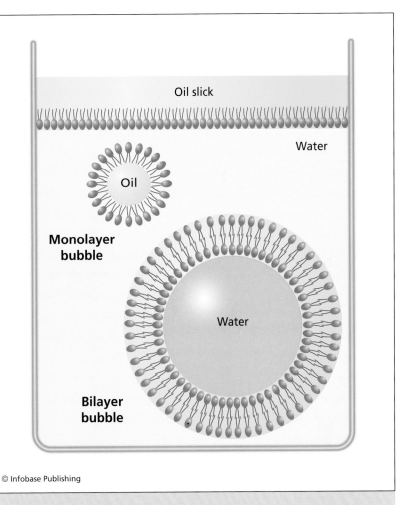

© Infobase Publishing

Phospholipid bubbles. Phospholipid molecules have a hydrophilic head-end (red ovals) and two hydrophobic tails that do not mix with water and will avoid being surrounded by it. In an oil slick, the hydrophobic tails mix with the oil, while the heads stay close to the water. In turbulence, phospholipids form two kinds of bubbles: a monolayer that can only capture a drop of oil and a bilayer that can capture a drop of water. The bilayer allows the hydrophobic tails to associate with themselves, while the heads associate with water on both the inside and outside surfaces of the bubble.

they improved the functional properties of their phospholipid "blanket" by adding cholesterol to it. The functional properties of phospholipids mixed with cholesterol are so important and so fundamental that to this day all cells are surrounded by a phospholipid membrane that contains cholesterol.

During the single-celled period of life on Earth, which spanned more than a billion years, the only downside to this arrangement was the necessity of finding, or synthesizing, enough phosphorous, lipid, and cholesterol for repairs, or to make new membranes when the cells divided. But then, about two billion years ago, multicellular creatures began to appear, and many of them, like birds and mammals, came to depend on an aqueous circulatory system to supply the various tissues and organs with nutrients. Since all of the cells in an animal's body require cholesterol and lipids (or fats) for their membranes, these materials had to be shipped to them by way of the circulatory system. Cholesterol and fats are not water soluble, so animals had to devise a special system in order to transport these compounds in the blood. The system they developed came in the form of two particles: LDL (mentioned above) and high-density lipoprotein (HDL), both of which can be transported in an aqueous environment.

In mammals, lipids and cholesterol are absorbed by the cells in the gut and sent to the liver as large lipoprotein complexes. The liver processes these complexes to produce LDL and HDL, which are then released into the blood. LDL is the main source of fats and cholesterol for all of the tissues in the body. This particle is essentially a monolayer phospholipid bubble containing cholesterol and fat (the two are linked together by a chemical bond). The vesicle is stabilized by apoprotein, which contains a recognition site for the LDL receptor. All cells have LDL receptors, located in special regions of the cell membrane known as coated-pits. The binding of LDL to the receptor activates endocytosis, a process by which the cell ingests and utilizes the LDL. HDL has a structure similar to that of LDL, but it is a smaller vesicle with a higher concentration of

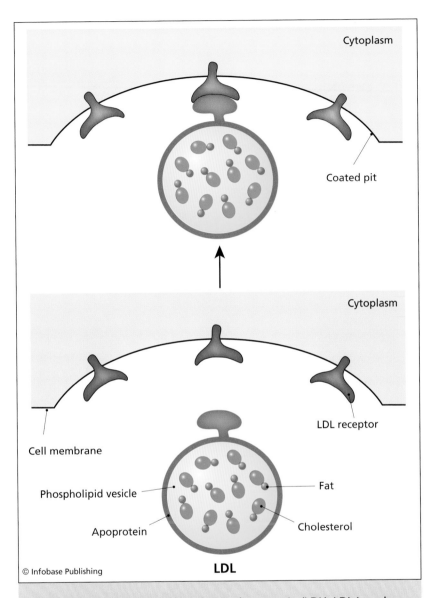

Structure and transport of low-density lipoprotein (LDL). LDL is a phospholipid vesicle (bubble) that transports cholesterol (combined with fat) from the liver to all the cells of the body. The vesicle is encased in apoprotein, which contains a recognition site for the LDL receptor. Binding of the apoprotein to the LDL receptor triggers the ingestion of the vesicle contents by a process known as receptor-mediated endocytosis.

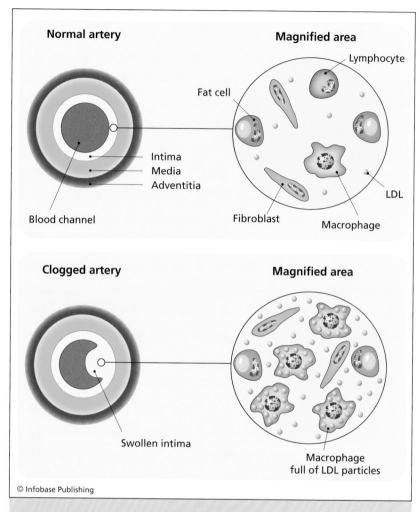

Normal and clogged coronary arteries. A normal coronary artery (shown in cross section) is a tri-layered tube consisting of the adventitia, media, and intima. The intima, covered in a thin layer of endothelium on the blood channel side, is a connective tissue consisting of fibroblasts, fat cells, and cells of the immune system (macrophages and lymphocytes). Excess LDL is taken up by the endothelium and collects in the intima. Oxidation of the LDL triggers an immune response that draws great numbers of macrophages and other immune cells into the area. Subsequent inflammation and faulty repair of the area leads to the formation of a swollen intima (plaque) that partially or completely blocks the artery.

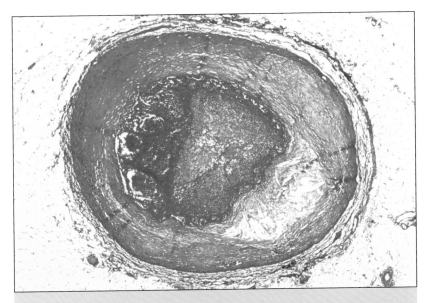

Degeneration of the arterial wall and narrowing of the lumen in the coronary artery. The artery is almost completely clogged in this image. *(Biophoto Associates/Photo Researchers, Inc.)*

fat and cholesterol. HDL's main job is that of a cholesterol regulator; it collects excess cholesterol, secreted by the cells, and transports it back to the liver.

This system worked well for humans until the advent of the modern lifestyle, characterized by high-fat diets and lack of exercise. When plasma levels of LDL are low (less than 60 mg per 100 ml of blood), all of the circulating LDL is taken up by cells and utilized. But when the plasma levels exceed 60 mg per ml, LDL tends to collect in the intima, or innermost lining of the coronary arteries. An unfortunate property of fats is that they tend to oxidize, or go rancid, just like butter left out on the counter for too long a time. The oxidation of the LDL fat is interpreted by the immune system as an attack by a foreign body.

White blood cells, macrophages in particular, converge on the coronary plaque and begin ingesting as much of the LDL as they can, so much so that under the microscope the interior of these cells look as though they are full of a yellow foam. In the meantime, other white blood cells such as T lymphocytes release a variety of signaling molecules to coordinate the immune attack. The immediate response of this attack is the initiation of inflammation: The plaque and surrounding tissue becomes hot, red, and swollen, just like a cut finger or any other wound on the skin or in the body. Cells located at the intima-media boundary respond to the inflammation by migrating up to the top of the plaque in a misguided attempt to "heal" the wound. This cap of cells isolates the plaque from the circulatory system, but it increases the overall size of the deposit, thus obstructing the artery even more. But the plaque rarely grows large enough to completely block the artery; pathologists have shown that of all the fatal heart attacks so far studied only 15 percent were caused by such a plaque. The remaining 85 percent were caused when the plaque ruptures, which leads to the formation of a large blood clot that completely blocks the artery.

Many treatments are available for cardiovascular disease, including surgical intervention, angioplasty, pharmaceuticals, diet, and exercise. The last three therapies are aimed at reducing plasma levels of LDL and promoting an increase in the amount of HDL. Plasma levels of LDL can be decreased with low-fat diets, regular exercise, and by not smoking cigarettes. Drugs, such as lovastatin, block the synthesis of cholesterol in the liver and have been used successfully to reduce plaque formation. Regular exercise and a glass of red wine a day are also known to increase plasma levels of HDL, which can reduce the rate of plaque formation substantially. But despite the success of these therapies, it is clear that while the onset of CVD is age-related it is mainly the result of lifestyle and not an inevitable consequence of age. A combination of adequate exercise and a healthy diet begun at an early age is the best treatment.

DIABETES

The appearance of life on Earth was made possible to a great extent by the presence of glucose in the oceans and the ability of the first cells to use this sugar as a source of energy. To this day glucose is central to energy metabolism in animals, plants, and microbes. In mammals defects in glucose metabolism and utilization are caused by a disease known as diabetes.

For microbes the process of acquiring glucose and extracting its energy is fairly straightforward. Each cell has receptors that import glucose from the environment, and biochemical pathways that break the sugar down to release the energy it contains. One of the pathways, consisting of a coordinated set of enzymes, is called glycolysis (meaning sugar splitting), and the other is called the Krebs cycle. These pathways convert the sugar's energy to ATP, which is used by all cells as an energy source.

Glucose metabolism is more complex in humans and other mammals. In mammals the uptake and utilization of glucose is coordinated by the endocrine system to ensure that the system as a whole has an adequate supply of energy. All cells in an animal's body have glucose receptors, but cells do not import glucose unless their receptors are bound to a hormone called insulin, which is produced by the pancreas, a large gland located just below the liver. The pancreas has two types of cells, called α (alpha) and β (beta). The α cells produce digestive enzymes that are secreted directly into the large intestine, and the β cells produce insulin. Glucose in the blood stimulates the β cells to make and release insulin; the amount of insulin released is directly proportional to the concentration of glucose in the blood.

One might wonder why the body bothers with such an indirect mechanism: Why not let each cell take up glucose whenever it can? The short answer to this question is that each cell would take up the glucose—a process that requires energy—whether it needed it or not. Dependence on insulin makes it possible for the endocrine system to regulate the uptake of glucose. For example, if the animal has a meal, but each cell already has plenty of ATP on hand, the endocrine system blocks the uptake of glucose everywhere but the liver, which is instructed to convert the glucose into glycogen, a molecule that serves as a storage depot.

Diabetes destroys the β cells' ability to manufacture insulin, leading to a buildup of glucose in the blood. A chronic elevation of blood glucose levels results in the inappropriate glycosylation (addition of sugar to proteins) of many proteins in the blood, including hemoglobin, the oxygen-carrying protein, as well as many other proteins associated with the cells and tissues. Systemwide protein glycosylation can lead to blindness, heart disease, kidney failure, and neurological disease. Diabetes is a major health problem in North America, where it affects more than 23 million people and causes approximately 500,000 deaths every year. Treatment is very expensive, amounting to about $170 billion annually.

There are two forms of this disease, known as type I and type II diabetes. Type I diabetes is an autoimmune disease, in which the white blood cells attack and destroy the β cells of the pancreas. This form of the disease is sometimes called juvenile diabetes because it occurs predominately in teenagers, although it can strike at any age. Type II diabetes affects older people, usually beginning when they are 50 to 60 years of age. In this case, the disease may be due to a genetic predisposition to short-lived β cells, or it may be due to beta cell burnout brought on by a lifelong preference for a diet that is heavy on sweets. This may account for the fact that more than 90 percent of those suffering from type II diabetes are overweight. At last count, 10 genetic loci were known to be associated with the onset of both types of diabetes.

OSTEOPOROSIS

Osteoporosis is a skeletal disorder characterized by weakened bone strength leading to an increased risk of fracture. Healthy bone structure depends on the following elements: mineral content, primarily calcium; the function of osteoblasts, the cells that produce the underlying bone matrix; and osteoclasts, cells that dissolve the bone matrix in preparation for bone remodeling. The steroid hormones estrogen and testosterone control the activity of these cells.

The age-related decline in the amount of these hormones increases the ratio of osteoclasts to osteoblasts and is believed to be the major cause of osteoporosis.

Although bone may seem like an inert material, it is in fact a living tissue like any other tissue or organ in the body. Osteoblasts, the bone-forming cells, are derived from fibroblasts, the principal cellular component of connective tissue. This tissue, consisting of a meshwork of collagen and elastin protein fibers, gives the body shape, holds organs together, and gives skin its elasticity and strength.

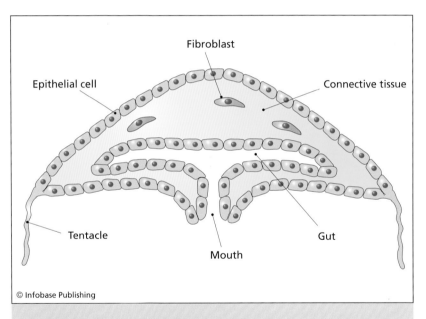

© Infobase Publishing

Connective tissue in a jellyfish. The importance of connective tissue is easy to see in a simple animal such as this. The shape of the creature is determined almost entirely by the jellylike connective tissue, which is produced and secreted by the fibroblasts. The internal organs, such as the gut and gonads (not shown), are embedded in the connective tissue. These properties of the connective tissue hold true for all animals, including humans. Note that the size of the epithelial cells, relative to the whole organism, is exaggerated for clarity.

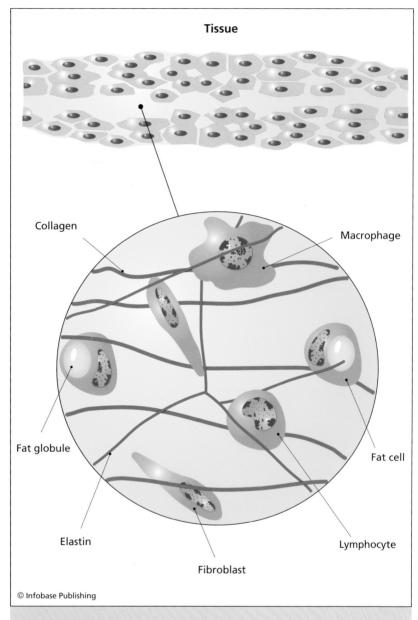

Tissue

Collagen

Macrophage

Fat globule

Fat cell

Elastin

Lymphocyte

Fibroblast

© Infobase Publishing

Connective tissue. All of the body's cells are embedded in connective tissue (colored yellow at the top in a sample of soft, loose tissue). A portion of the connective tissue is shown magnified at the bottom. This tissue consists of collagen fibers, elastin, and three principal cell types: fibroblasts, fat cells, and cells of the immune system (macrophages and lymphocytes).

Bone is nothing more than calcified connective tissue. Osteoblasts synthesize bone as a collection of calcified collagen rods, known as osteons, each of which consists of concentric rings. Blood vessels located in the Haversian canals at the center of each osteon supply the tissue with oxygen and nutrients. Every year, as one grows from an infant to an adult, new osteons are added and elongated. This process is so regular that barring traumas or starvation anthropologists have been able to estimate the age of an individual at the time of death by determining the number osteons in the bones.

The human skeleton is subjected to a great deal of stress and strain, which produces many hairline fractures and, in extreme cases, broken bones. Consequently, our bones are in a constant

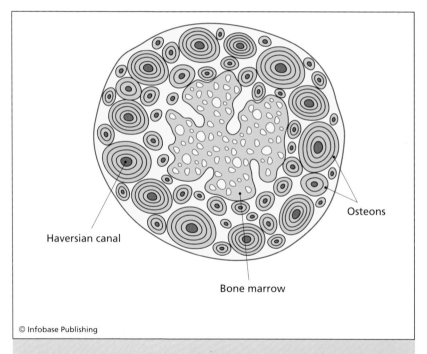

Osteons

Haversian canal

Bone marrow

© Infobase Publishing

Bone structure. Compact or dense bone is constructed from long tubular structures called osteons that are built up in concentric rings. The center of each osteon, called the Haversian canal, contains blood vessels that supply the bone with oxygen and nourishment. The central portion of the bone is porous and is called trabecular bone or, more commonly, bone marrow.

state of repair and remodeling. In the absence of fractures or broken bones, remodeling can strengthen specific areas of the skeleton that are subjected to repetitive stress. Estimates of bone replacement in humans range from 10 percent to nearly 20 percent per year, or a complete renewal of the skeleton every five to 10 years. Repair and remodeling are carried out in sequence by the osteoblasts and the osteoclasts. Osteoblasts regulate the process by releasing two growth factors at the appropriate time: macrophage-colony stimulating factor to stimulate the production of osteoclasts, and osteoprotegerin to inhibit osteoclast production. Osteoblasts are large cells with a variable shape that ranges from cuboidal to pyramidal. They have a large nucleus with a single prominent nucleolus and a very extensive endoplasmic reticulum. Osteoclasts are giant cells, about 50 micrometers in diameter, with a remarkable anatomy. These cells have several nuclei, a cytoplasm that is stuffed with organelles, and a cell membrane that is highly ruffled over half of the cell's surface. The ruffled membrane is brought into contact with the bone, where it secretes acids and hydrolases to dissolve away the bone matrix, after which the cavity is repaired by the osteoblasts. The complete repair cycle takes about 100 days. Osteoclasts function very much like macrophages, phagocytic cells of the immune system, which remove dead or dying cells as well as invading microbes from the tissues. Indeed, osteoclasts and macrophages are both derived from monocytes, a type of stem cell that gives rise to many cells of the immune system.

Bone mineral density (BMD) is a common criterion used to evaluate the onset of osteoporosis, which affects more than 20 million people in North America alone. BMD is usually determined with a special, dual-energy X-ray machine. Women are four times more likely to develop this disease than men. One out of every two women and one in eight men over 50 will have an osteoporosis-related fracture in her or his lifetime. Osteoporosis is caused primarily by hormonal changes that affect women and men as they

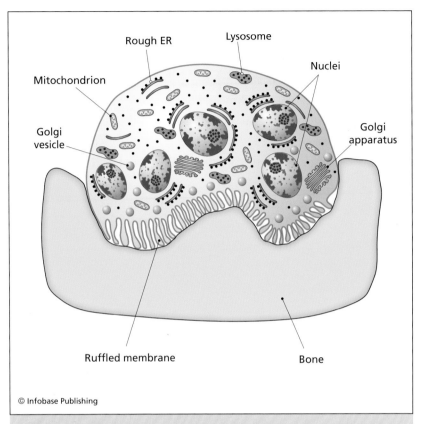

Osteoclast. The repair and remodeling of bone begins when osteoclasts dissolve away an area of bone by secreting acids and hydrolases, all along their ruffled membrane. Osteoclasts can bore deep into the bone, often forming long tunnels. Once the bone has been removed, osteoblasts move in to repair the area by secreting a new bone matrix.

approach their sixth decade. For women this involves a dramatic drop in estrogen levels at menopause, and for men a reduction in the levels of testosterone at a comparable age.

Osteoporosis is responsible for more than 1.5 million fractures annually, including 300,000 hip fractures, approximately 700,000 vertebral (spinal) fractures, 250,000 wrist fractures, and more than

300,000 fractures at other sites. In the presence of osteoporosis, fractures can occur from normal lifting and bending, as well as from falls. Osteoporotic fractures, particularly vertebral fractures, are usually associated with crippling pain. Hip fractures are by far the most serious and certainly the most debilitating. One in five patients dies one year following an osteoporotic hip fracture. Fifty percent of those people experiencing a hip fracture will be unable to walk without assistance, and about 30 percent will require long-term care.

Current treatments involve calcium and vitamin D supplements (at about 400 to 1,000 IU per day for vitamin D). The preferred calcium source is milk, cheese, or yogurt. Hormone replacement therapy, involving estrogen for women and testosterone for men, has proven to be very effective. Estrogen promotes bone growth by increasing the life span of osteoblasts. It also stimulates osteoblast production of osteoprotegrin (to inhibit osteoclast production) while weakening and killing osteoclasts directly. The effective estrogen dose was once believed to be low enough that cancer induction was not a serious concern, but a major study completed by the National Institutes of Health (NIH) indicated that this may not be so: Estrogen therapy does increase the risk of cancer development. As an alternative, scientists have synthesized a modified estrogen, called estren, which promotes bone growth in mice without simulating cellular growth in ovaries and testes. If these results are confirmed in human clinical trials, it will be possible to treat and prevent osteoporosis in men and women with a single hormone and without fear of cancer induction. Other promising therapies involve a family of drugs known as bisphosphonates (or diphosphonates) and parathyroid hormone.

Bisphosphonates are simple carbon compounds containing two phosphate groups and two variable groups attached to a single carbon atom. These drugs, the best studied of which are risedronate (Actonel) and alendronate (Fosamax), are taken up selectively by the osteoclasts for which they are toxic compounds. As a consequence, the ratio of osteoblasts to osteoclasts increases, and bone remodeling shifts toward bone building. Fosamax increases bone density by 10 percent during the first year and reduces the frequency of fractures by nearly 50 percent during the first three years of treatment. These numbers suggest that bisphosphonates are as effective as estrogen, but the long-term safety (beyond 10 years) of these drugs has not been determined.

Parathyroid hormone (PTH) is a small protein, or peptide, containing 800 amino acids that is normally involved in stimulating the release of calcium from bones and other calcium stores within the body. Thus, it was a surprise when scientists discovered that daily injections of a small amount of this hormone could increase bone density by 10 percent after one year with a 60 percent reduction in the risk of fractures. PTH seems to exert its effect by stimulating the release of insulinlike growth factor-1 (IGF-1) from the liver. IGF-1, in turn, exerts its effect by stimulating the production of osteoblasts. PTH was approved for general use by the U.S. Food and Drug Administration (FDA) in 2002 under the brand name Forteo. The long-term safety of this drug is yet to be determined. In male and female rats, the drug is known to cause osteosarcoma (malignant bone cancer), but currently the incidence of this cancer in patients taking Forteo is unknown.

In addition to drug therapies, regular exercise is recommended as a way to prevent the onset of this disease or to minimize its effects once it has started. A sedentary lifestyle has a devastating effect on bone mass since the induction of osteoblasts (bone-forming cells) is known to be dependent on physical activity. Consequently, a lifelong habit of avoiding exercise is known to be a major risk factor in the onset of osteoporosis.

7

Geriatrics

Geriatrics is a branch of the biomedical sciences devoted to helping the elderly (over 65 years old) deal with the effects of age. The geriatric approach does not try to reverse the aging process but rather to minimize its consequences by reducing or inhibiting the progression to disability. This effort, conducted in hospitals, clinics, and nursing homes, is based on a broad range of therapies that are grounded in the biological, psychological, and social sciences.

Treating and caring for the elderly is a complex endeavor. Because of their age, older people are usually suffering from several simultaneous disorders that cannot be treated with the drugs or therapies that are routine for younger individuals. Drug therapies assume a clearance time (physiological deactivation of the drug) provided by a healthy liver, which may not be found in an older patient. For example, drugs that are safely used to treat depression or cardiovascular disease in young patients can have devastating effects on the elderly. In addition, accurate medical histories are often difficult to obtain from elderly patients, either because of poor memory, or because of psychological compensation by which the patient ignores and minimizes danger signs and symptoms. Growing old is a time of loss: An elderly patient may have lost her husband, friends, physical abilities, and her family home may have been given up for a room in a nursing home or hospital ward. All of these elements complicate the diagnosis and the prognosis for a geriatrics patient.

The focus of this chapter is clinical geriatrics, which covers the many problems associated with the care and treatment of the elderly. The discussion begins with the demographics of North American society with respect to age distributions, epidemiology, and the capacity of health-care providers to deal with the ever-expanding geriatrics population.

OUR AGING SOCIETY

Between 1900 and 1990 the total U.S. population increased three-fold, while the number of elderly people increased tenfold. In 1990 more than 35 million Americans were over the age of 65, nearly twice as many as in 1960. This number reached 38 million in 2007 (10 percent of the population) and is expected to increase further to 88 million by 2050 (20 percent of the population). There are currently more than 5 million people who are among the very old (85 or older) and 96,548 centenarians (100 years or older), a number that is expected to increase to 600,000 by 2050. Women tend to live longer than men, so that among the very old, for every 100 woman there are only 41 men. Before the age of 85, the elderly usually live with relatives or a spouse, but after 85, 18 percent of men and 28 percent of women live in nursing homes or hospital wards.

Per capita costs for acute and long-term (chronic) health-care services are highest for the very old, so the growth of this group will have a profound affect on health-care costs. People over 65 currently represent just more than one in three of the patients seen by a primary care physician, and over the next 20 years this ratio is expected to increase to one in two. While the costs of caring for the elderly is expected to rise, this is due not just to the patient's age, but also to a general increase in the complexity and expense of diagnostic procedures and equipment. It is expected that as the proportion of older to younger people increases, less financial and social support will be available for the elderly. Medicare and Medicaid cover much of the financial burden of caring for the elderly in the United States. But even with these public services, the elderly still bear a considerable share of the expenses. Currently, geriatrics patients can expect to pay as much as 25 percent of their income for medical care.

EVALUATING THE GERIATRIC PATIENT

Evaluation of a geriatrics patient is much different from that of a younger individual. Young patients generally have a single complaint that the physician can focus on, and there is usually no reference to the patient's socioeconomic environment. But the approach to a geriatrics patient usually begins with the physician asking the patient to describe a typical day in his or her life. In this way the physician can best assess the elderly person's overall quality of life, liveliness of thought, and physical independence. This approach also helps develop a good patient-physician rapport, something that is especially important to elderly patients, who often take longer to answer questions, and may be shy because of it. In the initial interview, geriatricians are especially careful not to infantilize the patient by asking an attending relative questions pertaining to the patient's history or medical status. It is for this reason that geriatrics patients, unless suffering from dementia, are interviewed alone. During the initial evaluation and interview, the physician attempts to gather information about the patient's medical, drug, nutrition, and psychiatric histories.

Medical History

With an elderly patient the medical history may extend back to a time when society's disease profile was different than it is today. For example, rheumatic fever and tuberculosis were much more common in the mid 1900s than they are today. Consequently, the physician will ask about diseases that were common when the patient was young. The patient will also be asked about outdated treatments, such as mercury for syphilis or pneumothorax therapy for tuberculosis. Elderly people tend to underreport symptoms out of denial or a fear of illness, disability, and the dependence these conditions may bring. Aging can also alter the individual's response to certain diseases, such as a painless myocardial infarction or pneumonia without a cough.

Drug History

Although the physician will ask the patient, and the patient's relatives, about prescription drugs, some geriatricians have suggested that the best approach is the "brown bag" technique, whereby the patient is asked to empty his or her medicine cabinet into a brown paper bag and then to bring it to the evaluation interview. Often the complaints of older patients are traced to a drug or combination of drugs they have been taking. The drug history includes determining which drugs are used, at what dose, how often they are taken, who prescribed them, and for what reason. Topical drugs are included, such as eye drops for treating glaucoma, because there is the possibility that systemic absorption may cause unexpected side effects in the elderly. Over-the-counter drugs must be included because their overuse can have serious consequences, such as constipation from laxative use or salicylism from aspirin use. Patients are also asked to demonstrate their ability to read the labels (often printed in very small type) and to open the container, which may contain a child-resistant lid. Because older patients are often treated with multiple medications, they are at risk of noncompliance and adverse effects.

Nutrition History

The physician tries to determine the type, quantity, and frequency of food eaten, including the number of hot meals per week. Special diets, self-prescribed fad diets, alcohol consumption, over-the-counter vitamins, and dietary fiber are also determined. For the elderly, it is very important to determine the amount of money the patient has to spend on food each week, and whether suitable cooking facilities are available. The patient's ability to eat is assessed by examining the mouth and the condition of the teeth or dentures, if fitted. Poor vision, arthritis, immobility, or tremors may affect an old person's ability to prepare food. A patient who suffers from urinary incontinence may reduce fluid intake, which could also lead to poor food intake.

MANAGING AGE-RELATED DISORDERS

The most common disorders of the elderly are dementia, cardiovascular disease, osteoporosis, and incontinence. It is not unusual for elderly patients to suffer from all of these disorders simultaneously.

Dementia

Nearly half of all elderly patients suffer from various degrees of dementia. Two-thirds are caused by Alzheimer's disease (AD) and are currently irreversible. Reversible dementias are caused by strokes, neoplasms, or toxins such as alcohol, or those produced by infections. Although a complete cure for most dementias is not possible, optimal management can improve the ability of these patients to cope with basic tasks. In many cases, dementia is the result of one or more small strokes caused by hypertension. Thus the first step in managing dementia is aggressive treatment for high blood pressure. This is followed with pharmacological agents that enhance cognition and function, and treat associated problems, such as depression, paranoia, delusions, agitation, and even psychoses.

Where AD is suspected, the patient may be treated with cholinesterase inhibitors to maximize the half-life of brain neurotransmitters. There are three such drugs available: donepezil, rivastigmine, and galantamine. Clinical trials have shown that these drugs can improve cognitive function. But side effects, including nausea, vomiting, and diarrhea can lead to serious complications. Other drugs, such as estrogen (for women), vitamin E, ginkgo biloba, and nonsteroidal anti-inflammatory agents, are also used but their effectiveness is in doubt. While these agents may be ineffective as a treatment for advanced dementia, they may be useful in treating milder cases.

Cardiovascular Disease

Cardiac output and the response of the heart to exercise decreases with age. Ventricular contractions become weaker with each decade, a problem that is compounded by the age-related reduction in blood vessel elasticity. Hardening of the arteries is the prime cause of hypertension in the elderly, but it is not an unavoidable consequence of aging. The first stage in managing hypertension and cardiovascular disease is a change in lifestyle. Clinical trials have shown that even the very old can benefit by this approach, which involves maintaining an ideal body weight, no smoking, regular aerobic exercises, and a diet consisting of fruits, vegetables, and low-fat dairy products (all of which are rich in essential potassium, calcium, and magnesium). If these procedures fail to reduce blood pressure, drugs such as thiazide, beta-blockers, or calcium channel blockers may be used, but the diet and exercise regimen should be maintained.

Osteoporosis

Diminished bone mass can be determined most conveniently with special X-ray machines (dual energy X-ray absorptiometry) or with ultrasound densitometry. Both procedures determine the density as g/cm^2, which is compared to normal values from a younger population and is used to estimate the likelihood of fracture. The first attempts to manage this disease involve a diet rich in calcium and vitamin D, along with regular weight-bearing exercises. Hormone replacement therapy has also been recommended, for men and women, but as discussed in a previous chapter, this approach can lead to dangerous side effects. An alternative drug therapy involves the use of bisphosphonates, antiresorptive drugs that are known to increase bone mass. The bisphosphonate, alendronate, was shown to decrease the incidence of vertebral and nonvertebral fractures by more than 50 percent in postmenopausal women. The major side effects are gastrointestinal, and the drug must be taken on an empty stomach in an upright position.

Incontinence

Incontinence, or the involuntary loss of urine or stool, is very common in the geriatric population. About 33 percent of elderly women and 20 percent of elderly men suffer from this disorder. The prevalence may be as high as 80 percent in nursing homes or long-term care institutions. Incontinence may develop because of neurological damage sustained after a stroke, or it may be traced to age-related changes in the urinary system, in particular, the integrity of the urethra, and the holding volume of the bladder, which decreases with age. Delirium and the stress of being exposed to a new environment, such as recent admission to hospital or nursing home, can also lead to incontinence in the elderly. Simply modifying the patient's fluid intake and eliminating diuretics such as coffee or tea can often treat transient incontinence.

Persistent or acute incontinence is managed initially by ensuring the patient can reach a toilet quickly. It may also be necessary to provide the patient with incontinence undergarments and pads. Often with special care and training the problem can be resolved. In other cases it may be necessary to resort to drug therapy. A commonly used drug is a bladder relaxant, tolterodine, which is available in long-acting preparations. In severe cases surgery may be required to repair damaged sphincters that normally regulated urine flow through the urethra. It may also be necessary to fit the patient with a catheter that continually drains the bladder into a plastic bag. Chronic indwelling catherization is not advised, however, as it is associated with a high risk of developing urinary system infections.

DRUG THERAPY

Geriatric patients are often prescribed a large number of drugs to deal with the many disorders they suffer from. In many cases, there are effective nonpharmacological therapies available that should be attempted before resorting to drugs. All geriatric patients need a careful and thorough review of the drugs they are prescribed to ensure they are necessary and that there is no change of potentially dangerous drug interactions. Effective drug therapy is often hampered by faulty diagnosis. Older patients may underreport symptoms, or their complaints may be vague and multiple. In addition, symptoms of physical diseases may overlap with psychological illness. Consequently, making the correct diagnosis and prescribing the appropriate drugs is a very difficult task in geriatric medicine. Finally, the aging process alters the elderly patient's ability to deal with drugs physiologically. This deficit occurs primarily at the liver and at the kidneys.

The liver contains about 30 enzymes that are involved in the degradation of a wide variety of compounds that are consumed in an average diet. These enzymes can also handle more exotic compounds such as alcohol or pharmaceutical drugs. Age-related, or even alcohol-induced, deterioration of these enzymes make a safe drug dangerous when given to a geriatrics patient. Potentially fatal ventricular arrthymias have been caused by certain antihistamines when given to older patients with defective liver enzymes. The situation, however, is too complex for a physician to assume that an elderly patient with normal liver function tests will be able to metabolize a given drug as efficiently as a younger patient.

The kidneys also play an important role in ridding the body of foreign or unwanted chemicals and drugs. Drugs given to older patients are cleared more slowly by the kidneys and thus have a tendency to accumulate to high, possibly toxic, levels over the time-course of treatment. Thus drugs that have not been specifically tested for use on older subjects must be used with extreme caution. Medical servicing centers and pharmaceutical companies have developed computer algorithms and databases to help evaluate drug usage and to detect possibly dangerous drug combinations that are prescribed for geriatrics patients.

NURSING HOMES

The poor quality of care provided in nursing homes has been known for decades. There has been some improvement since the Institute of Medicine (IOM) released a critical report in 2000, but a recent report by congressional investigators shows that serious problems still exist. Quality of care is still generally poor in U.S. nursing homes. Chronic problems concerning residents' pain, pressure sores, malnutrition, and urinary incontinence have not been resolved.

Nursing homes are intended as places where the elderly can be cared for in their final years by a team of medical professionals who specialize in geriatric medicine. In many cases, however, logistic and economic restraints make this a very difficult goal to realize. Physician involvement in nursing home care is often limited to telephone conversations with the nursing staff. Restrictive Medicare and Medicaid reimbursement policies do not encourage physicians to make more than the required monthly or 60-day visits. Physician involvement in such essential services as attendance at the medical team conferences, family meetings, and counseling residents and surrogate decision makers on treatment plans in the event of terminal illness are usually not reimbursable at all. In addition, most nursing homes lack expensive diagnostic equipment, and thus many of the residents are sent to hospital emergency rooms, where they are evaluated by staff who lack training and interest in the care of frail elderly patients.

Despite these many problems, the effectiveness of nursing homes can be improved with more attention paid to the documentation of the resident's illness and treatment history, as well as the introduction of nurse practitioners and physician assistants. These medical practitioners could be very helpful in implementing some of the screening and monitoring that is needed to ensure proper care of the residents, and to this extent would function as an independent patient advocate. They could also have an important role in communicating with the staff, residents, and families when the physician is not in the facility.

The problems facing nursing homes over the next 40 years are tremendous. In a recent report the IOM noted the urgent need for research and data collection to obtain a better understanding and description of the various long-term-care arrangements throughout the country, including their size, the services provided and staffing levels and training, the characteristics of those receiving care, and the staffing and quality of care provided in the different settings and services. They also called for increased funding, concluding that "the amounts and ways we pay for long-term care are probably inadequate to support a workforce sufficient in numbers, skills, stability, and commitment to provide adequate clinical and personal services for the increasingly frail or complex populations using long-term care."

ETHICAL ISSUES

The basic ethical principles governing the care of the elderly were established in the 1970s in response to allegations that human subjects in biomedical clinical trials were poorly treated. Principles of respect for persons, beneficence, and informed consent apply equally well to elderly patients in a nursing home, or hospital ward, as they do to human subjects involved in clinical trials.

Respect for Persons

Respect for persons, in the context of clinical trials, demands that subjects enter into research voluntarily and with adequate information. This assumes the individuals are autonomous agents, that is, are competent to make up their own minds. There are, however, many instances of potential research subjects not really being autonomous: prisoners, patients in a mental institution, children, the elderly, and the infirm. All of these people require special protection to ensure they are not being coerced or fooled into volunteering as research subjects. Geriatrics patients are especially vulnerable because of their many medical disorders, which often affect their ability to understand what is being done to them.

Beneficence

It is not enough to respect a potential subject's decisions and to protect them from harm, but in addition it is necessary to do all that is possible to ensure their well-being. Beneficence is generally regarded as acts of kindness or charity, but in the case of geriatrics patients, weakened by illness and age, it is an obligation. In this sense, it is the natural extension of the Hippocratic oath that all physicians are expected to adhere to: *I will give no deadly medicine to anyone if asked, nor suggest any such counsel.* In other words, do no harm, and for those involved in biomedical research, never injure one person to benefit another. This is particularly relevant to prescribing drugs for the elderly, who are especially sensitive to this type of therapy.

Informed Consent

All participants in clinical trials must provide informed consent in writing. Moreover, steps must be taken to ensure the consent is, in fact, informed. This might involve an independent assessment of the individual's ability to understand the language on the consent form and any instructions or explanations the investigators have given. Geriatrics patients, many of whom suffer from dementia, cannot be expected to give informed consent under many circumstances. Consequently, it is necessary to proceed with extreme caution in such cases and to ensure that an action taken, such as moving an elderly person out of his or her home and into an institution, is really in their best interest and not simply a convenience.

8

Rejuvenation

The treatment of the aging process and of the diseases associated with it could lead to the rejuvenation of the body, life-extension, and immortality. Such an endeavor, however, would be extremely difficult, and the mere suggestion of it is highly controversial. Many scientists believe there is no such thing as a treatment that will reverse the aging process. Indeed, a coalition of 51 gerontologists and biologists, led by S. Jay Olshansky, took an unprecedented step of publishing a paper titled "No Truth to the Fountain of Youth," which was sharply critical of antiaging medicines and the companies that market them. The following is an excerpt from their position statement:

> There has been a resurgence and proliferation of health care providers and entrepreneurs who are promoting antiaging products and lifestyle changes that they claim will slow,

stop or reverse the processes of aging. Even though in most cases there is little or no scientific basis for these claims, the public is spending vast sums of money on these products and lifestyle changes, some of which may be harmful. Scientists are unwittingly contributing to the proliferation of these pseudoscientific antiaging products by failing to participate in the public dialogue about the genuine science of aging research. The purpose of this document is to warn the public against the use of ineffective and potentially harmful antiaging interventions.

Although there is some truth in this statement, the tone is such that it could discourage other scientists and the general public from seeking an authentic rejuvenation therapy. This debate continues to the present day and is currently focused not only on "entrepreneurs who are promoting antiaging products" but also on a critique of the British gerontologist Dr. Aubrey de Grey, who has chastised the biogerontology community for being too conservative in their approach to rejuvenation. De Grey has proposed what he calls "strategies for engineered negligible senescence" or SENS, which involves an aggressive battery of preventative and therapeutic treatments. Robert Butler, S. Jay Olshansky, George Martin, and other prominent members of the biogerontology community have dismissed the SENS protocol as mere science fantasy, and in a published statement they have declared that they "wish to dissociate ourselves from the cadre of those impressed by de Grey's ideas in their present state."

Many scientists who have entered the field of gerontology have done so with the stated intention of finding cures for age-related diseases, but not therapies to reverse the aging process. These scientists often shy away from any talk of rejuvenation for fear of being ridiculed by their colleagues. When Orville and Wilbur Wright were working secretly on their motorized kite at Kitty Hawk, North Carolina, most scientists thought the attempt to build a flying machine was pure folly and a complete waste of time. In the 1980s many scientists were equally contemptuous of any attempt to clone a mammal. Indeed, in 1984 James McGrath and Davor Solter, two leaders in the field of animal cloning, published an article in the journal *Science,* which claimed that cloning a mammal was biologically impossible. Just 12 years later, Ian Wilmut and his team proved them wrong.

This chapter will explore the controversial topic of rejuvenation and the science that could make it a practical reality. There is, of course, no way to reverse the aging process at the present time, but there are therapies available that treat age-related diseases. Some of these therapies, particularly those involving hormone supplements, can have dangerous side effects and should never be used without the supervision of a physician. But the goal of rejuvenation therapy is to treat and reverse the aging process itself, so that age-related diseases never occur in the first place. Accomplishing this feat will make the flight at Kitty Hawk seem like child's play and will dwarf all other scientific endeavors, including the exploration of Mars and the Human Genome Project. Nevertheless, the following discussion will show that the necessary theories, tools, and techniques are now at hand to produce a viable rejuvenation therapy within the next 20 years.

TURNING BACK THE CLOCK

The basic goal of any rejuvenation therapy is to reset the clock in aged cells or tissues in order to move them back to a preexisting, youthful state. Anti-aging medicines, such as estrogen or testosterone supplements, do not reverse the aging process, nor do they alleviate all of the symptoms associated with a loss of those hormones. This is due to the age-related changes that occur in all of the cells in the body. Old cells do not respond to hormones the same way they did when they were young. Hormone receptors in the membranes of every cell change with time, as does the translation machinery that uses mRNA to synthesize proteins. Success with treating age-related diseases, as described in chapter 9, will always be limited until the health of each cell in the body is restored.

The large number of aging theories suggests that rejuvenation would have to consist of many therapies designed to reverse the aging process simultaneously at the cell, tissue, and physiological levels—a task that would be almost impossible to accomplish. A better approach is to focus the therapy at the level of the cell nucleus, which is, after all, at the heart of the age-related changes that occur in humans and other animals. Nuclear rejuvenation therapy (NRT) would require a gene expression profile for every kind of cell in the body, as well as the identification of all gene regulatory molecules. With this information at hand, gene expression could be manipulated in order to rejuvenate the cells, which would lead automatically to the rejuvenation of the whole body.

Identification of all human genes, of which there are an estimated 30,000, is already under way. This information is being obtained by research laboratories in several countries around the world as part of the Human Genome Project (a brief history of the project is described in chapter 10). Once the genes are identified, several procedures can be applied in order to determine expression profiles, the identity of gene-regulatory molecules, and the manipulation of specific genes. These procedures include DNA microarray analysis, nuclear transfer technology, cell fusion technology, stem cell analysis, and gene therapy.

DNA MICROARRAY ANALYSIS

Based on information provided by the genome project, a short piece of every available gene can be spotted onto a solid support (usually, a specially treated glass microscope slide) to produce a microarray of gene fragments. The microarray can then be hybridized with labeled mRNA isolated from chosen cells. If a gene is active in the cell, its mRNA will bind to the piece of that gene attached to the microarray, effectively labeling that particular point, or pixel, on the

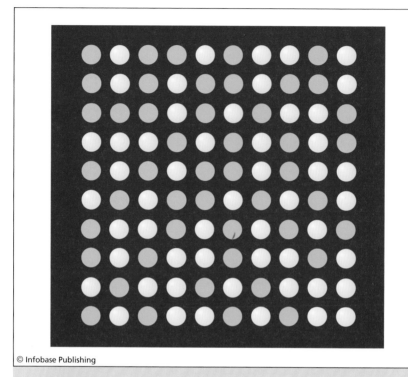

© Infobase Publishing

Microarray analysis of gene expression. Fragments of genes are spotted onto a glass microscope slide to produce a two-dimensional array. Labeled mRNA is hybridized to the array to determine which genes are active (yellow spots) and which are not (blue spots). This simulated array shows the expression of 100 genes.

array. Computers are used to compare the young and old cells, spot by spot, to gain a final estimate of expression for every gene represented on the array. Microarrays were used recently by University of Wisconsin scientists, who evaluated the activity of 20,000 genes in cells from the prostate gland, before and after the cells attained replicative senescence.

Microarray analysis provides an extremely powerful method for analyzing the aging process in an unbiased manner. That is, until the genome project was completed, gerontologists using available theories as a guide had to make an educated guess as to which genes might be involved in cellular senescence. Studies were then designed around these genes in a few of the animal's tissues or organs. It is clear now that such a limited approach is doomed to failure. Aging is a highly integrated phenomenon, involving all of the organs and tissues of the body. Some tissues or organs may age at their own rates, but they are all part of the same process.

NUCLEAR TRANSFER TECHNOLOGY

This technology involves the transfer of a nucleus from one cell into another cell that has had its own nucleus removed. This procedure has been used to clone amphibians and mammals and was originated by the great 19th-century German embryologist Hans Spemann to test two theories of cell differentiation. All animals originate from a single cell, which grows and divides in a process called embryogenesis to produce an animal consisting of billions of cells.

Embryogenesis is also associated with cellular differentiation. That is, as the embryo grows, some of the cells become neurons while others give rise to the heart, skin, bones, and all other cells and tissues of the body. If all the cells originate from the same cell, the egg, they must have the same genome (i.e., the same genes). But if that is the case, how can they differentiate? One theory suggests that cells differentiate by losing genes. A second theory states that all cells in an adult have the same genes, but some are repressed and thus nonfunctional. Spemann reasoned that if the second theory was true, a nucleus from an advanced embryo (containing 16 cells) should be able to support development when transferred into a 4-cell embryo. Spemann's experiment, using salamanders, produced two healthy embryos, thus supporting the second theory.

Full proof for the second theory, however, did not come until 1996, when Ian Wilmut and his team cloned Dolly the sheep. Wilmut's experiment differed from Spemann's in that the donor nuclei came from adult cells. If a nucleus from an adult cell can support embryonic development, leading to the birth of a normal lamb,

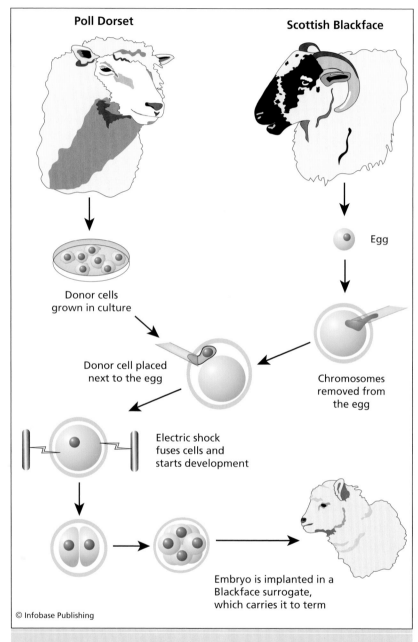

Poll Dorset

Scottish Blackface

Egg

Donor cells
grown in culture

Donor cell placed
next to the egg

Chromosomes
removed from
the egg

Electric shock
fuses cells and
starts development

Embryo is implanted in a
Blackface surrogate,
which carries it to term

© Infobase Publishing

Cloning sheep. The Poll Dorset provides the nucleus, which is obtained from cultured ovine mammary gland epithelial (OME) cells. The blackface provides the egg, which is subsequently enucleated. If the cloning process is successful, the clone will look like a Poll Dorset.

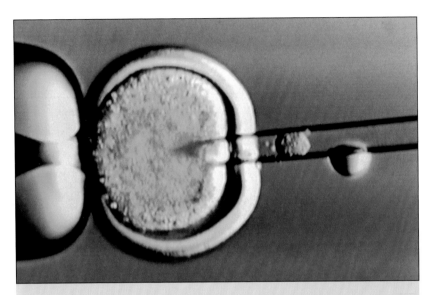

Cloning technique. Light micrograph of a sheep egg being injected with an embryonic cell during sheep cloning. The egg (at center) has had its DNA genetic material removed. At left a pipette holds the egg; at right a microneedle injects an embryonic sheep cell into it. The implanted egg is then stimulated to grow into a lamb by a spark of electricity, nourished in the womb of a surrogate sheep. In 1996 this research at the Roslin Institute in Edinburgh, Scotland, produced the world's first cloned (genetically identical) sheep. *(James King-Holmes/Photo Researchers, Inc.)*

then all cells in the body must have the full complement of genes, which are retained throughout the life span of the individual.

These cloning experiments not only proved the validity of the second theory of differentiation, but they also proved that it is possible to rejuvenate a nucleus, and that the molecules necessary to effect this dramatic transformation are located in the cytoplasm of the oocyte. In other words, animal cloning is a form of nuclear rejuvenation. When a nucleus from an adult cell is placed inside an enucleated egg, the environment of the egg reprograms, and rejuvenates, the older nucleus. Thus nuclear transfer, combined with microarray analysis, provides a powerful tool for developing a nuclear rejuvenation therapy.

CELL FUSION TECHNOLOGY

This technology is closely related to nuclear transfer in that the nucleus of one kind of cell is brought under the influence of the cytoplasm of a second type of cell. The two cells are exposed to a Sendai virus that stimulates fusion of the cells' membranes. This procedure was first used by cell biologists in the 1960s to study the reactivation of avian erythrocyte nuclei exposed to a HeLa cell (a type of cancer cell). The HeLa cell is a highly active, immortalized cell, with a large round nucleus composed of decondensed chromatin. By contrast, the avian erythrocyte is highly differentiated with a small, inactive nucleus, consisting mostly of condensed chromatin. Fusion of these two cells results in a dramatic transformation of the erythrocyte nuclei, characterized by a reduction in the amount of condensed chromatin and an increase in nuclear volume.

Scientists at Harvard University have reprogrammed somatic cell nuclei by fusing them with embryonic stem cells. Analysis of genome-wide transcriptional activity, along with additional tests, showed that the somatic genome was reprogrammed to an embryonic state. The use of stem cells in this way provides a very powerful method for identifying the factors responsible for nuclear rejuvenation.

STEM CELL ANALYSIS

Stem cells are capable of differentiating into many different kinds of cells and are currently being used to regenerate normal bone marrow in patients suffering from leukemia. Future applications involve therapies to treat damaged spinal cords, Parkinson's disease, Alzheimer's disease, and cardiovascular disease.

Stem cells may also be used to identify nuclear rejuvenation factors. This can be done in two ways: cell fusion experiments (described above) and directed differentiation, a process whereby cultured stem cells are induced to differentiate by exposing them to a variety of molecules. Experiments such as these will make it possible for scientists to identify cell-specific expression profiles. Studies have shown that stem cell differentiation to a neuron passes through several stages or levels, each of which is characterized by

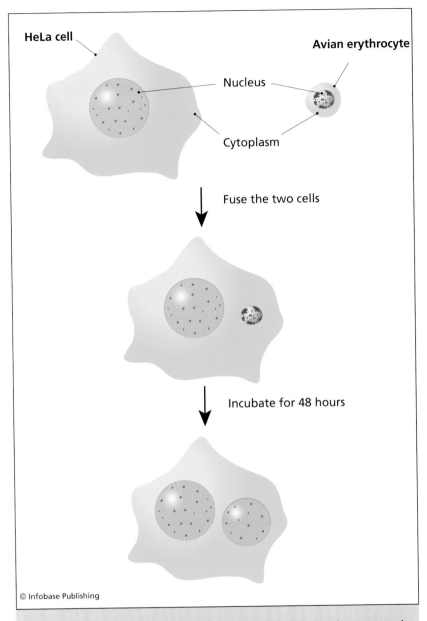

Cell Fusion. A HeLa cell was fused with an avian erythrocyte and allowed to incubate for 48 hours. Molecules in the HeLa cell cytoplasm induced a dramatic change in the erythrocyte nucleus, which included an increase in size, a decrease in the amount of condensed chromatin, and a reactivation of transcriptional activity.

Differentiation of embryonic stem cells. Embryonic stem cells are obtained from the inner cell mass of a blastocyst. When cultured, these cells can differentiate into many different kinds of cells, representing the three germ layers.

activation of a unique set of nuclear transcription factors (molecules that control gene expression). Aging is no doubt associated with a similar stage-specific set of nuclear factors. In this case a stage is

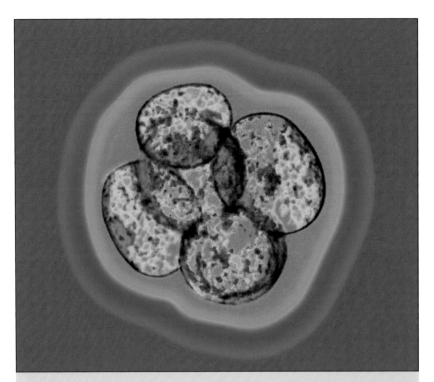

Micrograph of a human embryo soon after fertilization. The cells, or blastomeres, result from divisions of the fertilized egg and are surrounded by the protective zona pellucida layer. The cells of embryos like these are sometimes harvested as stem cells. *(Andrew Paul Leonard/Photo Researchers, Inc.)*

likely to be a period of about 10 years, so that each decade will be accompanied by a unique set of nuclear factors. Stem cell analysis, combined with cell fusion and cloning technologies, would provide a way to identify these factors, after which they could be used to reset the apparent age of a nucleus to any decade desirable.

GENE THERAPY

This therapy is used to modify or replace specific genes within the nucleus (see chapter 10 for details). Gene therapy would be used to correct random mutations that are likely to appear with age throughout the genome. Rejuvenating the nucleus with an age-specific set of transcription factors would not undo this damage. Indeed, genetic mutations could accelerate aging or trigger cancer development. Since the location of these mutations is expected to vary among individuals, it would be necessary to sequence the genome of every person who is interested in receiving rejuvenation therapy. Ultrafast sequencing machines are being developed now. The ultimate goal is a machine that can sequence the entire human genome in one day at a cost of about $1,000. These machines are expected to be available within the next 10 years.

THE FINAL PACKAGE

Delivery of rejuvenation therapy could be accomplished using liposomes. Each liposome would contain the factors necessary to rejuvenate one type of cell. As a consequence, it would be necessary to produce a separate liposome package for each of the 200 known cell types in the human body. Liposomes can be targeted to specific cells by embedding special recognition proteins in their membrane. Thus the liposomes would only bind to and enter specific cells. For example, a liposome package intended for cardiac muscle would have a cardiac muscle recognition protein embedded in its membrane. These recognition proteins can be designed to preclude cross-reactivity.

The exact contents of each liposome package would vary depending on the outcome of the above analysis for each individual. All individuals would receive the basic package needed to rejuvenate cells that have suffered age-related effects. But some patients may have a genetic predisposition for Alzheimer's disease, which would require the inclusion of a gene therapy vector for the affected neurons. Others may suffer from random genetic mutations, cardiovascular disease, osteoporosis, or diabetes, and thus would require special packages.

The liposome packages could rejuvenate an individual, but they would not stop the clock. Immediately after the therapy, the cells would begin to age again. Consequently, rejuvenation therapy would have to be repeated from time to time.

There would, of course, be many dangers associated with such a radical therapy. As the liposome packages are produced, they would have to be tested in a series of clinical trials before they could be used as a medical therapy. If the mosaic theory of the aging process holds true, only a fraction of the known cell types would have to be treated. In this case the 20-year estimate quoted above, to obtain a safe and effective therapy, would likely hold. On the other hand, if 200 packages had to be tested, then rejuvenation therapy of the kind described here would not be available for at least 50 years. At this rate 40 packages would have to be developed and tested every 10 years. This estimate assumes an accelerated pace in testing and validation procedures and an absence of serious complications in the trials themselves.

9

Clinical Trials

According to data provided by the National Institutes of Health (NIH), more than 3,000 clinical trials have been launched since the late 1990s to test potential therapies for age-related diseases such as Alzheimer's disease (AD), cardiovascular disease (CVD), osteoporosis, and Parkinson's disease. These trials typically enroll anywhere from 50 to 5,000 subjects and can last for just a few months to more than 50 years. The estimated cost of all of these trials is more than $20 billion, much of which comes from pharmaceutical companies. All of the trials discussed in this chapter were preceded by years of basic research involving mice or primates, which establishes the basic protocol for subsequent human trials. Alzheimer's disease, CVD, and osteoporosis are easily the subjects of the greatest number of trials, some of which have led to effective therapies. This chapter also describes clinical trials involving Parkinson's disease and the role of hormones, nutrition, and lifestyle in modulating the onset of age-related diseases.

ALZHEIMER'S DISEASE

Clinical trials involving AD have focused on therapies that might rejuvenate the damaged neurons and eliminate the beta-amyloid plaques that are associated with this disease. Three such therapies that have been tested are antioxidants, amyloid immunotherapy, and gene therapy.

Antioxidants

According to the free radical theory of the aging process, antioxidants should help reduce some of the symptoms associated with cellular senescence. In addition, research on longevity genes has shown that some of these genes code for proteins that minimize oxidative damage to cells and tissues. Several lines of evidence going back to the 1990s suggest that antioxidants, such as vitamin C and E, protect the brain from Alzheimer's disease and may even reverse some of the clinical symptoms in those patients already affected. Presumably, antioxidants block the formation of beta-amyloid and neurofibrillary tangles or they aid in the removal of these substances.

Peter Zandi and his associates have studied the effects of vitamin C and E, alone and in combination, on elderly subjects (age 65 or older) in Cache County, Utah. All participants in the study were given a standardized battery of tests to assess the prevalence of AD within the group. Of the original 4,740 subjects, 1,513 either died or withdrew before the trial was completed, leaving a total of 3,227 subjects. Participants consumed at least 400 IU of vitamin E and/or 500 milligrams (mg) of Vitamin C every two weeks. The results showed that vitamins C and E, when taken together, reduced the prevalence and incidence of AD. Neither vitamin, when taken alone, had any effect.

In 2006 the American National Institute of Aging (NIA), a part of NIH, launched a multicenter clinical trial to confirm and extend these results. This study, titled "Evaluation of the Safety, Tolerability and Impact on Biomarkers of Anti-Oxidant Treatment of Mild to Moderate Alzheimer's Disease" is a phase I clinical trial that enrolled 75 subjects, all of whom suffer from AD. The principal investigator is Douglas Galasko at the University of California, San Diego. All of the subjects were randomly sorted into three groups. One group received vitamin C, vitamin E, and an antioxidant, the second group received antioxidant only, and the third group was given a placebo. The treatment period is expected to last for five years. The effects of the two antioxidant treatments will be evaluated by determining the amount of beta-amyloid in the blood and cerebrospinal fluid (CSF) at the beginning and end of the period. A treatment that increases the removal of beta-amyloid from the brain is expected to decrease the level of this protein in general circulation and in the CSF.

Vitamin B has also been tested on patients suffering from AD. Scientists believe that this vitamin could slow the progression of AD by inhibiting the formation of homocystein, an amino acid that is elevated in people suffering from this disease. Dr. Paul Aisen and his team at the University of California, San Diego, studied the effects of vitamin B in 409 people with mild to moderate AD. These subjects were divided into two groups; one received the vitamin, and the other was given a placebo. Cognitive decline was then monitored over an 18-month period. The results showed that while the vitamin treatment did lower the levels of homocystein, it had no effect on reducing the incidence of cognitive decline and thus no effect on lowering the risk for AD. Moreover, the group receiving the vitamin was more prone to depression than were those receiving the placebo. These results were published in the October 15, 2008, issue of *JAMA* (the *Journal of the American Medical Association*).

Amyloid Immunotherapy

An alternative to removing beta-amyloid from the brain with antioxidants is to immunize the body against beta-amyloid. This approach was originated by scientists at Elan, a pharmaceutical company located in Dublin, Ireland, that develops treatments for neurological disorders. Preclinical research in the late 1990s demonstrated the effectiveness of this type of therapy. It was hypothesized that injection of a synthetic amyloid, AN-1792, into the bloodstream would lead to the formation of antibodies directed against AN-1792 as well as the native beta-amyloid, and that these antibodies would enhance clearance of beta-amyloid from the brain. Injection of AN-1792 appeared to stimulate clearance of the protein from the brains of experimental animals.

Elan initiated a phase I study of AN-1792 in 2000. This trial was designed to assess safety, tolerability, and immunogenicity (the amount of antibody produced by each subject) in response to injections of various doses of AN-1792. The trial also helped to identify doses and regimens that could be used in later studies. In 2001 Elan initiated a phase II trial to determine the clinical effectiveness of this therapy, but terminated it when four of the subjects developed encephalitis, one of whom died as a consequence. Despite these problems, the phase II trial provided evidence to support the beta-amyloid immunotherapy approach. After 12 months of treatment, several subjects responded with improved memory, attention, and concentration. Levels of the *Tau* protein in the cerebrospinal fluid decreased in the treated group, suggesting improved turnover and clearance. To overcome the problems associated with AN-1792, researchers at Elan adopted a different strategy by producing a monoclonal antibody called bapineuzumab (AAB-001) to beta-amyloid. This antibody was used in a subsequent phase I trial involving 30 subjects who were given a range of doses (0.5 mg per kg to 5.0 mg per kg). The trial was conducted for one year, and although one of the patients receiving the highest dose developed a fever, none developed serious clinical symptoms. A multicenter phase II trial was launched by NIA and Elan in April 2005 with 240 subjects enrolled. This trial is expected to run until 2010. The subjects, all between 50 to 85 years of age and diagnosed as probable AD cases, were randomly divided into two groups: one receiving the antibody and the other a placebo. The trial is double-blind, meaning that neither the subjects nor the personnel delivering the treatment know who is receiving the antibody or the placebo. Each patient's participation is scheduled to last for approximately two years.

Gene Therapy

Mark Tuszynski and his team at the University of California in San Diego have used gene therapy in a phase I clinical trial to treat AD. Preclinical research has shown that neural growth factor (NGF), could slow the progression of AD symptoms when injected into the brains of mice. Tuszynski's team began by isolating skin cells from each of the eight subjects enrolled in the trial, all of whom were diagnosed as suffering from AD. The skin cells were transfected with a viral vector containing the NGF gene and grown in tissue culture to confirm expression of the NGF gene. Cells testing positive for NGF were injected into the brains of the subjects from whom they were isolated. The first two patients received the injections under local anesthetic. One of these patients moved during the procedure and subsequently died from a brain hemorrhage. The remaining subjects were injected under a general anesthetic; all recovered fully from the operation. A follow-up in 2006 has shown that the extra NGF, being produced by the transgene, slowed the normal progression of the disease in six of the subjects. Memory tests indicated that cognitive decline was reduced by almost 50 percent. In addition, brain scans indicated increased activity levels over those obtained prior to the treatment. If these results are confirmed in other trials, it will be the first time a therapy actually prevented cell death in patients suffering from AD.

Ginkgo Biloba

Ginko biloba is a deciduous tree of ancient lineage that once grew in many parts of the world. Today it grows wild primarily in the Zhejiang province of eastern China. Ginkos are very hardy, and one specimen growing in China is said to be nearly 3,000 years old. The Chinese have long used an extract of the leaves as an herbal medicine to boost blood circulation and memory functions. It is also one of the top 10 natural pharmaceuticals used by Americans.

A ginkgo biloba extract has been tested by scientists at NIH for its ability to enhance memory in elderly subjects. Initial studies showed some promise, but a randomized controlled clinical trial concluded in 2008 that this herbal medicine is ineffective as a treatment for Alzheimer's disease. Moreover, the treatment failed to reduce the incidence of cardiovascular disease, stroke, and overall mortality. This trial enrolled more than 3,000 subjects who were followed for nearly seven years.

CARDIOVASCULAR DISEASE

CVD trials are observational and experimental. Observational trials study the lifestyle, diet, and natural progression of CVD in a selected population. The experimental trials have examined several possible therapies to treat atherosclerosis and damage to the heart muscle itself, which often occurs after a heart attack. The trials discussed in this section examined a large number of potential therapies for CVD, including an attempt to repair damaged heart muscle with gene therapy.

The Framingham Heart Study

In 1948 the American National Heart, Lung, and Blood Institute, a division of NIH, launched the Framingham heart study, the largest and most comprehensive CVD trial to date. At that time very little was known about CVD, but epidemiologists had noted that the disease, which began to appear in the early 1900s, had reached epidemic proportions by the 1940s. The objective of this observational study was to identify the common characteristics that contribute to CVD by following its development over a long period of time in a large group of subjects who had not yet developed overt symptoms of CVD or suffered a heart attack or stroke.

The researchers recruited more than 5,000 men and women between the ages of 30 and 62 from the town of Framingham, Massachusetts, for extensive physical examinations and lifestyle interviews that would be analyzed for their relevance to CVD. Since 1948 the subjects have returned to the study every two years for a detailed medical history, physical examination, and laboratory tests. In 1971 the study enrolled a second generation of subjects, consisting of the original participants' adult children and their spouses. The study was expanded to include a third generation when the grandchildren of the original cohort were enrolled and currently involves more than 4,000 participants.

Analysis of the data produced by the Framingham trial has identified several *risk factors* (a term that was coined by the trial researchers): high blood pressure, high blood cholesterol, smoking, obesity, diabetes, and physical inactivity. In addition, the trial collected a great deal of information on the effects of related factors, such as blood triglyceride and HDL cholesterol levels, age, gender, and psychosocial issues. Although the Framingham cohort is primarily white, the importance of the risk factors identified in this group have been shown in other studies to apply to all racial and ethnic groups. The many and varied results obtained by the Framingham study have been the subject of more than 1,200 articles in science and medical journals. Over the past 10 years the identification of CVD risk factors has become the focus of many experimental trials that have led to the development of effective therapies and preventive strategies.

The Women's Health Initiative (WHI)

The Women's Health Initiative (WHI), sponsored by NIH, was a long-term study of health issues involving postmenopausal women. This initiative consisted of an experimental clinical trial and an observational study (OS) with a combined enrollment of more than 160,000 women at 40 clinics in the United States. The clinical trial, with an enrollment of more than 68,000 women, was divided into three components: dietary modification (DM), calcium and vitamin D supplementation (Cal-VDS), and hormone therapy (HT).

The HT trial tested the effects of hormones, specifically equine (horse) estrogen and progestin (a synthetic progesterone), on the age-related progression of breast cancer, colon cancer, and heart disease. The Cal-VDS trial (discussed in a later section) examined the role of calcium and vitamin D supplements on the development of osteoporosis and colon cancer, and the DM trial determined the effect of a low-fat, high fruit and vegetables diet on CVD and colon cancer. The OS tracked the medical history and health habits of women who were not receiving a WHI intervention.

The results of this initiative were surprising and disappointing. The HT trial was terminated prematurely when the results began to show that the treatment was doing more harm than good: It actually increased the incidence of CVD rather than reducing it. A similar result was obtained with a second group of women treated with equine estrogen only. The results of the DM trial, like the HT trial, failed to show any benefit. Contrary to prevailing wisdom, reducing total fat intake and increasing one's consumption of fruits and vegetables did not reduce the risk of developing CVD.

As thorough as these studies were, they have been criticized on several points:

1. Using equine (horse) estrogen instead of 17β-estradiol (human estrogen) in the HT trial. These two forms of estrogen are not identical, and critics have pointed to a small clinical trial, concluded in 2001, that showed a reduction in the incidence of atherosclerosis among postmenopausal women receiving 17β-estradiol instead of the placebo.

2. Failure to ensure a reasonable level of physical activity in all subjects, whether they received the placebo or the HT. Interactions between physical activity and hormonal environment are known to be important in maintaining a healthy cardiovascular system. Variations in this study parameter could have negated any beneficial effects of the treatment.

3. Focusing on total fat rather than the type of fat in the DM trial. Medical researchers have known for decades that saturated fats from meat and dairy products can be harmful, whereas unsaturated fats, such as those found in olive oil, can be beneficial. All of the subjects had to reduce total fat intake, but the results are flawed if some of the women received their entire daily fat quota from dairy products instead of olive oil or whole grains. Critics point to a small clinical trial, conducted by Ramon Estruch of the University of Barcelona, Spain, which showed that a high-fat Mediterranean diet (i.e., fat from olive oil, fruits, and nuts) was better for the cardiovascular system than a typical North American low-fat diet (all fat obtained from meat and dairy products). Thus the type of fat is the critical factor, not total fat. The results of this study were published in the *Annals of Internal Medicine* on July 4, 2006.

HORMONE REPLACEMENT THERAPY (HRT)

Several prominent hormones, such as estrogen, testosterone, thyroid hormone, and growth hormone (GH) decrease dramatically as people reach their sixth decade. One example is the drop in estrogen levels when a woman goes through menopause. Men experience a similar, though more gradual, decline in testosterone levels when they reach a comparable age (referred to as andropause). The effect of this decline on human physiology is profound. As described in chapter 4, the problem is not simply a drop in the hormone level but the change in the estrogen/testosterone ratio that occurs in both sexes. A disturbance in this ratio weakens our bones, our immune system, and places us at an elevated risk of developing cancer, arthritis, osteoporosis and other diseases.

Estrogen and testosterone supplementation, which has been a routine medical procedure, is known to reverse the onset of osteoporosis and can alleviate the symptoms of osteoarthritis. The great concern associated with the use of these steroids is their suspected role in cancer induction. The results of the Women's Health Initiative, described above, showed an increased risk in the group receiving HRT for heart attacks, breast cancer, and stroke. But the effect was relatively small. For example, the study suggested that of 10,000 women getting hormone therapy for a year, eight more will develop invasive breast cancer and seven more will have heart attacks than a similar group not taking hormones. The benefits would be six fewer cases of colorectal cancer and five fewer hip fractures. A follow-up study in 2009 confirmed the increased risk of breast cancer in women receiving estrogen supplements. The American researchers concluded that a 50 percent drop in the number of women taking HRT means 1,000 fewer cases of breast cancer each year. Nevertheless, many physicians believe HRT is still an appropriate therapy in many cases.

Human growth hormone (hGH) is another hormone that has been used in an effort to reverse the symptoms of age. The first clinical trial to test the effects of growth hormone supplements on the elderly was conducted in the early 1990s by Dr. Daniel Rudman and his colleagues at the Medical College of Wisconsin. The trial ran for 21 months and enrolled 45 men, all of whom were 65 years of age or older. Half of the group received daily injections of synthetic hGH, and the other half received no treatment. At the end of the trial period, the experimental group showed an increase in bone density, lean muscle mass, and skin thickness, and a reduction in the amount of subcutaneous fat tissue.

Since the Rudman trial, several companies have begun selling hGH as an anti-aging miracle drug. But this hormone is much more dangerous to use than are the sex steroids. Growth hormone, as its name implies, promotes growth in children and adolescents, but in a fully mature individual, GH takes care of many other physiological chores, including the daily mobilization of energy reserves and amino acids. The adult chores require much less hGH than would be present in a child or an adolescent. Replacement therapies often produce dangerously high concentrations of hGH in the blood, which can lead to a condition known as acromegaly. This disease, first described in the 1930s, is the result of excessive GH production in an adult, leading to severe disfigurement of the face, hands, and feet, as well as overgrowth of soft tissue, leading to thickening of the skin and visceral organs.

In recent years acromegaly has occurred in laboratory-bred transgenic salmon, containing an extra GH gene. Initially, these fish simply grow faster than their cohorts, but as they approach sexual maturity, they suffer extreme deformities of the head and spine, making it difficult for them to feed and swim (these fish are produced for research purposes only). Because of its dangerous side effects, companies that attempt to sell hGH as a medicinal drug face the imposition of very stiff fines from the FDA.

Researchers at Washington University School of Medicine, St. Louis, Missouri, have shown an increase in bone density with a reduction in fat content in 74-year-old men and women being treated with dehydroepiandrosterone (DHEA). The effect was similar in magnitude to that observed in the Rudman trial. This hormone, discussed in chapter 3, is a precursor of testosterone and estrogen and is known to decrease with age in both men and women. The trial ran for six months, and the experimental group, consisting of 10 women and eight men, received oral DHEA replacement at 50 mg per day.

Scientists in the United Kingdom (UK) have shown that the cognitive function of elderly men (55 to 75 years old) can be improved by inhibiting the synthesis of cortisol. Test subjects received carbenoxolone three times daily for four weeks. Carbenoxolone is a drug that inhibits the synthesis of cortisol from circulating inert cortisone. Subjects receiving carbenoxolone showed a marked improvement in verbal skills and memory function.

Researchers at the University of Washington have studied the effect of GH on mental acuity. This trial enrolled 89 adults, all of whom were over 65 years of age. Unlike the Rudman trial, the experimental group in this trial received regular injections of growth hormone-releasing hormone (GHRH) rather than GH itself. The results not only confirmed the earlier GH trial, but also suggested that the age-related decline in the amount of GH is due to an age-related change in the hypothalamus, where GHRH is synthesized.

NUTRITION AND LIFESTYLE

A variety of studies dating back to the 1980s have shown that a proper diet, regular exercise, moderate alcohol consumption, and abstinence from smoking can reduce the incidence of age-related diseases and conditions, such as CVD, cancer, and AD.

A comprehensive trial titled "Healthy Ageing: a Longitudinal study in Europe (HALE)" examined the benefits of a Mediterranean diet on the prevention of coronary heart disease, cardiovascular disease, and cancer. The study, which ran from 1998 to 2004, enrolled more than 1,000 men and women, aged 70 to 90 years, in 11 European countries. The decision to focus on a Mediterranean diet was based on preliminary studies showing that such a diet was associated with extreme longevity and a healthy elderly population. Jeanne Calment, the longest-lived human to date, is a famous example of this relationship.

The Mediterranean diet, as practiced in southern Italy, southern France, Greece, Portugal, and Spain, is characterized by a high consumption of fruit and vegetables, bread and other cereals, olive oil, fish, and regular but moderate quantities of red wine. This diet was first described in 1945 by Ancel Keys, an American physician who noted that while North Americans and Mediterraneans consume an equivalent amount of fat, Mediterraneans experience lower rates of CVD, cancer, and other age-related diseases. Subsequent analysis of the Mediterranean diet has shown that the fat, obtained primarily from olive oil, is unsaturated and contains a high concentration of powerful antioxidants, which, as explained in chapter 4, protect organs and cells from the damaging effects of free radicals. In addition, unlike the animal fat that is typical of a North American diet, olive oil lowers cholesterol levels in the blood and is resistant to oxidation; two features that could be directly responsible for the lower incidence of CVD in European populations.

In the HALE study, subjects adhering to a Mediterranean diet had a 50 percent lower rate of cancer and CVD, thus confirming the benefits of a healthy diet in general, and the Mediterranean diet in particular. Whether the Mediterranean diet can increase the mean human life span, the way caloric restriction increases the mean rodent life span, is yet to be determined. A starvation diet appears to be the only sure way to increase the mean life span of a mammal. It has been shown to work in mice, rats, and Rhesus monkeys. In these cases, caloric restriction is associated with a reduction in the amount of low-density lipoprotein (LDL), a lower body weight, and a more youthful appearance. On the other hand, these animals, by necessity, are less active and much more boring than the control group.

Caloric restriction is important from a theoretical point of view, but it is never likely to form a practical therapy. North Americans in general find it difficult maintaining even modest shifts in eating habits. The typical CR diet, which reduces caloric intake to one-third of normal levels, is not likely to attract a large following. Nevertheless, CR experiments highlight the importance of diet on the rate of aging, and this could at least encourage healthier, low caloric eating habits.

Several clinical trials have studied the benefits of physical activity in the elderly. One of the earliest of these trials was conducted in 1994 on 100 frail nursing home patients with an age range of 72 to 98 years. This trial was funded by the National Institute of Aging and conducted in Boston, Massachusetts. Half of the subjects, chosen at random, engaged in daily weight lifting exercise (resistance training) on a cable-pulley machine three days per week, 45 minutes per session, for 10 weeks. The control group engaged in three activities of their choice offered by the recreational-therapy service of the facility. No resistance training was allowed, but aerobic or flexibility exercises were permitted. Typical activities were walking, calisthenics while the subject was seated, board games, crafts, concerts, and group discussions. At the end of the trial, the experimental group showed a dramatic improvement in muscle strength (113 percent versus 3 percent in the control group). Gait velocity improved by 12 percent in the exercisers, but declined by 1 percent in the control group. Stair-climbing power improved by 28 percent in the exercisers, but only by 4 percent in the nonexercisers. On a qualitative level, the researchers noted an increase in the level of spontaneous physical activity among the experimental group, but not among the controls. The results also indicated that muscles in the elderly, even in the very elderly, could respond to weight-bearing exercise.

Since the Massachusetts trial, many recent studies have shown that exercise not only improves the overall physical well-being of the elderly, but it reduces the incidence of CVD, cancer, diabetes, and AD. Studies around the world have consistently shown that people who reach a healthy advanced age (85 or older) invariably have had a life-long habit of engaging in physical activity and generally adhere to a Mediterranean diet or something similar to it.

OSTEOPOROSIS

Many trials have been conducted to test a variety of treatments for osteoporosis. The most successful treatments to have come out of these trials include the bisphosphonates, parathyroid hormone, and estrogen.

Bisphosphonates

Risedronate (Actonel), alendronate (Fosamax) and ibandronate (Boniva) have been approved by the FDA for the treatment of osteoporosis. Only the first two are available in oral formulations and thus figure prominently in the clinical trials discussed below. Actonel and Fosamax are usually administered with calcium and vitamin D supplements.

Five placebo-controlled clinical trials have shown that Actonel and Fosamax substantially reduce the risk of vertebral fractures. In one trial, known as the hip intervention program (HIP), Actonel reduced hip and other nonvertebral fractures in 70- to 79-year-old women, who already had severe osteoporosis, by more than 60 percent. Similar results were obtained with Fosamax in a separate trial. A large multi-center trial known as the Vertebral Efficacy with Risedronate Therapy (VERT) study showed that Actonel is just as effective at preventing vertebral fractures (a reduction of 65 percent). A companion study known as the Fracture Intervention Trial (FIT) showed that Fosamax reduced the incidence of bone fractures by 47 percent in elderly women who had already suffered vertebral fractures. The VERT trial, HIP, and FIT were three-year trials designed to test the effectiveness of Actonel and Fosamax on postmenopausal osteoporosis, which is the most severe form of this disease. It is important to note that these drugs not only increase bone mineral density (BMD), but also reduce the risk of secondary fractures, which are often the most debilitating.

Parathyroid Hormone

Several recent trials have shown that daily injections of a recombinant human parathyroid hormone called Forteo reduced the risk of vertebral fractures by 65 to 69 percent, and the risk of nonvertebral fractures by 40 percent. The long-term effects of this treatment are unknown; as a consequence, this drug is approved for a maximum of two years of use, and only for patients with severe osteoporosis who are at high risk of developing fractures.

Estrogen

The Women's Health Initiative (WHI), described above in relation to CVD, also studied the effects of hormone therapy on osteoporosis. The analysis concluded that hormone therapy reduced the risk of vertebral and hip fractures by one-third as compared with a placebo. Subsequent concerns regarding long-term estrogen therapy, coupled with the success of the bisphosphonates, led to the recommendation that estrogen not be used to treat or prevent osteoporosis.

PARKINSON'S DISEASE

Most research concerning Parkinson's disease is still at the preclinical stage. The primary treatment for this disorder is a drug known as levodopa, a precursor to dopamine. This drug alleviates some of the symptoms of PD, but only for a limited time. In 2006 the FDA approved a new drug call Azilect for the treatment of this disease. The effectiveness of this new drug was established in three 18- to 26-week, randomized, placebo-controlled trials. In one of these trials Azilect was given as initial monotherapy and in the other two as adjunctive therapy to levodopa. The studies, which included more than 1,500 patients, showed that Azilect slowed the progression of PD while also demonstrating good tolerability.

Azilect, produced by Teva Neuroscience, a pharmaceutical company based in Israel, exerts its effect by inhibiting an enzyme called monoamine oxidase (MAO), which in turn is responsible for destroying dopamine. Inhibition of MAO leads to a buildup of dopamine, which helps alleviate many of the symptoms associated with PD. Azilect is prescribed as a daily monotherapy, and as an addition to levodopa in more advanced cases.

Many scientists believe that vitamin deficiencies could exacerbate the progression of PD. Researchers at the Emory University School of Medicine in Atlanta, Georgia, tested this assumption in a trial consisting of 100 Parkinson's patients, 97 Alzheimer's patients, and 99 healthy people matched for age and other factors. The results showed that the subjects suffering from PD had the lowest concentration of vitamin D (31.9 nanograms per milliliter of blood), compared with 34.8 nanograms among Alzheimer's patients and 37 nanograms among the healthy controls. Thus it may be possible that chronically low levels of vitamin D may increase the risk of developing PD. This study was published in the October 2008 issue of the *Archives of Neurology*. Future studies will determine whether the maintenance of normal Vitamin D levels will improve the symptoms associated with Parkinson's disease.

10

Resource Center

Studying the aging process is a complex endeavor that depends on an understanding of cell biology and a variety of research techniques known as biotechnology. This chapter provides an introduction to these topics as well as brief discussions of gene therapy, the human genome project, and the design of clinical trials.

CELL BIOLOGY

A cell is a microscopic life-form made from a variety of nature's building blocks. The smallest of these building blocks are sub-atomic particles known as quarks and leptons that form protons, neutrons, and electrons, which in turn form atoms. Scientists have identified more than 200 atoms, each of which represents a fundamental element of nature; carbon, oxygen, and nitrogen are common examples. Atoms, in their turn, can associate with one another to form another kind of building block known as a molecule. Sugar,

Multicellular organisms

Plants, animals, and fungi

↑

Cells

Prokaryotes and eukaryotes

↑

Macromolecules

Protein, RNA, DNA, phospholipids, and polysaccharides

↑

Molecules

Sugar, phosphate, glycerol, fatty acids, amino acids, and nucleotides

↑

Atoms

Oxygen, hydrogen, nitrogen, phosphorous, and carbon

© Infobase Publishing

Nature's building blocks. Particles known as quarks and leptons, created in the heat of the big bang, formed the first atoms, which combined to form molecules in the oceans of the young Earth. Heat and electrical storms promoted the formation of macromolecules, providing the building blocks for cells, which in turn went on to form multicellular organisms.

for example, is a molecule constructed from carbon, oxygen, and hydrogen, while ordinary table salt is a molecule consisting of just two elements: sodium and chloride. Molecules can link up with one another to form yet another kind of building block known as a macromolecule. Macromolecules, present in the atmosphere of the young Earth, gave rise to cells, which in turn went on to form multicellular organisms; in forming those organisms, cells became a new kind of building block.

The Origin of Life

Molecules essential for life are thought to have formed spontaneously in the oceans of the primordial Earth about 4 billion years ago. Under the influence of a hot stormy environment, the molecules combined to produce macromolecules, which in turn formed microscopic bubbles that were bounded by a sturdy macromolecular membrane analogous to the skin on a grape. It took about half a billion years for the prebiotic bubbles to evolve into the first cells, known as prokaryotes, and another 1 billion years for those cells to evolve into the eukaryotes. Prokaryotes, also known as bacteria, are small cells (about five micrometers in diameter) that have a relatively simple structure and a genome consisting of about 4,000 genes. Eukaryotes are much larger (about 30 micrometers in diameter), with a complex internal structure and a very large genome, often exceeding 20,000 genes. These genes are kept in a special organelle called the nucleus (*eukaryote* means "true nucleus"). Prokaryotes are all single-cell organisms, although some can form short chains or temporary fruiting bodies. Eukaryotes, on the other hand, gave rise to all of the multicellular plants and animals that now inhabit the Earth.

A Typical Eukaryote

Eukaryotes assume a variety of shapes that are variations on the simple spheres from which they originated. Viewed from the side, they often have a galactic profile, with a central bulge (the nucleus), tapering to a thin perimeter. The internal structure is complex, being dominated by a large number of organelles.

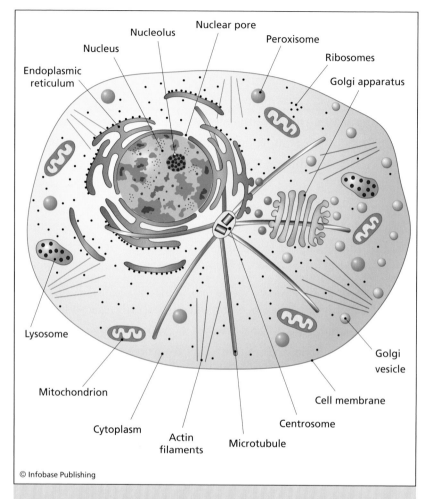

© Infobase Publishing

The eukaryote cell. The structural components shown here are present in organisms as diverse as protozoans, plants, and animals. The nucleus contains the DNA genome and an assembly plant for ribosomal subunits (the nucleolus). The endoplasmic reticulum (ER) and the Golgi work together to modify proteins, most of which are destined for the cell membrane. These proteins travel from the ER to the Golgi and from the Golgi to their final destination in transport vesicles (red and yellow spheres). Mitochondria provide the cell with energy in the form of ATP. Ribosomes, some of which are attached to the ER, synthesize proteins. Lysosomes and peroxisomes recycle cellular material. The microtubules and centrosome form the spindle apparatus for moving chromosomes to the daughter cells during cell division. Actin and other protein filaments form a weblike cytoskeleton.

The functional organization of a eukaryote is analogous to a carpentry shop, which is usually divided into two main areas: the shop floor where the machinery, building materials, and finishing rooms are kept, and the shop office, where the work is coordinated and where the blueprints are stored for everything the shop makes. Carpentry shops keep a blueprint on file for every item that is made. When the shop receives an order, perhaps for a chair, someone in the office makes a copy of the chair's blueprint and delivers it to the carpenters on the shop floor. In this way the master copy is kept out of harm's way, safely stored in the filing cabinet. The carpenters, using the blueprint copy and the materials and tools at hand, build the chair, and then they send it into a special room where it is painted. After the chair is painted, it is taken to another room where it is polished and then packaged for delivery. The energy for all of this activity comes through the electrical wires, which are connected to a power generator somewhere in the local vicinity. The shop communicates with other shops and its customers by using the telephone, e-mail, or postal service.

In the cell the shop floor is called the cytoplasm, and the shop office is the nucleus. Eukaryotes make a large number of proteins, and they keep a blueprint for each one, only in this case the blueprints are not pictures on pieces of paper but molecules of deoxyribonucleic acid (DNA) that are kept in the nucleus. A cellular blueprint is called a gene, and a typical cell has thousands of them. A human cell, for example, has 30,000 genes, all of which are kept on 46 separate DNA molecules known as chromosomes (23 from each parent). When the cell decides to make a protein, it begins by making a ribonucleic acid (RNA) copy of the protein's gene. This blueprint copy, known as messenger RNA, is made in the nucleus and delivered to the cell's carpenters in the cytoplasm. These carpenters are enzymes that control and regulate all of the cell's chemical reactions. Some of the enzymes are part of a complex protein-synthesizing machine known as a ribosome. Cytoplasmic enzymes and the ribosomes synthesize proteins using mRNA as the template, after which many of the proteins are sent to a compartment, known as the endoplasmic reticulum (ER), where they are glycosylated or "painted" with sugar molecules. From there they are shipped to another compartment called the Golgi apparatus, where the glycosylation is refined before the finished products, now looking like molecular trees, are loaded into transport bubbles and shipped to their final destination.

The shape of the cell is maintained by an internal cytoskeleton comprising actin and intermediate filaments. Mitochondria, once free-living prokaryotes, provide the cell with energy in the form of adenosine triphosphate (ATP). The production of ATP is carried out by an assembly of metal-containing proteins, called the electron transport chain, located in the mitochondrion inner membrane. Lysosomes and peroxisomes process and recycle cellular material and molecules. The cell communicates with other cells and the outside world through a forest of glycoproteins, known as the glycocalyx, that covers the cell surface. Producing and maintaining the glycocalyx is the principal function of the ER and Golgi apparatus and a major priority for all eukaryotes.

Cells are biochemical entities that synthesize many thousands of molecules. Studying these chemicals, as well as the biochemistry of the cell, would be extremely difficult were it not for the fact that most of the chemical variation is based on six types of molecules that are assembled into just five types of macromolecules. The six basic molecules are: amino acids, phosphate, glycerol, sugars, fatty acids, and nucleotides. The five macromolecules are: proteins, DNA, RNA, phospholipids, and sugar polymers called polysaccharides.

Molecules of the Cell

Amino acids have a simple core structure consisting of an amino group, a carboxyl group, and a variable R group attached to a carbon atom. There are 20 different kinds of amino acids, each with a unique R group. The simplest and most ancient amino acid is glycine, with an R group that consists only of hydrogen. The chemistry of the various amino acids varies considerably: Some carry a positive electric charge, while others are negatively charged or

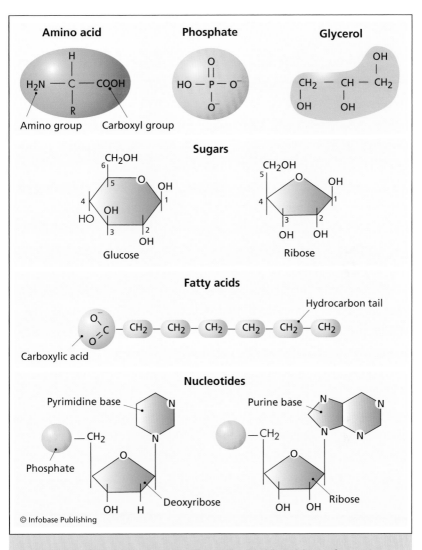

Molecules of the cell. Amino acids are the building blocks for proteins. Phosphate is an important component of many other molecules and is added to proteins to modify their behavior. Glycerol is an alcohol that is an important ingredient in cell membranes and fat. Sugars, like glucose, are a primary energy source for most cells and also have many structural functions. Fatty acids are involved in the production of cell membranes and storage of fat. Nucleotides are the building blocks for DNA and RNA. Note that the sugar carbon atoms are numbered. P: Phosphate, C: Carbon, H: Hydrogen, O: Oxygen, N: Nitrogen, R: Variable molecular group.

electrically neutral; some are water soluble (hydrophilic), while others are hydrophobic.

Phosphates are extremely important molecules that are used in the construction, or modification, of many other molecules. They are also used to store chemical-bond energy in the form of adenosine triphosphate (ATP). The production of phosphate-to-phosphate chemical bonds for use as an energy source is an ancient cellular process, dating back at least 2 billion years.

Glycerol is a simple three-carbon alcohol that is an important component of cell membranes and fat reservoirs. This molecule may have stabilized the membranes of prebiotic bubbles. Interestingly, it is often used today as an ingredient in a solution for making long-lasting soap bubbles.

Sugars are versatile molecules, belonging to a general class of compounds known as carbohydrates that serve a structural role as well as providing energy for the cell. Glucose, a six-carbon sugar, is the primary energy source for most cells and the principal sugar used to glycosylate the proteins and lipids that form the outer coat of all cells. Plants have exploited the structural potential of sugars in their production of cellulose; wood, bark, grasses, and reeds are all polymers of glucose and other monosaccharides. Ribose, a five-carbon sugar, is a component of nucleic acids as well as the cell's main energy depot, ATP. The numbering convention for sugar carbon atoms is shown in the figure on page 157. Ribose carbons are numbered as 1′ (1 prime), 2′, and so on. Consequently, references to nucleic acids, which include ribose, often refer to the 3′ or 5′ carbon.

Fatty acids consist of a carboxyl group (the hydrated form is called carboxylic acid) linked to a hydrophobic hydrocarbon tail. These molecules are used in the construction of cell membranes and fat. The hydrophobic nature of fatty acids is critically important to the normal function of the cell membrane since it prevents the passive entry of water and water-soluble molecules.

Nucleotides are building blocks for DNA and RNA. These molecules consist of three components: a phosphate, a ribose sugar, and a nitrogenous (nitrogen-containing) ring compound that behaves as a base in solution (a base is a substance that can accept a proton in solution). Nucleotide bases appear in two forms: a single-ring nitrogenous base, called a pyrimidine, and a double-ringed base, called a purine. There are two kinds of purines (adenine and guanine), and three pyrimidines (uracil, cytosine, and thymine). Uracil is specific to RNA, substituting for thymine. In addition, RNA nucleotides contain ribose, whereas DNA nucleotides contain deoxyribose (hence the origin of their names). Ribose has a hydroxyl (OH) group attached to both the 2′ and 3′ carbons, whereas deoxyribose is missing the 2′ hydroxyl group.

Macromolecules of the Cell

The six basic molecules are used by all cells to construct five essential macromolecules: proteins, RNA, DNA, phospholipids, and polysaccharides. Macromolecules have primary, secondary, and tertiary structural levels. The primary structural level refers to the chain that is formed by linking the building blocks together. The secondary structure involves the bending of the linear chain to form a three-dimensional object. Tertiary structural elements involve the formation of chemical bonds between some of the building blocks in the chain to stabilize the secondary structure. A quaternary structure can also occur when two identical molecules interact to form a dimer or double molecule.

Proteins are long chains or polymers of amino acids. The primary structure is held together by peptide bonds that link the carboxyl end of one amino acid to the amino end of a second amino acid. Thus once constructed, every protein has an amino end and a carboxyl end. An average protein consists of about 400 amino acids. There are 21 naturally occurring amino acids; with this number the cell can produce an almost infinite variety of proteins. Evolution and

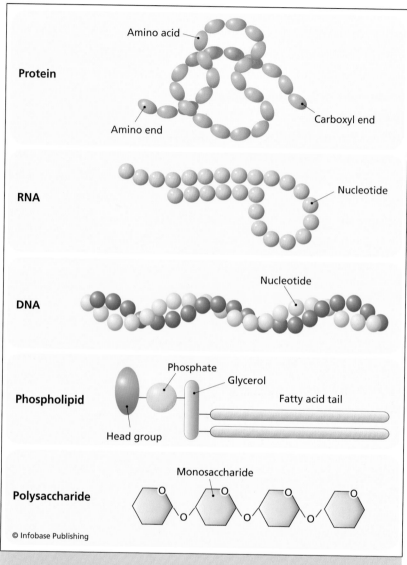

Macromolecules of the cell. Protein is made from amino acids linked together to form a long chain that can fold up into a three-dimensional structure. RNA and DNA are long chains of nucleotides. RNA is generally single-stranded, but can form localized double-stranded regions. DNA is a double-stranded helix, with one strand coiling around the other. A phospholipid is composed of a hydrophilic headgroup, a phosphate, a glycerol molecule and two hydrophobic fatty acid tails. Polysaccharides are sugar polymers.

natural selection, however, have weeded out most of these, so that eukaryote cells function well with 10,000 to 30,000 different proteins. In addition, this select group of proteins has been conserved over the past 2 billion years (i.e., most of the proteins found in yeast can also be found, in modified form, in humans and other higher organisms) The secondary structure of a protein depends on the amino acid sequence and can be quite complicated, often producing three-dimensional structures possessing multiple functions.

RNA is a polymer of the ribonucleotides adenine, uracil, cytosine and guanine. RNA is generally single stranded, but it can form localized double-stranded regions by a process known as complementary base pairing, whereby adenine forms a bond with uracil and cytosine pairs with guanine. RNA is involved in the synthesis of proteins and is a structural and enzymatic component of ribosomes.

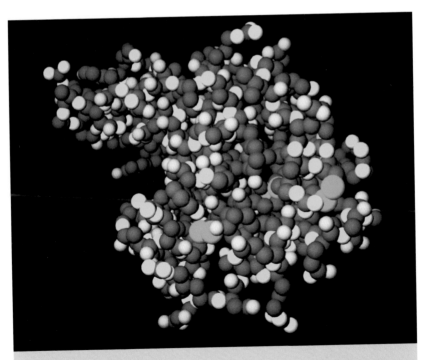

Computer-generated model of lysozyme, an enzyme found in tears and mucus that protects against bacterial infection by literally dissolving the bacteria. *(Kenneth Eward/BioGrafx/Photo Researchers, Inc.)*

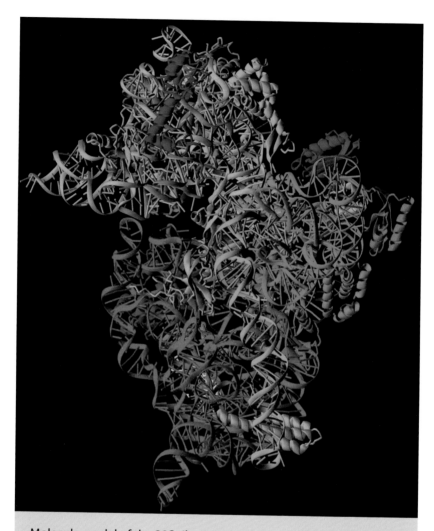

Molecule model of the 30S ribosomal subunit, which consists of protein (corkscrew structures) and RNA (coiled ladders). The overall shape of the molecule is determined by the RNA, which is also responsible for the catalytic function of the ribosome. (V. Ramakrishnan, MRC Laboratory of Molecular Biology, Cambridge)

DNA is a double-stranded nucleic acid. This macromolecule encodes cellular genes and is constructed from adenine, thymine, cytosine, and guanine deoxyribonucleotides. The two

DNA strands coil around each other like strands in a piece of rope, creating a double helix. The two strands are complementary throughout the length of the molecule: adenine pairs with thymine, and cytosine pairs with guanine. Thus if the sequence of one strand is known to be ATCGTC, the sequence of the other strand must be TAGCAG.

Phospholipids are the main component in cell membranes; these macromolecules are composed of a polar head group (usually an alcohol), a phosphate, glycerol, and two hydrophobic fatty acid tails. Fat that is stored in the body as an energy reserve has a structure similar to a phospholipid, being composed of three fatty acid chains attached to a molecule of glycerol. The third fatty acid takes the place of the phosphate and head group of a phospholipid.

Polysaccharides are sugar polymers consisting of two or more monosaccharides. Disaccharides (two monosaccharides), and oligosaccharides (about three to 12 monosaccharides), are attached to proteins and lipids destined for the cell surface or the extracellular matrix. Polysaccharides, such as glycogen and starch, may contain several hundred monosaccharides, and are stored in cells as an energy reserve.

Basic Cellular Functions

There are six basic cellular functions: DNA replication, DNA maintenance, gene expression, power generation, cell division, and cell communication. DNA replication usually occurs in conjunction with cell division, but there are exceptions known as polyploidization (see the Glossary). Gene expression refers to the process whereby the information stored in a gene is used to synthesize RNA or protein. The production of power is accomplished by extracting energy from food molecules and then storing that energy in a form that is readily available to the cell. Cells communicate with their environment and with other cells. The communication hardware consists of a variety of special macromolecules that are embedded in the cell membrane.

DNA Replication

Replication is made possible by the complementarity of the two DNA strands. Since adenine (A) always pairs with thymine (T) and guanine (G) always pairs with cytosine (C), replication enzymes are able to duplicate the molecule by treating each of the original strands as templates for the new strands. For example, if a portion of the template strand reads: ATCGTTGC, the new strand will be TAGCAACG.

DNA replication requires the coordinated effort of a team of enzymes, led by DNA helicase and primase. The helicase separates the two DNA strands at the astonishing rate of 1,000 nucleotides every second. This enzyme gets its name from the fact that it unwinds the DNA helix as it separates the two strands. The enzyme that is directly responsible for reading the template strand, and for synthesizing the new daughter strand, is called DNA polymerase. This enzyme also has an editorial function; it checks the preceding nucleotide to make sure it is correct before it adds a nucleotide to the growing chain. The editor function of this enzyme introduces an interesting problem. How can the polymerase add the very first nucleotide, when it has to check a preceding nucleotide before adding a new one? A special enzyme, called primase, which is attached to the helicase, solves this problem. Primase synthesizes short pieces of RNA that form a DNA-RNA double-stranded region. The RNA becomes a temporary part of the daughter strand, thus priming the DNA polymerase by providing the crucial first nucleotide in the new strand. Once the chromosome is duplicated, DNA repair enzymes, discussed below, remove the RNA primers and replace them with DNA nucleotides.

DNA Maintenance

Every day in a typical human cell, thousands of nucleotides are being damaged by spontaneous chemical events, environmental pollutants, and radiation. In many cases it takes only a single defective nucleotide within the coding region of a gene to produce an inactive, mutant protein. The most common forms of DNA damage are depurination and deamination. Depurination is the loss of a purine base (guanine or adenine), resulting in a gap in the DNA sequence, referred to as a "missing tooth." Deamination converts cytosine to uracil, a base that is normally found only in RNA.

About 5,000 purines are lost from each human cell every day, and over the same time period 100 cytosines are deaminated per cell. Depurination and deamination produce a great deal of damage, and in either case the daughter strand ends up with a missing nucleotide, and possibly a mutated gene, as the DNA replication machinery simply bypasses the uracil or the missing tooth. If left unrepaired, the mutated genes will be passed on to all daughter cells, with catastrophic consequences for the organism as a whole.

DNA damage caused by depurination is repaired by special nuclear proteins that detect the missing tooth, excise about 10 nucleotides on either side of the damage, and then, using the complementary strand as a guide, reconstruct the strand correctly. Deamination is dealt with by a special group of DNA repair enzymes known as base-flippers. These enzymes inspect the DNA one nucleotide at a time. After binding to a nucleotide, a base-flipper breaks the hydrogen bonds holding the nucleotide to its complementary partner. It then performs the maneuver for which it gets its name. Holding onto the nucleotide, it rotates the base a full 180 degrees, inspects it carefully, and, if it detects any damage, cuts the base out and discards it. In this case the base-flipper leaves the final repair to the missing-tooth crew that detects and repairs the gap as described previously. If the nucleotide is normal, the base-flipper rotates it back into place and reseals the hydrogen bonds. Scientists have estimated that these maintenance crews inspect and repair the entire genome of a typical human cell in less than 24 hours.

Gene Expression

Genes encode proteins and several kinds of RNA. Extracting the coded information from DNA requires two sequential processes known as transcription and translation. A gene is said to be expressed when either or both of these processes have been completed. Transcription, catalyzed by the enzyme RNA polymerase, copies one strand of the DNA into a complementary strand of mRNA, which is sent to the cytoplasm, where it joins with a ribosome. Translation is a process that is orchestrated by the ribosomes. These particles synthesize proteins using mRNA and the genetic code as guides. The ribosome can synthesize any protein specified by the mRNA, and the mRNA can be translated many times before it is recycled. Some RNAs, such as ribosomal RNA and transfer RNA, are never translated. Ribosomal RNA (rRNA) is a structural and enzymatic component of ribosomes. Transfer RNA (tRNA), though separate from the ribosome, is part of the translation machinery.

The genetic code provides a way for the translation machinery to interpret the sequence information stored in the DNA molecule and represented by mRNA. DNA is a linear sequence of four different kinds of nucleotides, so the simplest code could be one in which each nucleotide specifies a different amino acid; that is, adenine coding for the amino acid glycine, cytosine for lysine, and so on. The earliest cells may have used this coding system, but it is limited to the construction of proteins consisting of only four different kinds of amino acids. Eventually a more elaborate code evolved in which a combination of three out of the four possible DNA nucleotides, called codons, specifies a single amino acid. With this scheme it is possible to have a unique code for each of the 20 naturally occurring amino acids. For example, the codon AGC specifies the amino acid serine, whereas TGC specifies the amino acid cysteine. Thus a gene may be viewed as a long continuous sequence of codons. However, not all codons specify an amino acid. The sequence TGA signals the end of the gene, and a special codon, ATG, signals the start site, in addition to specifying the amino acid methionine. Consequently, all proteins begin with this amino acid, although it is sometimes removed once construction of the protein is complete. As mentioned above, an average protein may consist of 300 to 400 amino acids; since the codon consists of three nucleotides for each amino acid, a typical gene may be 900 to 1,200 nucleotides long.

Power Generation

Dietary fats, sugars, and proteins, not targeted for growth, storage, or repairs, are converted to ATP by the mitochondria. This process requires a number of metal-binding proteins, called the respiratory chain (also known as the electron transport chain), and a special ion channel-enzyme called ATP synthase. The respiratory chain consists of three major components: NADH dehydrogenase, cytochrome b, and cytochrome oxidase. All of these components are protein complexes with an iron (NADH dehydrogenase, cytochrome b) or a copper core (cytochrome oxidase), and together with the ATP synthase are located in the inner membrane of the mitochondria.

The respiratory chain is analogous to an electric cable that transports electricity from a hydroelectric dam to our homes, where it is used to turn on lights or to run stereos. The human body, like that of all animals, generates electricity by processing food molecules through a metabolic pathway called the Krebs cycle, also located within the mitochondria. The electrons (electricity) so generated are transferred to hydrogen ions, which quickly bind to a special nucleotide called nicotinamide adenine dinucleotide (NAD). Binding of the hydrogen ion to NAD is noted by abbreviating the resulting molecule as NADH. The electrons begin their journey down the respiratory chain when NADH binds to NADH dehydrogenase, the first component in the chain. This enzyme does just what its name implies: It removes the hydrogen from NADH, releasing the stored electrons, which are conducted through the chain by the iron and copper as though they were traveling along an electric wire. As the electrons travel from one end of the chain to the other, they energize the synthesis of ATP, which is released from the mitochondria for use by the cell. All electrical circuits must have a ground, that is, the electrons need someplace to go once they have completed the circuit. In the case of the respiratory chain, the ground is oxygen. After passing through cytochrome oxidase, the last component in the chain, the electrons are picked up by oxygen, which combines with hydrogen ions to form water.

The Cell Cycle

Free-living single cells divide as a way of reproducing their kind. Among plants and animals, cells divide as the organism grows from a seed, or an embryo, into a mature individual. This form of cell division, in which the parent cell divides into two identical daughter cells, is called mitosis. A second form of cell division, known as meiosis, is intended for sexual reproduction and occurs exclusively in gonads.

Cell division is part of a grander process known as the cell cycle, which consists of two phases: interphase and M phase (meiosis or mitosis). Interphase is divided into three subphases called Gap 1 (G_1), S phase (a period of DNA synthesis) and Gap 2 (G_2). The conclusion of interphase, and with it the termination of G_2, occurs with division of the cell and a return to G_1. Cells may leave the cycle by entering a special phase called G_0. Some cells, such as postmitotic neurons in an animal's brain, remain in G_0 for the life of the organism. For most cells, the completion of the cycle, known as the generation time, can take 30 to 60 minutes.

Cells grow continuously during interphase while preparing for the next round of division. Two notable events are the duplication of the spindle (the centrosome and associated microtubules), a structure that is crucial for the movement of the chromosomes during cell division, and the appearance of an enzyme called maturation promoting factor (MPF) at the end of G_2. MPF phosphorylates histones, proteins that bind to the DNA, and when phosphorylated compact (or condense) the chromosomes in preparation for cell

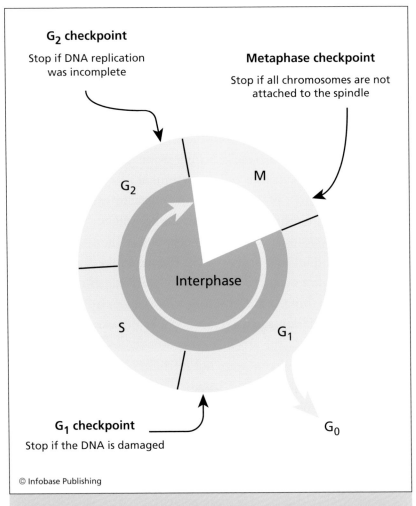

G₂ checkpoint

Stop if DNA replication
was incomplete

Metaphase checkpoint

Stop if all chromosomes are not
attached to the spindle

M

G₂

Interphase

S

G₁

G₁ checkpoint

Stop if the DNA is damaged

G₀

© Infobase Publishing

The cell cycle. Many cells spend their time cycling between interphase and M phase (cell division by mitosis or meiosis). Interphase
is divided into three subphases: Gap 1(G_1), S phase (DNA synthesis),
and Gap 2 (G_2). Cells may exit the cycle by entering G_0. The cell cycle
is equipped with three checkpoints to ensure the daughter cells are
identical and that there is no genetic damage. The yellow arrow indicates the direction of the cycle.

division. MPF is also responsible for the breakdown of the nuclear
membrane. When cell division is complete, MPF disappears, allowing the chromosomes to decondense and the nuclear envelope to

reform. Completion of a normal cell cycle always involves the division of a cell into two daughter cells, either meiotically or mitotically.

Cell division is such a complex process that many things can, and do, go wrong. Cell cycle monitors, consisting of a team of enzymes, check to make sure that everything is going well each time a cell divides, and if it is not, those monitors stop the cell from dividing until the problem is corrected. If the damage cannot be repaired, a cell remains stuck in midstream for the remainder of its life. If this happens to a cell in an animal's body, it is forced to commit suicide, in a process called apoptosis, by other cells in the immediate neighborhood or by the immune system.

The cell cycle includes three checkpoints: The first is a DNA damage checkpoint that occurs in G_1. The monitors check for damage that may have occurred as a result of the last cell cycle or were caused by something in the environment, such as UV radiation or toxic chemicals. If damage is detected, DNA synthesis is blocked until it can be repaired. The second checkpoint occurs in G_2, where the monitors make sure errors were not introduced when the chromosomes were duplicated during S-phase. The G_1 and G_2 checkpoints are sometimes referred to collectively as DNA damage checkpoints. The third and final checkpoint occurs in M-phase, to ensure that all of the chromosomes are properly attached to the spindle. This checkpoint is intended to prevent gross abnormalities in the daughter cells with regard to chromosome number. If a chromosome fails to attach to the spindle, one daughter cell will end up with too many chromosomes, while the other will have too few.

Mitosis

Mitosis is divided into four stages: prophase, metaphase, anaphase, and telophase. The behavior and movement of the chromosomes characterize each stage. At prophase, DNA replication has already occurred and the nuclear membrane begins to break down. Condensation of the duplicated chromosomes initiates the phase (i.e. the very long, thin chromosomes are folded up to produce short, thick chromosomes that are easy to move and maneuver). Under the microscope the chromosomes become visible as X-shaped structures, which are the two duplicated chromosomes, often called sister chromatids. A special region of each chromosome, called a centromere, holds the chromatids together. Proteins bind to the centromere to form a structure called the kinetochore. The centrosome is duplicated, and the two migrate to opposite ends of the cell.

During metaphase the chromosomes are sorted out and aligned between the two centrosomes. By this time the nuclear membrane has completely broken down. The two centrosomes and the microtubules fanning out between them form the mitotic spindle. The area in between the spindles, where the chromosomes are aligned, is known as the metaphase plate. Some of the microtubules make contact with the kinetochores, while others overlap, with motor proteins situated in between.

Anaphase begins when the duplicated chromosomes move to opposite poles of the cell. The first step is the release of an enzyme that breaks the bonds holding the kinetochores together, thus allowing the sister chromatids to separate from each other while remaining bound to their respective microtubules. Motor proteins, using energy supplied by ATP, move along the microtubule dragging the chromosomes to opposite ends of the cell.

During telophase the daughter chromosomes arrive at the spindle poles and decondense to form the relaxed chromosomes characteristic of interphase nuclei. The nuclear envelope begins forming around the chromosomes, marking the end of mitosis. By the end of telophase individual chromosomes are no longer distinguishable and are referred to as chromatin. While the nuclear membrane reforms, a contractile ring, made of the proteins myosin and actin, begins pinching the parental cell in two. This stage, separate from mitosis, is called cytokinesis, and leads to the formation of two daughter cells, each with one nucleus.

Meiosis

Many eukaryotes reproduce sexually through the fusion of gametes (eggs and sperm). If gametes were produced mitotically, a catastrophic growth in the number of chromosomes would occur each time a sperm fertilized an egg. Meiosis is a special form of cell division that prevents this from happening by producing haploid gametes, each possessing half as many chromosomes as the diploid cell. When haploid gametes fuse, they produce an embryo with the correct number of chromosomes.

Unlike mitosis, which produces two identical daughter cells, meiosis produces four genetically unique daughter cells that have half the number of chromosomes found in the parent cell. This is possible because meiosis consists of two rounds of cell division, called meiosis I and meiosis II, with only one round of DNA synthesis. Microbiologists discovered meiosis almost 100 years ago by comparing the number of chromosomes in somatic cells and germ cells. The roundworm, for example, was found to have four chromosomes in its somatic cells, but only two in its gametes. Many other studies also compared the amount of DNA in nuclei from somatic cells and gonads, always with the same result: The amount of DNA in somatic cells is at least double the amount in fully mature gametes.

Meiotic divisions are divided into the four mitotic stages discussed above. Indeed, meiosis II is virtually identical to a mitotic division. Meiosis I resembles mitosis, but close examination shows two important differences: Gene swapping occurs between homologous chromosomes in prophase, producing recombinant chromosomes, and the distribution of maternal and paternal chromosomes to different daughter cells. At the end of meiosis I, one of the daughter cells contains a mixture of normal and recombinant maternal chromosomes, and the other contains normal and recombinant paternal chromosomes. During meiosis II, the duplicated chromosomes are distributed to different daughter cells, yielding four, genetically unique cells: paternal, paternal recombinant, maternal, and maternal recombinant. Mixing genetic material in this way is unique to meiosis, and it is one of the reasons sexual reproduction has been such a powerful evolutionary force.

Cell Communication

A forest of glycoproteins and glycolipids covers the surface of every cell like trees on the surface of the Earth. The cell's forest is called the glycocalyx, and many of its trees function like sensory antennae. Cells use these antennae to communicate with their environment and with other cells. In multicellular organisms the glycocalyx also plays an important role in holding cells together. In this case the antennae of adjacent cells are connected to one another through the formation of chemical bonds.

The sensory antennae, also known as receptors, are linked to a variety of secondary molecules that serve to relay messages to the interior of the cell. These molecules, some of which are called second messengers, may activate machinery in the cytoplasm, or they may enter the nucleus to activate gene expression. The signals that a cell receives are of many different kinds, but generally fall into one of five categories: 1) proliferation, which stimulates the cell to grow and divide; 2) activation, which is a request for the cell to synthesize and release specific molecules; 3) deactivation, which serves as a brake for a previous activation signal; 4) navigation, which helps direct the cell to a specific location (this is very important for free-living cells hunting for food and for immune system cells that are hunting for invading microorganisms); 5) termination, which is a signal that orders the cell to commit suicide. This death signal occurs during embryonic development (e.g. the loss of webbing between the fingers and toes) and during an infection. In some cases the only way the immune system can deal with an invading pathogenic microbe is to order some of the infected cells to commit suicide. This process is known as apoptosis.

BIOTECHNOLOGY

Biotechnology (also known as recombinant DNA technology) consists of several procedures that are used to study the structure and function of genes and their products. Central to this technology is the ability to clone specific pieces of DNA and to construct libraries of these DNA fragments that represent the genetic repertoire of an entire organism or a specific cell type. With these libraries at hand, scientists have been able to study the cell and whole organisms in unprecedented detail. The information so gained has revolutionized biology as well as many other disciplines, including medical science, pharmacology, psychiatry, and anthropology, to name but a few.

DNA Cloning

In 1973 scientists discovered that restriction enzymes (enzymes that can cut DNA at specific sites), DNA ligase (an enzyme that can join two pieces of DNA together), and bacterial plasmids could be used to clone DNA molecules. Plasmids are small (about 3,000 base pairs) circular minichromosomes that occur naturally in bacteria and are often exchanged between cells by passive diffusion. A bacterium is said to be transfected when it acquires a new plasmid. For bacteria, the main advantage to swapping plasmids is that they often carry antibiotic resistance genes, so that a cell sensitive to ampicillin can become resistant simply by acquiring the right plasmid. For scientists, plasmid swapping provided an ideal method for amplifying or cloning a specific piece of DNA.

The first cloning experiment used a plasmid from the bacterium *Escherichia coli* that was cut with the restriction enzyme *Eco*RI. The plasmid had a single *Eco*RI site, so the restriction enzyme simply opened the circular molecule. Foreign DNA, cut with the same restriction enzyme, was incubated with the plasmid. Because the plasmid and foreign DNA were both cut with *Eco*RI, the DNA could insert itself into the plasmid to form a hybrid, or recombinant plasmid, after which DNA ligase sealed the two together. The reaction mixture was added to a small volume of *E. coli* so that some of the

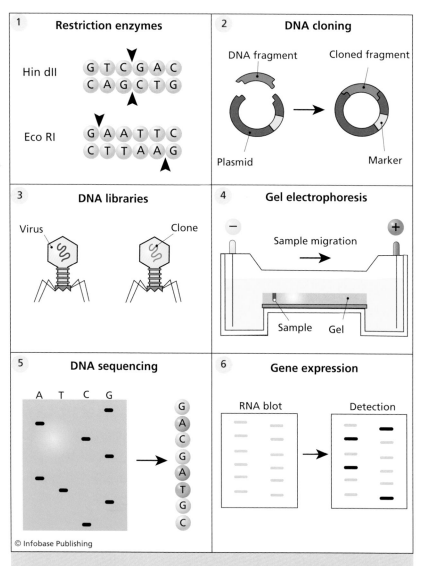

1 Restriction enzymes	2 DNA cloning
3 DNA libraries	4 Gel electrophoresis
5 DNA sequencing	6 Gene expression

© Infobase Publishing

Biotechnology. This technology consists of six basic steps: 1) digestion of DNA with restriction enzymes in order to isolate specific DNA fragments; 2) cloning of restriction fragments in circular bacterial minichromosomes to increase their numbers; 3) storing the fragments for further study in viral-based DNA libraries; 4) isolation and purification of DNA fragments from gene libraries using gel electrophoresis; 5) sequencing cloned DNA fragments; 6) determining the expression profile of selected DNA clones using RNA blots and radioactive detection procedures.

cells could take up the recombinant plasmid before being transferred to a nutrient broth containing streptomycin. Only those cells carrying the recombinant plasmid, which contained an antistreptomycin gene, could grow in the presence of this antibiotic. Each time the cells divided, the plasmid DNA was duplicated along with the main chromosome. After the cells had grown overnight, the foreign DNA had been amplified billions of times and was easily isolated for sequencing or expression studies. In this procedure the plasmid is known as a cloning vector because it serves to transfer the foreign DNA into a cell.

DNA Libraries

The basic cloning procedure described above not only provides a way to amplify a specific piece of DNA, but it can also be used to construct DNA libraries. In this case, however, the cloning vector is a bacteriophage called lambda. The lambda genome is double-stranded DNA of about 40,000 base pairs (bp), much of which can be replaced by foreign DNA without sacrificing the ability of the virus to infect bacteria. This is the great advantage of lambda over a plasmid. Lambda can accommodate very long pieces of DNA, often long enough to contain an entire gene, whereas a plasmid cannot accommodate foreign DNA that is larger than 2,000 base pairs. Moreover, a bacteriophage has the natural ability to infect bacteria, so that the efficiency of transfection is 100 times greater than it is for plasmids.

The construction of a DNA library begins with the isolation of genomic DNA and its digestion with a restriction enzyme to produce fragments of 1,000 to 10,000 bp. These fragments are ligated into lambda genomes, which are subjected to a packaging reaction to produce mature viral particles, most of which carry a different piece of the genomic DNA. This collection of viruses is called a genomic library and is used to study the structure and organization of specific genes. Clones from a library such as this contain the coding sequences, in addition to noncoding sequences such as introns, intervening sequences, promoters, and enhancers. An alternative form of a DNA library can be constructed by isolating messenger RNA (mRNA) from a specific cell type. This RNA is converted to the complementary DNA (cDNA) using an RNA-dependent DNA polymerase called reverse transcriptase. The cDNA is ligated to lambda genomes and packaged as for the genomic library. This collection of recombinant viruses is known as a cDNA library and contains genes that were being expressed by the cells when the mRNA was extracted. It does not include introns or controlling elements as these are lost during transcription and the processing that occurs in the cell to make mature mRNA. Thus a cDNA library is intended for the purpose of studying gene expression and the structure of the coding region only.

Labeling Cloned DNA

Many of the procedures used in biotechnology were inspired by the events that occur during DNA replication (described above). This includes the labeling of cloned DNA for use as probes in expression studies, DNA sequencing, and PCR (described below). DNA replication involves duplicating one of the strands (the parent, or template strand) by linking nucleotides in an order specified by the template and depends on a large number of enzymes, the most important of which is DNA polymerase. This enzyme, guided by the template strand, constructs a daughter strand by linking nucleotides together. One such nucleotide is deoxyadenine triphosphate (dATP). Deoxyribonucleotides have a single hydroxyl group located at the $3'$ carbon of the sugar group while the triphosphate is attached to the $5'$ carbon.

The procedure for labeling DNA probes, developed in 1983, introduces radioactive nucleotides into a DNA molecule. This method supplies DNA polymerase with a single-stranded DNA template, a primer, and the four nucleotides in a buffered solution to induce in vitro replication. The daughter strand, which becomes the labeled probe, is made radioactive by including a ^{32}P-labeled nucleotide in the reaction mix. The radioactive nucleotide is usually deoxycytosine triphosphate (dCTP) or dATP. The ^{32}P is always part of the α (alpha) phosphate (the phosphate closest to the 5′ carbon), as this is the one used by the polymerase to form the phosphodiester bond between nucleotides. Nucleotides can also be labeled with a fluorescent dye molecule.

Single-stranded DNA hexamers (six bases long) are used as primers, and these are produced in such a way that they contain all possible permutations of four bases taken six at a time. Randomizing the base sequence for the primers ensures that there will be at least one primer site in a template that is only 50 bp long. Templates used in labeling reactions such as this are generally 100 to 800 bp long. This strategy of labeling DNA is known as random primer labeling.

Gel Electrophoresis

This procedure is used to separate DNA and RNA fragments by size in a slab of agarose (highly refined agar) or polyacrylamide subjected to an electric field. Nucleic acids carry a negative charge and thus will migrate toward a positively charged electrode. The gel acts as a sieving medium that impedes the movement of the molecules. Thus the rate at which the fragments migrate is a function of their size; small fragments migrate more rapidly than large fragments. The gel containing the samples is run submerged in a special pH-regulated solution, or buffer on page 175. Agarose gels are run horizontal as shown in the figure. But DNA sequencing gels, made of polyacrylamide, are much bigger and are run in a vertical tank.

DNA Sequencing

A sequencing reaction developed by the British biochemist Dr. Fred Sanger in 1976, is a technique that takes its inspiration from the natural process of DNA replication. DNA polymerase requires a primer with a free 3′ hydroxyl group. The polymerase adds the first nucleotide to this group, and all subsequent bases are added to the 3′ hydroxyl of the previous base. Sequencing by the Sanger method is usually performed with the DNA cloned into a special sequencing plasmid. This simplifies the choice of the primers since their sequence can be derived from the known plasmid sequence. Once the primer binds to the primer site, the cloned DNA may be replicated.

Sanger's innovation involved the synthesis of chain-terminating nucleotide analogues lacking the 3′ hydroxyl group. These analogues, also known as dideoxynucleotides (ddATP, ddCTP, ddGTP and ddTTP), terminate the growth of the daughter strand at the point of insertion, and this can be used to determine the distance of each base on the daughter strand from the primer. These distances can be visualized by separating the Sanger reaction products on a polyacrylamide gel, and then exposing the gel to X-ray film to produce an autoradiogram. The DNA sequence is read directly from this film, beginning with the smallest fragment at the bottom of the gel (the nucleotide closest to the primer), and ending with the largest fragment at the top. A hypothetical autoradiogram and the derived DNA sequence are shown in the figure on page 175 (panel 5). The smallest fragment in this example is the "C" nucleotide at the bottom of lane 3. The next nucleotide in the sequence is the "G" nucleotide in lane 4, then the "T" nucleotide in lane 2, and so on to the top of the gel.

Automated versions of the Sanger sequencing reaction use fluorescent-labeled dideoxynucleotides, each with a different color, so a computer can record the sequence of the template as the reaction mix passes a sensitive photocell. Machines such as this were used to sequence the human genome, a job that cost many millions of dollars and took years to complete. Recent advances in DNA sequencing technology will make it possible to sequence the human genome in less than a week at a cost of $1,000.

Gene Expression

The production of a genomic or cDNA library, followed by the sequencing of isolated clones, is a very powerful method for characterizing genes and the genomes from which they came. But the icing on the cake is the ability to determine the expression profile for a gene: That is, to determine which cells express the gene and exactly when the gene is turned on and off. Typical experiments may wish to determine the expression of specific genes in normal versus cancerous tissue, or tissues obtained from groups of different ages. There are essentially three methods for doing this: RNA blotting, Fluorescent In Situ Hybridization (FISH), and the Polymerase Chain Reaction.

RNA Blotting

This procedure consists of the following steps:

1. Extract mRNA from the cells or tissue of interest.
2. Fractionate (separate by size) the mRNA sample using gel electrophoresis.
3. Transfer the fractionated sample to a nylon membrane (the blotting step).
4. Incubate the membrane with a gene fragment (usually a cDNA clone) that has been labeled with a radioisotope.
5. Expose the membrane to X-ray film to visualize the signal.

The RNA is transferred from the gel to a nylon membrane using a vacuum apparatus or a simple dish containing a transfer buffer topped by a large stack of ordinary paper towels and a weight. The paper towels pull the transfer buffer through the gel, eluting the RNA from the gel and trapping it on the membrane. The location of specific mRNAs can be determined by hybridizing the membrane to a radiolabeled cDNA or genomic clone. The hybridization procedure involves placing the membrane in a buffer solution containing a labeled probe. During a long incubation period, the probe binds to the target sequence immobilized on the membrane. A-T and G-C base pairing (also known as hybridization) mediate the binding between the probe and target. The double-stranded molecule that is formed is a hybrid, being formed between the RNA target, on the membrane, and the DNA probe.

Fluorescent In Situ Hybridization (FISH)

Studying gene expression does not always depend on RNA blots and membrane hybridization. In the 1980s scientists found that cDNA probes could be hybridized to DNA or RNA in situ, that is, while located within cells or tissue sections fixed on a microscope slide. In this case the probe is labeled with a fluorescent dye molecule, rather than a radioactive isotope. The samples are then examined and photographed under a fluorescent microscope. FISH is an extremely powerful variation on RNA blotting. This procedure gives precise information regarding the identity of a cell that expresses a specific gene, information that usually cannot be obtained with membrane hybridization. Organs and tissues are generally composed of many different kinds of cells, which cannot be separated from one another using standard biochemical extraction procedures. Histological sections, however, show clearly the various cell types, and when subjected to FISH analysis, provide clear information as to which cells express specific genes. FISH is also used in clinical laboratories for the diagnosis of genetic abnormalities.

Polymerase Chain Reaction (PCR)

PCR is simply repetitive DNA replication over a limited, primer defined, region of a suitable template. It provides a way of amplifying a short segment of DNA without going through the cloning procedures described above. The region defined by the primers is amplified to such an extent that it can be easily isolated for further study. The reaction exploits the fact that a DNA duplex, in a low-salt buffer, will melt (i.e., separate into two single strands) at 167°F (75°C), but will reanneal (rehybridize) at 98.6°F (37°C).

The reaction is initiated by melting the template, in the presence of primers and polymerase in a suitable buffer, cooling quickly to 98.6°F (37°C), and allowing sufficient time for the polymerase to replicate both strands of the template. The temperature is then increased to 167°F (75°C) to melt the newly formed duplexes and then cooled to 98.6°F (37°C). At the lower temperature more primer will anneal to initiate another round of replication. The heating-cooling cycle is repeated 20 to 30 times, after which the reaction products are fractionated on an agarose gel, and the region containing the amplified fragment is cut out of the gel and purified for further study. The DNA polymerase used in these reactions is isolated from thermophilic bacteria that can withstand temperatures of 158°F (70°C) to 176°F (80°C). PCR applications are nearly limitless. It is used to amplify DNA from samples containing at times no more than a few cells. It is being used in the development of ultrafast DNA sequencers, identification of tissue samples in criminal investigations, amplification of ancient DNA obtained from fossils, and the identification of genes that are turned on or off during embryonic development or during cellular transformation (cancer formation).

GENE THERAPY

An illness is often due to invading microbes that destroy or damage cells and organs in our body. Cholera, smallpox, measles, diphtheria, AIDS, and the common cold are all examples of what is called an infectious disease. Such diseases may be treated with a drug that will in some cases remove the microbe from the body, thus curing the disease. Unfortunately, most diseases are not of the infectious kind. In such cases there are no microbes to fight, no drugs to apply. Instead, physicians are faced with a far more difficult problem, for this type of disease is an ailment that damages a gene. Gene therapy attempts to cure these diseases by replacing, or supplementing, the damaged gene.

When a gene is damaged, it usually is caused by a point mutation, a change that affects a single nucleotide. Sickle-cell anemia, a disease affecting red blood cells, was the first genetic disorder of this kind to be described. The mutation occurs in a gene that codes for the β (beta) chain of hemoglobin, converting the codon GAG to GTG, which substitutes the amino acid valine at position 6, for glutamic acid. This single amino-acid substitution is enough to cripple the hemoglobin molecule, making it impossible for it to carry enough oxygen to meet the demands of a normal adult. Scientists have identified several thousand genetic disorders that are known to be responsible for diseases such as breast cancer, colon cancer, hemophilia, and two neurological disorders, Alzheimer's disease and Parkinson's disease.

Gene therapy is made possible by recombinant DNA technology (biotechnology). Central to this technology is the use of viruses to clone specific pieces of DNA. That is, the DNA is inserted into a viral chromosome and is amplified as the virus multiplies. Viruses are parasites that specialize in infecting bacterial and animal cells. Consequently, scientists realized that a therapeutic gene could be inserted into a patient's cells by first introducing it into a virus and then letting the virus carry it into the affected cells. In this context the virus is referred to as gene therapy delivery vehicle or vector (in recombinant technology it is referred to as a cloning vector).

Commonly used viruses are the retrovirus and the adenovirus. A retrovirus gets its name from the fact that it has an RNA genome that is copied into DNA after it infects a cell. Corona viruses (which cause the common cold) and the AIDS virus are common examples of retroviruses. The adenovirus (from "adenoid," a gland from which the virus was first isolated) normally infects the upper respiratory tract, causing colds and flulike symptoms. This virus, unlike the retrovirus, has a DNA genome. Artificial vectors, called liposomes,

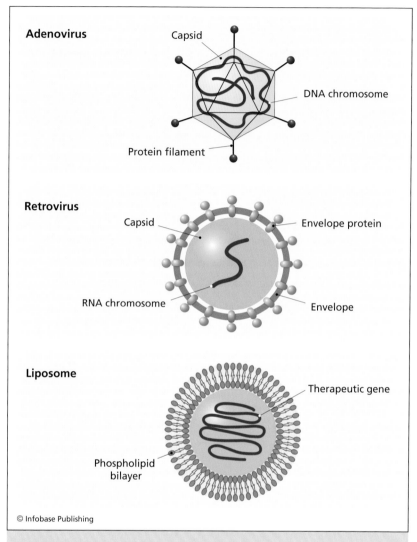

Adenovirus

Capsid

DNA chromosome

Protein filament

Retrovirus

Capsid

Envelope protein

RNA chromosome

Envelope

Liposome

Therapeutic gene

Phospholipid bilayer

© Infobase Publishing

Vectors used in gene therapy. Adenoviruses have a DNA genome, contained in a crystalline protein capsid, and normally infect cells of the upper respiratory tract, causing colds and flulike symptoms. The protein filaments are used to infect cells. Retroviruses have an RNA genome that is converted to DNA when a cell is infected. The capsid is enclosed in a phospholipid envelope, studded with proteins that are used to infect cells. The AIDS virus is a common example of a retrovirus. Artificial vectors have also been used, consisting of a phospholipid bilayer enclosing the therapeutic gene.

have also been used that consist of a phospholipid vesicle (bubble), containing the therapeutic gene.

Gene therapy vectors are prepared by cutting the viral chromosome and the therapeutic gene with the same restriction enzyme, after which the two are joined together with a DNA ligase. This recombinant chromosome is packaged into viral particles to form the final vector. The vector may be introduced into cultured cells suffering from a genetic defect and then returned to the patient from whom they were derived (ex vivo delivery). Alternatively, the vector may be injected directly into the patient's circulatory system (in vivo delivery). The ex vivo procedure is used when the genetic defect appears in white blood cells, or stem cells that may be harvested from the patient and grown in culture. The in vivo procedure is used when the genetic defect appears in an organ, such as the liver, brain, or pancreas. This is the most common form of gene therapy, but it is also potentially hazardous because the vector, being free in the circulatory system, may infect a wide range of cells, thus activating an immune response that could lead to widespread tissue and organ damage.

The first gene therapy trial, conducted in 1990, used ex vivo delivery. This trial cured a young patient named Ashi deSilva of an immune deficiency (adenosine deaminase deficiency) that affects white blood cells. Other trials since then have either been ineffective or were devastating failures. Such a case occurred in 1999, when Jesse Gelsinger, an 18-year-old patient suffering from a liver disease, died while participating in a gene therapy trial. His death was caused by multiorgan failure brought on by the viral vector. In 2002 two children being treated for another form of immune deficiency developed vector-induced leukemia (cancer of the white blood cells). Subsequent studies, concluded in 2009, appear to have resolved these problems. Gene therapy holds great promise as a medical therapy. In the United States alone, there are currently more than 900 trials in progress to treat a variety of genetic disorders.

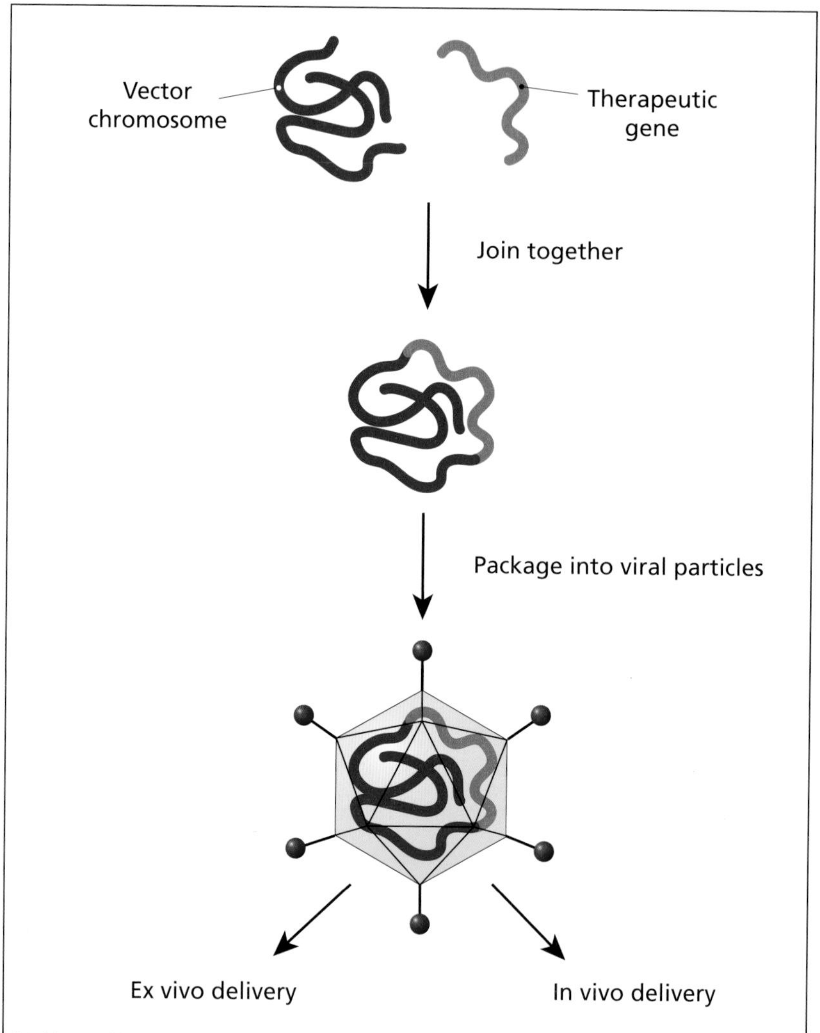

Vector chromosome

Therapeutic gene

Join together

Package into viral particles

Ex vivo delivery

In vivo delivery

© Infobase Publishing

Vector preparation and delivery. A viral chromosome and a therapeutic gene are cut with the same restriction enzyme, and the two are joined together, after which, the recombinant chromosome is packaged into viral particles to form the vector. The vector may be introduced into cultured cells and then returned to the patient from whom they were derived (ex vivo delivery), or the vector may be injected directly into the patient's circulatory system (in vivo delivery).

THE HUMAN GENOME PROJECT

Sequencing the entire human genome is an idea that grew over a period of 20 years, beginning in the early 1980s. At that time the DNA-sequencing method invented by the British biochemist Fred Sanger, then at the University of Cambridge, was but a few years old and had only been used to sequence viral or mitochondrial genomes. Indeed, one of the first genomes to be sequenced was that of bacteriophage G4, a virus that infects the bacterium *Escherichia coli (E. coli)*. The G4 genome consists of 5,577 nucleotide pairs (or base pairs, abbreviated bp) and was sequenced in Dr. Sanger's laboratory in 1979. By 1982 the Sanger protocol was used by others to sequence the genome of the animal virus SV40 (5,224 bp), the human mitochondrion (16,569 bp), and bacteriophage lambda (48,502 bp). Besides providing invaluable data, these projects demonstrated the feasibility of sequencing very large genomes.

The possibility of sequencing the entire human genome was first discussed at scientific meetings organized by the U.S. Department of Energy (DOE) between 1984 and 1986. A committee appointed by the U.S. National Research Council endorsed the idea in 1988 but recommended a broader program to include the sequencing of the genes of humans, bacteria, yeast, worms, flies, and mice. They also called for the establishment of research programs devoted to the ethical, legal, and social issues raised by human genome research. The program was formally launched in late 1990 as a consortium consisting of coordinated sequencing projects in the United States, Britain, France, Germany, Japan, and China. At about the same time, the Human Genome Organization (HUGO) was founded to provide a forum for international coordination of genomic research.

By 1995 the consortium had established a strategy, called hierarchical shotgun sequencing, which they applied to the human genome as well as to the other organisms mentioned. With this strategy, genomic DNA is cut into one-megabase (Mb) fragments (i.e., each fragment consists of 1 million bases) that are cloned into bacterial artificial chromosomes (BACs) to form a library of DNA fragments. The BAC fragments are partially characterized, then organized into an overlapping assembly called a contig. Clones are selected from the contigs for shotgun sequencing. That is, each shotgun clone is digested into small 1,000 bp fragments, sequenced, and then assembled into the final sequence with the aid of computers. Organizing the initial BAC fragments into contigs greatly simplifies the final assembly stage.

Sequencing of the human genome was divided into two stages. The first stage, completed in 2001, was a rough draft that covered about 80 percent of the genome with an estimated size of more than 3 billion bases (also expressed as 3 gigabases, or 3 Gb). The final draft, completed in April 2003, covers the entire genome and refines the data for areas of the genome that were difficult to sequence. It also filled in many gaps that occurred in the rough draft. The final draft of the human genome gives us a great deal of information that may be divided into three categories: gene content, gene origins, and gene organization.

Gene Content

Analysis of the final draft has shown that the human genome consists of 3.2 Gb of DNA that encodes about 30,000 genes (estimates range between 25,000 to 32,000). The estimated number of genes is surprisingly low; many scientists had believed the human genome contained 100,000 genes. By comparison, the fruit fly has 13,338 genes and the simple roundworm, *Caenorhabditis elegans (C. elegans)*, has 18,266. The genome data suggests that human complexity, as compared to the fruit fly or the worm, is not simply due to the absolute number of genes but involves the complexity of the proteins that are encoded by those genes. In general, human proteins tend to be much more complex than those of lower organisms. Data from the final draft and other sources provides a detailed overview of the functional profile of human cellular proteins.

Gene Origins

Fully one-half of human genes originated as transposable elements, also known as jumping genes (these will be discussed at length in a following section). Equally surprising is the fact that 220 of our genes were obtained by horizontal transfer from bacteria, rather than ancestral, or vertical, inheritance. In other words, humans obtained these genes directly from bacteria, probably during episodes of infection, in a kind of natural gene therapy, or gene swapping. Scientists know this to be the case because while these genes occur in bacteria, they are not present in yeast, fruit flies, or any other eukaryotes that have been tested.

The function of most of the horizontally transferred genes is unclear, although a few may code for basic metabolic enzymes. A notable exception is a gene that codes for an enzyme called monoamine oxidase (MAO). Monoamines are neurotransmitters, such as dopamine, norepinephrine, and serotonin, which are needed for neural signaling in the human central nervous system. Monoamine oxidase plays a crucial role in the turnover of these neurotransmitters. How MAO, obtained from bacteria, could have developed such an important role in human physiology is a great mystery.

Gene Organization

In prokaryotes, genes are simply arranged in tandem along the chromosome, with little if any DNA separating one gene from the other. Each gene is transcribed into messenger RNA (mRNA), which is translated into protein. Indeed, in prokaryotes, which have no nucleus, translation often begins even before transcription is complete. In eukaryotes, as one might expect, gene organization is more complex. Data from the genome project shows clearly that eukaryote genes are split into subunits, called exons, and that each exon is separated by a length of DNA, called an intron. A gene, consisting of introns and exons, is separated from other genes by long stretches of noncoding DNA called intervening sequences.

Eukaryote genes are transcribed into a primary RNA molecule that includes exon and intron sequences. The primary transcript never leaves the nucleus and is never translated into protein. Nuclear enzymes remove the introns from the primary transcript, after which the exons are joined together to form the mature mRNA. Thus only the exons carry the necessary code to produce a protein.

UNDERSTANDING CLINICAL TRIALS

Clinical trials are conducted in four phases and are always preceded by research conducted on experimental animals such as mice, rats, or monkeys. The format for preclinical research is informal; it is conducted in a variety of research labs around the world, with the results being published in scientific journals. Formal approval from a governmental regulatory body is not required.

Phase I Clinical Trial

Pending the outcome of the preclinical research, investigators may apply for permission to try the experiments on human subjects. Applications in the United States are made to the Food and Drug Administration (FDA), the National Institutes of Health (NIH), and the Recombinant DNA Advisory Committee (RAC). RAC was set up by NIH to monitor any research, including clinical trials, dealing with cloning, recombinant DNA, or gene therapy. Phase I trials are conducted on a small number of adult volunteers, usually between two and 20, who have given informed consent. That is, the investigators explain the procedure, the possible outcomes, and especially, the dangers associated with the procedure before the subjects sign a consent form. The purpose of the Phase I trial is to determine the overall effect the treatment has on humans. A treatment that works well in monkeys or mice may not work at all on humans. Similarly, a treatment that appears safe in lab animals may be toxic, even deadly, when given to humans. Since most clinical trials are testing a new drug of some kind, the first priority is to determine a safe dosage for humans. Consequently, subjects in the Phase I trial are given a range of doses, all of which, even the high dose, are less than the highest dose given to experimental animals. If the results from the Phase I trial are promising, the investigators may apply for permission to proceed to Phase II.

Phase II Clinical Trial

Having established the general protocol, or procedure, the investigators now try to replicate the encouraging results from Phase I but with a much larger number of subjects (100–300). Only with a large number of subjects is it possible to prove the treatment has an effect. In addition, dangerous side effects may have been missed in Phase I because of a small sample size. The results from Phase II will determine how safe the procedure is and whether it works or not. If the statistics show the treatment is effective and toxicity is low, the investigators may apply for permission to proceed to Phase III.

Phase III Clinical Trial

Based on Phase II results, the procedure may look very promising, but before it can be used as a routine treatment, it must be tested on thousands of patients at a variety of research centers. This is the expensive part of bringing a new drug or therapy to market, costing millions, sometimes billions, of dollars. It is for this reason that Phase III clinical trials invariably have the financial backing of large pharmaceutical or biotechnology companies. If the results of the Phase II trial are confirmed in Phase III, the FDA will approve the use of the drug for routine treatment. The use of the drug or treatment now passes into an informal Phase IV trial.

Phase IV Clinical Trial

Even though the treatment has gained formal approval, its performance is monitored for very long-term effects, sometimes stretching on for 10 to 20 years. In this way the FDA retains the power to recall the drug long after it has become a part of standard medical procedure. It can happen that in the long term, the drug costs more than an alternative, in which case health insurance providers may refuse to cover the cost of the treatment.

GENE AND PROTEIN NOMENCLATURE

Scientists who were, in effect, probing around in the dark have discovered many genes and their encoded proteins. Once discovered, the new genes or proteins had to be named. Usually the "name" is nothing more than a lab-book code or an acronym suggested by the system under study at the time. Sometimes it turns out, after further study, that the function observed in the original study is a minor aspect of the gene's role in the cell. It is for this reason that gene and protein names sometimes seem absurd and poorly chosen.

In 2003 an International Committee on Standardized Genetic Nomenclature agreed to unify the rules and guidelines for gene and protein names for the mouse and rat. Similar committees have attempted to standardize gene-naming conventions for human, frog, zebrafish, and yeast genes. In general, the gene name is expected to be brief and to begin with a lowercase letter unless it is a person's name. The gene symbols are acronyms taken from the gene name and are expected to be three to five characters long and not more than 10. The symbols must be written with Roman letters and Arabic numbers. The same symbol is used for orthologs (i.e. the same gene) among different species, such as human, mouse, or rat. Thus the gene sonic hedgehog is symbolized as shh, and the gene myelocytomatosis is symbolized as myc.

Unfortunately, the various committees were unable to agree on a common presentation for the gene and protein symbols. A human gene symbol, for example, is italicized, uppercase letters, and the protein is uppercase and not italicized. A frog gene symbol is lowercase, and the protein is uppercase, while neither is italicized. Thus the myc gene and its protein, for example, are written as *MYC* and MYC in humans, myc and MYC in frogs, and *Myc* and Myc in mice and rats. The latter convention, *Myc* and Myc, is used throughout the New Biology set, regardless of the species.

WEIGHTS AND MEASURES

The following table presents some common weights, measures, and conversions that appear in this book and other volumes of the New Biology set.

QUANTITY	EQUIVALENT
Length	1 meter (m) = 100 centimeters (cm) = 1.094 yards = 39.37 inches 1 kilometer (km) = 1,000 m = 0.62 miles 1 foot = 30.48 cm 1 inch = 1/12 foot = 2.54 cm 1 cm = 0.394 inch = 10^{-2} (or 0.01) m 1 millimeter (mm) = 10^{-3} m 1 micrometer (μm) = 10^{-6} m 1 nanometer (nm) = 10^{-9} m 1 angstrom (Å) = 10^{-10} m
Mass	1 gram (g) = 0.0035 ounce 1 pound = 16 ounces = 453.6 grams 1 kilogram (kg) = 2.2 pounds (lb) 1 milligram (mg) = 10^{-3} g 1 microgram (μg) = 10^{-6} g
Volume	1 liter (l) = 1.06 quarts (US) = 0.264 gallon (US) 1 quart (US) = 32 fluid ounces = 0.95 liter 1 milliliter (ml) = 10^{-3} liter = 1 cubic centimeter (cc)
Temperature	°C = 5/9 (°F – 32) °F = (9/5 × °C) + 32
Energy	Calorie = the amount of heat needed to raise the temperature of 1 gram of water by 1°C. Kilocalorie = 1,000 calories. Used to describe the energy content of foods.

 **Glossary**

acetyl A chemical group derived from acetic acid that is important in energy metabolism and for the modification of proteins.

acetylcholine A neurotransmitter released at axonal terminals by cholinergic neurons, found in the central and peripheral nervous systems and released at the vertebrate neuromuscular junction.

acetyl-CoA A water-soluble molecule, coenzyme A (CoA) that carries acetyl groups in cells.

acid A substance that releases protons when dissolved in water; carries a net negative charge.

actin filament A protein filament formed by the polymerization of globular actin molecules; forms the cytoskeleton of all eukaryotes and part of the contractile apparatus of skeletal muscle.

action potential A self-propagating electrical impulse that occurs in the membranes of neurons, muscles, photoreceptors, and hair cells of the inner ear.

active transport Movement of molecules across the cell membrane, using the energy stored in ATP.

adenylate cyclase A membrane-bound enzyme that catalyzes the conversion of ATP to cyclic AMP; an important component of cell-signaling pathways.

adherens junction A cell junction in which the cytoplasmic face of the membrane is attached to actin filaments.

adipocyte A fat cell.

adrenaline (epinephrine) A hormone released by chromaffin cells in the adrenal gland; prepares an animal for extreme activity by increasing the heart rate and blood sugar levels.

adult stem cells   Stem cells isolated from adult tissues, such as bone marrow or epithelium.

aerobic   Refers to a process that either requires oxygen or occurs in its presence.

agar   A polysaccharide isolated from seaweed that forms a gel when boiled in water and cooled to room temperature; used by microbiologists as a solid culture medium for the isolation and growth of bacteria and fungi.

agarose   A purified form of agar that is used to fractionate (separate by size) biomolecules.

allele   An alternate form of a gene. Diploid organisms have two alleles for each gene, located at the same locus (position) on homologous chromosomes.

allogeneic transplant   A cell, tissue, or organ transplant from an unrelated individual.

alpha helix   A common folding pattern of proteins in which a linear sequence of amino acids twists into a right-handed helix stabilized by hydrogen bonds.

amino acid   An organic molecule containing amino and carboxyl groups that is a building block of protein.

aminoacyl tRNA   An amino acid linked by its carboxyl group to a hydroxyl group on tRNA.

aminoacyl-tRNA synthetase   An enzyme that attaches the correct amino acid to a tRNA.

amino terminus   The end of a protein or polypeptide chain that carries a free amino group.

amphipathic   Having both hydrophilic and hydrophobic regions, as in a phospholipid.

anabolism   A collection of metabolic reactions in a cell whereby large molecules are made from smaller ones.

anaerobic   A cellular metabolism that does not depend on molecular oxygen.

anaphase   A mitotic stage in which the two sets of chromosomes move away from each other toward opposite spindle poles.

anchoring junction   A cell junction that attaches cells to each other.

angiogenesis   Sprouting of new blood vessels from preexisting ones.

angstrom A unit of length, equal to 10^{-10} meter or 0.1 nanometer (nM), that is used to measure molecules and atoms.

anterior A position close to or at the head end of the body.

antibiotic A substance made by bacteria, fungi, and plants that is toxic to microorganisms. Common examples are penicillin and streptomycin.

antibody A protein made by B cells of the immune system in response to invading microbes.

anticodon A sequence of three nucleotides in tRNA that is complementary to a messenger RNA codon.

antigen A molecule that stimulates an immune response, leading to the formation of antibodies.

antigen-presenting cell A cell of the immune system, such as a monocyte, that presents pieces of an invading microbe (the antigen) to lymphocytes.

antiparallel The relative orientation of the two strands in a DNA double helix; the polarity of one strand is oriented in the opposite direction to the other.

antiporter A membrane carrier protein that transports two different molecules across a membrane in opposite directions.

apoptosis Regulated or programmed form of cell death that may be activated by the cell itself or by the immune system to force cells to commit suicide when they become infected with a virus or bacterium.

archaea The archaea are prokaryotes that are physically similar to bacteria (both lack a nucleus and internal organelles), but they have retained a primitive biochemistry and physiology that would have been commonplace 2 billion years ago.

asexual reproduction The process of forming new individuals without gametes or the fertilization of an egg by a sperm. Individuals produced this way are identical to the parent and referred to as a clone.

aster The star-shaped arrangement of microtubules that is characteristic of a mitotic or meiotic spindle.

ATP (adenosine triphosphate) A nucleoside consisting of adenine, ribose, and three phosphate groups that is the main carrier of chemical energy in the cell.

ATPase   Any enzyme that catalyzes a biochemical reaction by extracting the necessary energy from ATP.

ATP synthase   A protein located in the inner membrane of the mitochondrion that catalyzes the formation of ATP from ADP and inorganic phosphate using the energy supplied by the electron transport chain.

autogeneic transplant   A patient receives a transplant of his or her own tissue.

autologous   Refers to tissues or cells derived from the patient's own body.

autoradiograph (autoradiogram)   X-ray film that has been exposed to X-rays or to a source of radioactivity; used to visualize internal structures of the body and radioactive signals from sequencing gels and DNA or RNA blots.

autosome   Any chromosome other than a sex chromosome.

axon   A long extension of a neuron's cell body that transmits an electrical signal to other neurons.

axonal transport   The transport of organelles, such as Golgi vesicles, along an axon to the axonal terminus. Transport also flows from the terminus to the cell body.

bacteria   One of the most ancient forms of cellular life (the other is the archaea). Bacteria are prokaryotes, and some are known to cause disease.

bacterial artificial chromosome (BAC)   A cloning vector that accommodates DNA inserts of up to 1 million base pairs.

bacteriophage   A virus that infects bacteria. Bacteriophages were used to prove that DNA is the cell's genetic material and are now used as cloning vectors.

base   A substance that can accept a proton in solution. The purines and pyrimidines in DNA and RNA are organic bases and are often referred to simply as bases.

base pair   Two nucleotides in RNA or DNA that are held together by hydrogen bonds. Adenine bound to thymine or guanine bound to cytosine are examples of base pairs

B cell (B lymphocyte)   A white blood cell that makes antibodies and is part of the adaptive immune response.

benign   Tumors that grow to a limited size and do not spread to other parts of the body.

beta sheet   Common structural motif in proteins in which different strands of the protein run alongside one another and are held together by hydrogen bonds.

biopsy   The removal of cells or tissues for examination under a microscope. When only a sample of tissue is removed, the procedure is called an incisional biopsy or core biopsy. When an entire lump or suspicious area is removed, the procedure is called an excisional biopsy. When a sample of tissue or fluid is removed with a needle, the procedure is called a needle biopsy or fine-needle aspiration.

biosphere   The world of living organisms.

biotechnology   A set of procedures that are used to study and manipulate genes and their products.

blastomere   A cell formed by the cleavage of a fertilized egg. Blastomeres are the totipotent cells of the early embryo.

blotting   A technique for transferring DNA (southern blotting), RNA (northern blotting), or proteins (western blotting) from an agarose or polyacrylamide gel to a nylon membrane.

BRCA1 (breast cancer gene 1)   A gene on chromosome 17 that may be involved in regulating the cell cycle. A person who inherits an altered version of the BRCA1 gene has a higher risk of getting breast, ovarian, or prostate cancer.

BRCA2 (breast cancer gene 2)   A gene on chromosome 13 that, when mutated, increases the risk of getting breast, ovarian, or prostate cancer.

budding yeast   The common name for the baker's yeast *Saccharomyces cerevisiae,* a popular experimental organism that reproduces by budding off a parental cell.

buffer   A pH-regulated solution with a known electrolyte (salt) content; used in the isolation, manipulation, and storage of biomolecules and medicinal products.

cadherin   Belongs to a family of proteins that mediates cell-cell adhesion in animal tissues.

calorie   A unit of heat. One calorie is the amount of heat needed to raise the temperature of one gram of water by 1°C. Kilocalories (1,000 calories) are used to describe the energy content of foods.

capsid   The protein coat of a virus, formed by autoassembly of one or more proteins into a geometrically symmetrical structure.

carbohydrate   A general class of compounds that includes sugars, containing carbon, hydrogen, and oxygen.

carboxyl group   A carbon atom attached to an oxygen and a hydroxyl group.

carboxyl terminus   The end of a protein containing a carboxyl group.

carcinogen   A compound or form of radiation that can cause cancer.

carcinogenesis   The formation of a cancer.

carcinoma   Cancer of the epithelium, representing the majority of human cancers.

cardiac muscle   Muscle of the heart; composed of myocytes that are linked together in a communication network based on free passage of small molecules through gap junctions.

caspase   A protease involved in the initiation of apoptosis.

catabolism   Enzyme regulated breakdown of large molecules for the extraction of chemical-bond energy. Intermediate products are called catabolites.

catalyst   A substance that lowers the activation energy of a reaction.

CD28   Cell-surface protein located in T-cell membranes, necessary for the activation of T-cells by foreign antigens.

cDNA (complementary DNA)   DNA that is synthesized from mRNA, thus containing the complementary sequence; cDNA contains coding sequence, but not the regulatory sequences that are present in the genome. Labeled probes are made from cDNA for the study of gene expression.

cell adhesion molecule (CAM)   A cell surface protein that is used to connect cells to one another.

cell body   The main part of a cell containing the nucleus, Golgi complex, and endoplasmic reticulum; used in reference to neurons that have long processes (dendrites and axons) extending some distance from the nucleus and cytoplasmic machinery.

cell coat   (see **glycocalyx**)

cell-cycle control system   A team of regulatory proteins that governs progression through the cell cycle.

cell-division-cycle gene (*cdc* gene)   A gene that controls a specific step in the cell cycle.

cell fate   The final differentiated state that a pluripotent embryonic cell is expected to attain.

cell-medicated immune response   Activation of specific cells to launch an immune response against an invading microbe.

cell nuclear transfer   Animal cloning technique whereby a somatic cell nucleus is transferred to an enucleated oocyte; synonymous with somatic cell nuclear transfer.

celsius   A measure of temperature. This scale is defined such that 0°C is the temperature at which water freezes and 100°C is the temperature at which water boils.

central nervous system (CNS)   That part of a nervous system that analyzes signals from the body and the environment. In animals, the CNS includes the brain and spinal cord.

centriole   A cylindrical array of microtubules that is found at the center of a centrosome in animal cells.

centromere   A region of a mitotic chromosome that holds sister chromatids together. Microtubules of the spindle fiber connect to an area of the centromere called the kinetochore.

centrosome   Organizes the mitotic spindle and the spindle poles; in most animal cells it contains a pair of centrioles.

chiasma (plural **chiasmata**)   An X-shaped connection between homologous chromosomes that occurs during meiosis I, representing a site of crossing-over, or genetic exchange between the two chromosomes.

chromatid   A duplicate chromosome that is still connected to the original at the centromere. The identical pair are called sister chromatids.

chromatin   A complex of DNA and proteins (histones and non-histones) that forms each chromosome and is found in the nucleus of all eukaryotes. Decondensed and threadlike during interphase.

chromatin condensation   Compaction of different regions of interphase chromosomes that is mediated by the histones.

chromosome   One long molecule of DNA that contains the organism's genes. In prokaryotes, the chromosome is circular and naked; in eukaryotes, it is linear and complexed with histone and nonhistone proteins.

chromosome condensation   Compaction of entire chromosomes in preparation for cell division.

clinical breast exam   An exam of the breast performed by a physician to check for lumps or other changes.

cnidoblast   A stinging cell found in the Cnidarians (jellyfish).

cyclic adenosine monophosphate (cAMP)   A second messenger in a cell-signaling pathway that is produced from ATP by the enzyme adenylate cyclase.

cyclin   A protein that activates protein kinases (cyclin-dependent protein kinases, or Cdk) that control progression from one stage of the cell cycle to another.

cytochemistry   The study of the intracellular distribution of chemicals.

cytochrome   Colored, iron-containing protein that is part of the electron transport chain.

cytotoxic T cell   A T lymphocyte that kills infected body cells.

dendrite   An extension of a nerve cell that receives signals from other neurons.

dexrazoxane   A drug used to protect the heart from the toxic effects of anthracycline drugs such as doxorubicin. It belongs to the family of drugs called chemoprotective agents.

dideoxynucleotide   A nucleotide lacking the 2' and 3' hydroxyl groups.

dideoxy sequencing   A method for sequencing DNA that employs dideoxyribose nucleotides; also known as the Sanger sequencing method, after Fred Sanger, a chemist who invented the procedure in 1976.

diploid   A genetic term meaning two sets of homologous chromosomes, one set from the mother and the other from the father. Thus, diploid organisms have two versions (alleles) of each gene in the genome.

DNA (deoxyribonucleic acid)   A long polymer formed by linking four different kinds of nucleotides together likes beads on a string. The sequence of nucleotides is used to encode an organism's genes.

DNA helicase   An enzyme that separates and unwinds the two DNA strands in preparation for replication or transcription.

DNA library   A collection of DNA fragments that are cloned into plasmids or viral genomes.

DNA ligase   An enzyme that joins two DNA strands together to make a continuous DNA molecule.

DNA microarray   A technique for studying the simultaneous expression of a very large number of genes.

DNA polymerase   An enzyme that synthesizes DNA using one strand as a template.

DNA primase   An enzyme that synthesizes a short strand of RNA that serves as a primer for DNA replication.

dorsal   The backside of an animal; also refers to the upper surface of anatomical structures, such as arms or wings.

dorsalventral   The body axis running from the backside to the front-side or the upperside to the underside of a structure.

double helix   The three-dimensional structure of DNA in which the two strands twist around each other to form a spiral.

doxorubicin   An anticancer drug that belongs to a family of antitumor antibiotics.

Drosophila melanogaster   Small species of fly, commonly called a fruit fly, that is used as an experimental organism in genetics, embryology, and gerontology.

ductal carcinoma in situ (DCIS)   Abnormal cells that involve only the lining of a breast duct. The cells have not spread outside the duct to other tissues in the breast; also called intraductal carcinoma.

dynein   A motor protein that is involved in chromosome movements during cell division.

dysplasia   Disordered growth of cells in a tissue or organ, often leading to the development of cancer.

ectoderm   An embryonic tissue that is the precursor of the epidermis and the nervous system.

electrochemical gradient   A differential concentration of an ion or molecule across the cell membrane that serves as a source of potential energy and may polarize the cell electrically.

electron microscope   A microscope that uses electrons to produce a high-resolution image of the cell.

electrophoresis   The movement of a molecule, such as protein, DNA, or RNA, through an electric field. In practice, the molecules migrate through a slab of agarose or polyacrylamide that is immersed in a special solution and subjected to an electric field.

elution   To remove one substance from another by washing it out with a buffer or solvent.

embryogenesis   The development of an embryo from a fertilized egg.

embryonic stem cell (ES cell)   A pluripotent cell derived from the inner cell mass (the cells that give rise to the embryo instead of the placenta) of a mammalian embryo.

endocrine cell   A cell that is specialized for the production and release of hormones. Such cells make up hormone-producing tissue such as the pituitary gland or gonads.

endocytosis   Cellular uptake of material from the environment by invagination of the cell membrane to form a vesicle called an endosome. The endosome's contents are made available to the cell after it fuses with a lysosome.

endoderm   An embryonic tissue layer that gives rise to the gut.

endoplasmic reticulum (ER)   Membrane-bounded chambers that are used to modify newly synthesized proteins with the addition of sugar molecules (glycosylation). When finished, the glycosylated proteins are sent to the Golgi apparatus in exocytotic vesicles.

enhancer   A DNA-regulatory sequence that provides a binding site for transcription factors capable of increasing the rate of transcription for a specific gene; often located thousands of base pairs away from the gene it regulates.

enveloped virus   A virus containing a capsid that is surrounded by a lipid bilayer originally obtained from the membrane of a previously infected cell.

enzyme   A protein or RNA that catalyzes a specific chemical reaction.

epidermis   The epithelial layer, or skin, that covers the outer surface of the body.

ER marker sequence   The amino terminal sequence that directs proteins to enter the endoplasmic reticulum (ER). This sequence is removed once the protein enters the ER.

erythrocyte   A red blood cell that contains the oxygen-carrying pigment hemoglobin; used to deliver oxygen to cells in the body.

Escherichia coli (E. coli)   Rod-shape, gram-negative bacterium that inhabits the intestinal tract of most animals and is used as an experimental organism by geneticists and biomedical researchers.

euchromatin   Lightly staining portion of interphase chromatin, in contrast to the darkly staining heterochromatin (condensed chromatin). Euchromatin contains most, if not all, of the active genes.

eukaryote (eucaryote)   A cell containing a nucleus and many membrane-bounded organelles. All life-forms, except bacteria and viruses, are composed of eukaryote cells.

exocytosis   The process by which molecules are secreted from a cell. Molecules to be secreted are located in Golgi-derived vesicles that fuse with the inner surface of the cell membrane, depositing the contents into the intercellular space.

exon   Coding region of a eukaryote gene that is represented in messenger RNA and thus directs the synthesis of a specific protein.

expression studies   Examination of the type and quantity of mRNA or protein that is produced by cells, tissues, or organs.

fat   A lipid material, consisting of triglycerides (fatty acids bound to glycerol), that is stored adipocytes as an energy reserve.

fatty acid   A compound that has a carboxylic acid attached to a long hydrocarbon chain. A major source of cellular energy and a component of phospholipids.

fertilization   The fusion of haploid male and female gametes to form a diploid zygote.

fibroblast   The cell type that, by secreting an extracellular matrix, gives rise to the connective tissue of the body.

filopodium   A fingerlike projection of a cell's cytoplasmic membrane, commonly observed in amoeba and embryonic nerve cells.

filter hybridization   The detection of specific DNA or RNA molecules, fixed on a nylon filter (or membrane), by incubating the filter with a labeled probe that hybridizes to the target sequence; also known as membrane hybridization.

fixative   A chemical that is used to preserve cells and tissues. Common examples are formaldehyde, methanol, and acetic acid.

flagellum (plural **flagella**)   Whiplike structure found in prokaryotes and eukaryotes that is used to propel cells through water.

fluorescein   Fluorescent dye that produces a green light when illuminated with ultraviolet or blue light.

fluorescent dye   A dye that absorbs UV or blue light and emits light of a longer wavelength, usually as green or red light.

fluorescent in situ hybridization (FISH)   A procedure for detecting the expression of a specific gene in tissue sections or smears through the use of DNA probes labeled with a fluorescent dye.

fluorescent microscope   A microscope that is equipped with special filters and a beam splitter for the examination of tissues and cells stained with a fluorescent dye.

follicle cell   Cells that surround and help feed a developing oocyte.

G$_0$ G "zero" refers to a phase of the cell cycle; state of withdrawal from the cycle as the cell enters a resting or quiescent stage; occurs in differentiated body cells, as well as in developing oocytes.

G$_1$ Gap 1 refers to the phase of the cell cycle that occurs just after mitosis and before the next round of DNA synthesis.

G$_2$ The Gap 2 phase of the cell cycle follows DNA replication and precedes mitosis.

gap junction   A communication channel in the membranes of adjacent cells that allows free passage of ions and small molecules.

gel electrophoresis   A procedure that is used to separate biomolecules by forcing them to migrate through a gel matrix (agarose or polyacrylamide) subjected to an electric field.

gene   A region of the DNA that specifies a specific protein or RNA molecule that is handed down from one generation to the next. This region includes both the coding, noncoding, and regulatory sequences.

gene regulatory protein   Any protein that binds to DNA and thereby affects the expression of a specific gene.

gene repressor protein   A protein that binds to DNA and blocks transcription of a specific gene.

gene therapy   A method for treating disease whereby a defective gene, causing the disease, is either repaired, replaced, or supplemented with a functional copy.

genetic code   A set of rules that assigns a specific DNA or RNA triplet, consisting of a three-base sequence, to a specific amino acid.

genome   All of the genes that belong to a cell or an organism.

genomic library   A collection of DNA fragments, obtained by digesting genomic DNA with a restriction enzyme, that are cloned into plasmid or viral vectors.

genomics   The study of DNA sequences and their role in the function and structure of an organism.

genotype   The genetic composition of a cell or organism.

germ cell   Cells that develop into gametes, either sperm or oocytes.

glucose   Six-carbon monosaccharide (sugar) that is the principal source of energy for many cells and organisms; stored as glycogen in animal cells and as starch in plants. Wood is an elaborate polymer of glucose and other sugars.

glycerol   A three-carbon alcohol that is an important component of phospholipids.

glycocalyx   A molecular "forest," consisting of glycosylated proteins and lipids, that covers the surface of every cell. The glycoproteins and glycolipids, carried to the cell membrane by Golgi-derived vesicles, have many functions including the formation of ion channels, cell-signaling receptors, and transporters.

glycogen   A polymer of glucose, used to store energy in an animal cell.

glycolysis   The degradation of glucose with production of ATP.

glycoprotein   Any protein that has a chain of glucose molecules (oligosaccharide) attached to some of the amino acid residues.

glycosylation   The process of adding one or more sugar molecules to proteins or lipids.

glycosyl transferase   An enzyme in the Golgi complex that adds glucose to proteins.

Golgi complex (Golgi apparatus)   Membrane-bounded organelle in eukaryote cells that receives glycoproteins from the ER, which are modified and sorted before being sent to their final destination. The Golgi complex is also the source of glycolipids that are destined for the cell membrane. The glycoproteins and glycolipids leave the Golgi by exocytosis. This organelle is named after the Italian histologist Camillo Golgi, who discovered it in 1898.

Gram stain   A bacterial stain that detects different species of bacteria based on the composition of their cell wall. Bacteria that retain the Gram stain are colored blue (Gram positive), whereas those that do not are colored orange (Gram negative).

granulocyte   A type of white blood cell that includes the neutrophils, basophils, and eosinophils.

growth factor   A small protein (polypeptide) that can stimulate cells to grow and proliferate.

haploid   Having only one set of chromosomes; a condition that is typical in gametes, such as sperm and eggs.

HeLa cell   A tumor-derived cell line, originally isolated from a cancer patient in 1951; currently used by many laboratories to study the cell biology of cancer and carcinogenesis.

helix-loop-helix   A structural motif common to a group of gene-regulatory proteins.

helper T cell   A type of T lymphocyte that helps stimulate B cells to make antibodies directed against a specific microbe or antigen.

hemoglobin   An iron-containing protein complex, located in red blood cells, that picks up oxygen in the lungs and carries it to other tissues and cells of the body.

hemopoiesis   Production of blood cells, occurring primarily in the bone marrow.

hematopoietic   Refers to cells, derived form the bone marrow, that give rise to red and white blood cells.

hematopoietic stem cell transplantation (HSCT)   The use of stem cells isolated from the bone marrow to treat leukemia and lymphoma.

hepatocyte   A liver cell.

heterochromatin   A region of a chromosome that is highly condensed and transcriptionally inactive.

histochemistry   The study of chemical differentiation of tissues.

histology   The study of tissues.

histone   Small nuclear proteins, rich in the amino acids arginine and lysine, that form the nucleosome in eukaryote nuclei, a beadlike structure that is a major component of chromatin.

HIV   The human immunodeficiency virus that is responsible for AIDS.

homolog   One of two or more genes that have a similar sequence and are descended from a common ancestor gene.

homologous   Organs or molecules that are similar in structure because they have descended from a common ancestor; used primarily in reference to DNA and protein sequences.

homologous chromosomes   Two copies of the same chromosome, one inherited from the mother and the other from the father.

hormone   A signaling molecule, produced and secreted by endocrine glands; usually released into general circulation for coordination of an animal's physiology.

housekeeping gene   A gene that codes for a protein that is needed by all cells, regardless of the cell's specialization. Genes encoding enzymes involved in glycolysis and Krebs cycle are common examples.

hybridization   A term used in molecular biology (recombinant DNA technology) meaning the formation a double-stranded nucleic acid through complementary base-pairing; a property that is exploited in filter hybridization; a procedure that is used to screen gene libraries and to study gene structure and expression.

hydrolysis   The breaking of a covalent chemical bond with the subsequent addition of a molecule of water.

hydrophilic   A polar compound that mixes readily with water.

hydrophobic   A nonpolar molecule that dissolves in fat and lipid solutions, but not in water.

hydroxyl group (-OH)   Chemical group consisting of oxygen and hydrogen that is a prominent part of alcohol.

image analysis   A computerized method for extracting information from digitized microscopic images of cells or cell organelles.

immunofluorescence   Detection of a specific cellular protein with the aid of a fluorescent dye that is coupled to an antibody.

immunoglobulin (Ig)   An antibody made by B cells as part of the adaptive immune response.

incontinence   Inability to control the flow of urine from the bladder (urinary incontinence) or the escape of stool from the rectum (fecal incontinence).

insertional mutagenesis   Damage suffered by a gene when a virus or a jumping gene inserts itself into a chromosome.

in situ hybridization   A method for studying gene expression, whereby a labeled cDNA or RNA probe hybridizes to a specific mRNA in intact cells or tissues. The procedure is usually carried out on tissue sections or smears of individual cells.

insulin   Polypeptide hormone secreted by β (beta) cells in the vertebrate pancreas. Production of this hormone is regulated directly by the amount of glucose that is in the blood.

interleukin   A small protein hormone, secreted by lymphocytes, to activate and coordinate the adaptive immune response.

interphase   The period between each cell division, which includes the G_1, S, and G_2 phases of the cell cycle.

intron   A section of a eukaryotic gene that is noncoding. It is transcribed but does not appear in the mature mRNA.

in vitro   Refers to cells growing in culture or a biochemical reaction occurring in a test tube (Latin for "in glass").

in vivo   A biochemical reaction, or a process, occurring in living cells or a living organism (Latin for "in life").

ion   An atom that has gained or lost electrons, thus acquiring a charge. Common examples are Na^+ and Ca^{++} ions.

ion channel   A transmembrane channel that allows ions to diffuse across the membrane down their electrochemical gradient.

ischemia   An inadequate supply of blood to a part of the body caused by degenerative vascular disease.

Jak-STAT signaling pathway   One of several cell signaling pathways that activates gene expression. The pathway is activated through cell surface receptors and cytoplasmic Janus kinases (Jaks) and signal transducers and activators of transcription (STATs).

karyotype   A pictorial catalogue of a cell's chromosomes, showing their number, size, shape, and overall banding pattern.

keratin   Proteins produced by specialized epithelial cells called keratinocytes. Keratin is found in hair, fingernails, and feathers.

kilometer   One thousand meters, which is equal to 0.621 miles.

kinesin   A motor protein that uses energy obtained from the hydrolysis of ATP to move along a microtubule.

kinetochore   A complex of proteins that forms around the centromere of mitotic or meiotic chromosomes, providing an attachment site for microtubules. The other end of each microtubule is attached to a chromosome.

Krebs cycle (citric acid cycle)   The central metabolic pathway in all eukaryotes and aerobic prokaryotes; discovered by the German chemist Hans Krebs in 1937. The cycle oxidizes acetyl groups derived from food molecules. The end products are CO_2, H_2O, and high-energy electrons, which pass via NADH and FADH2 to the respiratory chain. In eukaryotes, the Krebs cycle is located in the mitochondria.

labeling reaction   The addition of a radioactive atom or fluorescent dye to DNA or RNA for use as a probe in filter hybridization.

lagging strand   One of the two newly synthesized DNA strands at a replication fork. The lagging strand is synthesized discontinuously and therefore its completion lags behind the second, or leading, strand.

lambda bacteriophage   A viral parasite that infects bacteria; widely used as a DNA cloning vector.

leading strand   One of the two newly synthesized DNA strands at a replication fork. The leading strand is made by continuous synthesis in the 5' to 3' direction.

leucine zipper   A structural motif of DNA binding proteins, in which two identical proteins are joined together at regularly spaced leucine residues, much like a zipper, to form a dimer.

leukemia   Cancer of white blood cells.

lipid bilayer   Two closely aligned sheets of phospholipids that form the core structure of all cell membranes. The two layers are aligned such that the hydrophobic tails are interior, while the hydrophilic head groups are exterior on both surfaces.

liposome   An artificial lipid bilayer vesicle used in membrane studies and as an artificial gene therapy vector.

locus   A term from genetics that refers to the position of a gene along a chromosome. Different alleles of the same gene occupy the same locus.

long-term potentiation (LTP)   A physical remodeling of synaptic junctions that receive continuous stimulation.

lumen   A cavity completely surrounded by epithelial cells.

lymphocyte   A type of white blood cell that is involved in the adaptive immune response. There are two kinds of lymphocytes: T lymphocytes and B lymphocytes. T lymphocytes (T cells) mature in the thymus and attack invading microbes directly. B lymphocytes (B cells) mature in the bone marrow and make antibodies that are designed to immobilize or destroy specific microbes or antigens.

lysis   The rupture of the cell membrane followed by death of the cell.

lysosome   Membrane-bounded organelle of eukaryotes that contains powerful digestive enzymes.

macromolecule   A very large molecule that is built from smaller molecular subunits. Common examples are DNA, proteins, and polysaccharides.

magnetic resonance imaging (MRI)   A procedure in which radio waves and a powerful magnet linked to a computer are used to create detailed pictures of areas inside the body. These pictures can show the difference between normal and diseased tissue. MRI makes better images of organs and soft tissue than other scanning techniques, such as CT or X-ray. MRI is especially useful for imaging the brain, spine, the soft tissue of joints, and the inside of bones. Also called nuclear magnetic resonance imaging.

major histocompatibility complex   Vertebrate genes that code for a large family of cell-surface glycoproteins that bind foreign antigens and present them to T cells to induce an immune response.

malignant   Refers to the functional status of a cancer cell that grows aggressively and is able to metastasize, or colonize, other areas of the body.

mammography   The use of X-rays to create a picture of the breast.

MAP-kinase (mitogen-activated protein kinase)   A protein kinase that is part of a cell proliferation–inducing signaling pathway.

M-cyclin   A eukaryote enzyme that regulates mitosis.

meiosis   A special form of cell division by which haploid gametes are produced. This is accomplished with two rounds of cell division, but only one round of DNA replication.

melanocyte   A skin cell that produces the pigment melanin.

membrane   The lipid bilayer and the associated glycocalyx that surround and enclose all cells.

membrane channel   A protein complex that forms a pore or channel through the membrane for the free passage of ions and small molecules.

membrane potential   A buildup of charged ions on one side of the cell membrane establishes an electrochemical gradient that is measured in millivolts (mV); an important characteristic of neurons as it provides the electrical current, when ion channels open, that enable these cells to communicate with one another.

mesoderm   An embryonic germ layer that gives rise to muscle, connective tissue, bones, and many internal organs.

messenger RNA (mRNA)   An RNA transcribed from a gene that is used as the gene template by the ribosomes and other components of the translation machinery to synthesize a protein.

metabolism   The sum total of the chemical processes that occur in living cells.

metaphase   The stage of mitosis at which the chromosomes are attached to the spindle but have not begun to move apart.

metaphase plate   Refers to the imaginary plane established by the chromosomes as they line up at right angles to the spindle poles.

metaplasia   A change in the pattern of cellular behavior that often precedes the development of cancer.

metastasis   Spread of cancer cells from the site of the original tumor to other parts of the body.

meter   Basic unit in the metric system; equal to 39.4 inches or 1.09 yards.

methyl group (-CH$_3$)   Hydrophobic chemical group derived from methane; occurs at the end of a fatty acid.

micrograph   Photograph taken through a light, or electron, microscope.

micrometer (μm or micron)   Equal to 10^{-6} meters.

microtubule   A fine cylindrical tube made of the protein tubulin, forming a major component of the eukaryote cytoskeleton.

millimeter (mm)   Equal to 10^{-3} meters.

mitochondrion (plural mitochondria)   Eukaryote organelle, formerly free living, that produces most of the cell's ATP.

mitogen   A hormone or signaling molecule that stimulates cells to grow and divide.

mitosis   Division of a eukaryotic nucleus; from the Greek *mitos,* meaning a thread, in reference to the threadlike appearance of interphase chromosomes.

mitotic chromosome   Highly condensed duplicated chromosomes held together by the centromere. Each member of the pair is referred to as a sister chromatid.

mitotic spindle   Array of microtubules, fanning out from the polar centrioles, and connecting to each of the chromosomes.

molecule   Two or more atoms linked together by covalent bonds.

monoclonal antibody   An antibody produced from a B cell–derived clonal line. Since all of the cells are clones of the original B cell, the antibodies produced are identical.

monocyte   A type of white blood cell that is involved in the immune response.

motif   An element of structure or pattern that may be a recurring domain in a variety of proteins.

M phase   The period of the cell cycle (mitosis or meiosis) when the chromosomes separate and migrate to the opposite poles of the spindle.

multipass transmembrane protein   A membrane protein that passes back and forth across the lipid bilayer.

multipotency   The property by which an undifferentiated animal cell can give rise to many of the body's cell types.

mutant   A genetic variation within a population.

mutation   A heritable change in the nucleotide sequence of a chromosome.

myelin sheath   Insulation applied to the axons of neurons. The sheath is produced by oligodendrocytes in the central nervous system and by Schwann cells in the peripheral nervous system.

myeloid cell   White blood cells other than lymphocytes.

myoblast   Muscle precursor cell; many myoblasts fuse into a syncytium, containing many nuclei, to form a single muscle cell.

myocyte   A muscle cell.

NAD (nicotine adenine dinucleotide)   Accepts a hydride ion (H^-), produced by the Krebs cycle, forming NADH, the main carrier of electrons for oxidative phosphorylation.

NADH dehydrogenase   Removes electrons from NADH and passes them down the electron transport chain.

nanometer (nm)   Equal to 10^{-9} meters or 10^{-3} microns.

National Institutes of Health (NIH)   A biomedical research center that is part of the U.S. Department of Health and Human Services. NIH consists of more than 25 research institutes, including the National Institute of Aging (NIA) and the National Cancer Institute (NCI). All of the institutes are funded by the federal government.

natural killer cell (NK cell)   A lymphocyte that kills virus-infected cells in the body; also kills foreign cells associated with a tissue or organ transplant.

neuromodulator   A chemical released by neurons at a synapse that modifies the behavior of the targeted neuron(s).

neuromuscular junction   A special form of synapse between a motor neuron and a skeletal muscle cell.

neuron   A cell specially adapted for communication that forms the nervous system of all animals.

neurotransmitter   A chemical released by the synapse that activates the targeted neuron.

non–small cell lung cancer   A group of lung cancers that includes squamous cell carcinoma, adenocarcinoma, and large cell carcinoma. The small cells are endocrine cells.

northern blotting   A technique for the study of gene expression. Messenger RNA (mRNA) is fractionated on an agarose gel and then transferred to a piece of nylon filter paper (or membrane). A specific mRNA is detected by hybridization with a labeled DNA or RNA probe. The original blotting technique invented by E. M. Southern inspired the name. Also known as RNA blotting.

nuclear envelope   The double membrane (two lipid bilayers) enclosing the cell nucleus.

nuclear localization signal (NLS)   A short amino acid sequence located on proteins that are destined for the cell nucleus, after they are translated in the cytoplasm.

nucleic acid   DNA or RNA, a macromolecule consisting of a chain of nucleotides.

nucleolar organizer   Region of a chromosome containing a cluster of ribosomal RNA genes that gives rise to the nucleolus.

nucleolus   A structure in the nucleus where ribosomal RNA is transcribed and ribosomal subunits are assembled.

nucleoside   A purine or pyrimidine linked to a ribose or deoxyribose sugar.

nucleosome   A beadlike structure, consisting of histone proteins.

nucleotide   A nucleoside containing one or more phosphate groups linked to the 5' carbon of the ribose sugar. DNA and RNA are nucleotide polymers.

nucleus   Eukaryote cell organelle that contains the DNA genome on one or more chromosomes.

oligodendrocyte   A myelinating glia cell of the vertebrate central nervous system.

oligo labeling   A method for incorporating labeled nucleotides into a short piece of DNA or RNA. Also known as the random-primer labeling method.

oligomer   A short polymer, usually consisting of amino acids (oligopeptides), sugars (oligosaccharides), or nucleotides (oligonucleotides); taken from the Greek word *oligos,* meaning few or little.

oncogene   A mutant form of a normal cellular gene, known as a proto-oncogene, that can transform a cell to a cancerous phenotype.

oocyte   A female gamete or egg cell.

operator   A region of a prokaryote chromosome that controls the expression of adjacent genes.

operon   Two or more prokaryote genes that are transcribed into a single mRNA.

organelle   A membrane-bounded structure, occurring in eukaryote cells, that has a specialized function. Examples are the nucleus, Golgi complex, and endoplasmic reticulum.

osmosis   The movement of solvent across a semipermeable membrane that separates a solution with a high concentration of solutes from one with a low concentration of solutes. The membrane must be permeable to the solvent but not to the solutes. In the context of cellular osmosis, the solvent is always water, the solutes are ions and molecules, and the membrane is the cell membrane.

osteoblast   Cells that form bones.

ovulation   Rupture of a mature follicle with subsequent release of a mature oocyte from the ovary.

oxidative phosphorylation   Generation of high-energy electrons from food molecules that are used to power the synthesis of ATP from ADP and inorganic phosphate. The electrons are eventually transferred to oxygen, to complete the process; occurs in bacteria and mitochondria.

p53   A tumor suppressor gene that is mutated in about half of all human cancers. The normal function of the *p53* protein is to block passage through the cell cycle when DNA damage is detected.

parthenogenesis   A natural form of animal cloning whereby an individual is produced without the formation of haploid gametes and the fertilization of an egg.

pathogen   An organism that causes disease.

PCR (polymerase chain reaction)   A method for amplifying specific regions of DNA by temperature cycling a reaction mixture containing the template, a heat-stable DNA polymerase, and replication primers.

peptide bond The chemical bond that links amino acids together to form a protein.

pH Measures the acidity of a solution as a negative logarithmic function (p) of H^+ concentration (H). Thus, a pH of 2.0 (10^{-2} molar H^+) is acidic, whereas a pH of 8.0 (10^{-8} molar H^+) is basic.

phagocyte A cell that engulfs other cells or debris by phagocytosis.

phagocytosis A process whereby cells engulf other cells or organic material by endocytosis. A common practice among protozoans and cells of the vertebrate immune system; from the Greek *phagein*, "to eat."

phenotype Physical characteristics of a cell or organism.

phosphokinase An enzyme that adds phosphate to proteins.

phospholipid The kind of lipid molecule used to construct cell membranes. Composed of a hydrophilic head-group, phosphate, glycerol, and two hydrophobic fatty acid tails.

phosphorylation A chemical reaction in which a phosphate is covalently bonded to another molecule.

photoreceptor A molecule or cell that responds to light.

photosynthesis A biochemical process in which plants, algae, and certain bacteria use energy obtained from sunlight to synthesize macromolecules from CO_2 and H_2O.

phylogeny The evolutionary history of a group of organisms, usually represented diagrammatically as a phylogenetic tree.

pinocytosis A form of endocytosis whereby fluid is brought into the cell from the environment.

pixel One element in a data array that represents an image or photograph.

placebo An inactive substance that looks the same and is administered in the same way as a drug in a clinical trial.

plasmid A minichromosome, often carrying antibiotic-resistant genes, that occurs naturally among prokaryotes; used extensively as a DNA cloning vector.

platelet A cell fragment derived from megakaryocytes and lacking a nucleus that is present in the bloodstream and is involved in blood coagulation.

ploidy The total number of chromosomes (n) that a cell has. Ploidy is also measured as the amount of DNA (C) in a given cell, relative to a haploid nucleus of the same organism. Most organisms are diploid, having two sets of chromosomes, one from each parent, but there is great variation among plants and animals. The silk gland of the moth *Bombyx mori,* for example, has cells that are extremely polyploid, reaching values of 100,000C, flowers are often highly polyploid, and vertebrate hepatocytes may be 16C.

pluripotency The property by which an undifferentiated animal cell can give rise to most of the body's cell types.

poikilotherm An animal incapable of regulating its body temperature independent of the external environment. It is for this reason that such animals are restricted to warm tropical climates.

point mutation A change in DNA, particularly in a region containing a gene, that alters a single nucleotide.

polarization A term used to describe the reestablishment of a sodium ion gradient across the membrane of a neuron. Polarization followed by depolarization is the fundamental mechanism by which neurons communicate with one another.

polyacrylamide A tough polymer gel that is used to fractionate DNA and protein samples.

polyploid Possessing more than two sets of homologous chromosomes.

polyploidization DNA replication in the absence of cell division; provides many copies of particular genes and thus occurs in cells that highly active metabolically (see **ploidy**).

portal system A system of liver vessels that carries liver enzymes directly to the digestive tract.

post-mitotic Refers to a cell that has lost the ability to divide.

probe Usually a fragment of a cloned DNA molecule that is labeled with a radioisotope or fluorescent dye, and used to detect specific DNA or RNA molecules on southern or northern blots.

progenitor cell A cell that has developed from a stem cell but can still give rise to a limited variety of cell types.

proliferation A process whereby cells grow and divide.

promoter A DNA sequence to which RNA polymerase binds to initiate gene transcription.

prophase The first stage of mitosis; the chromosomes are duplicated and are beginning to condense but are attached to the spindle.

protein   A major constituent of cells and organisms. Proteins, made by linking amino acids together, are used for structural purposes and regulate many biochemical reactions in their alternative role as enzymes. Proteins range in size from just a few amino acids to more than 200.

protein glycosylation   The addition of sugar molecules to a protein.

proto-oncogene   A normal gene that can be converted to a cancer-causing gene (oncogene) by a point mutation or through inappropriate expression.

protozoa   Free-living, single-cell eukaryotes that feed on bacteria and other microorganisms. Common examples are *Paramecium* and *Amoeba*. Parasitic forms inhabit the digestive and urogenital tract of many animals, including humans.

P-site   The binding site on the ribosome for the growing protein (or peptide) chain.

purine   A nitrogen-containing compound that is found in RNA and DNA. Two examples are adenine and guanine.

pyrimidine   A nitrogen-containing compound found in RNA and DNA. Examples are cytosine, thymine, and uracil (RNA only).

radioactive isotope   An atom with an unstable nucleus that emits radiation as it decays.

randomized clinical trial   A study in which the participants are assigned by chance to separate groups that compare different treatments; neither the researchers nor the participants can choose which group. Using chance to assign people to groups means that the groups will be similar and that the treatments they receive can be compared objectively. At the time of the trial, it is not known which treatment is best.

random primer labeling   A method for incorporating labeled nucleotides into a short piece of DNA or RNA.

reagent   A chemical solution designed for a specific biochemical or histochemical procedure.

recombinant DNA   A DNA molecule that has been formed by joining two or more fragments from different sources.

refractive index   A measure of the ability of a substance to bend a beam of light expressed in reference to air that has, by definition, a refractive index of 1.0.

regulatory sequence A DNA sequence to which proteins bind that regulate the assembly of the transcriptional machinery.

replication bubble Local dissociation of the DNA double helix in preparation for replication. Each bubble contains two replication forks.

replication fork The Y-shaped region of a replicating chromosome; associated with replication bubbles.

replication origin (origin of replication, ORI) The location at which DNA replication begins.

respiratory chain (electron transport chain) A collection of iron- and copper-containing proteins, located in the inner mitochondrion membrane, that use the energy of electrons traveling down the chain to synthesize ATP.

restriction enzyme An enzyme that cuts DNA at specific sites.

restriction map The size and number of DNA fragments obtained after digesting with one or more restriction enzymes.

retrovirus A virus that converts its RNA genome to DNA once it has infected a cell.

reverse transcriptase An RNA-dependent DNA polymerase. This enzyme synthesizes DNA by using RNA as a template, the reverse of the usual flow of genetic information from DNA to RNA.

ribosomal RNA (rRNA) RNA that is part of the ribosome and serves both a structural and functional role, possibly by catalyzing some of the steps involved in protein synthesis.

ribosome A complex of protein and RNA that catalyzes the synthesis of proteins.

rough endoplasmic reticulum (rough ER) Endoplasmic reticulum that has ribosomes bound to its outer surface.

Saccharomyces Genus of budding yeast that are frequently used in the study of eukaryote cell biology.

sarcoma Cancer of connective tissue.

Schwann cell Glia cell that produces myelin in the peripheral nervous system.

screening Checking for disease when there are no symptoms.

senescence Physical and biochemical changes that occur in cells and organisms with age; from the Latin word *senex,* meaning "old man" or "old age."

signal transduction   A process by which a signal is relayed to the interior of a cell where it elicits a response at the cytoplasmic or nuclear level.

smooth muscle cell   Muscles lining the intestinal tract and arteries; lack the striations typical of cardiac and skeletal muscle, giving a smooth appearance when viewed under a microscope.

somatic cell   Any cell in a plant or animal except those that produce gametes (germ cells or germ cell precursors).

somatic cell nuclear transfer   Animal cloning technique whereby a somatic cell nucleus is transferred to an enucleated oocyte. Synonymous with cell nuclear transfer or replacement.

Southern transfer   The transfer of DNA fragments from an agarose gel to a piece of nylon filter paper. Specific fragments are identified by hybridizing the filter to a labeled probe; invented by the Scottish scientist E. M. Southern, in 1975; also known as DNA blotting.

stem cell   Pluripotent progenitor cell found in embryos and various parts of the body that can differentiate into a wide variety of cell types.

steroid   A hydrophobic molecule with a characteristic four-ringed structure. Sex hormones, such as estrogen and testosterone, are steroids.

structural gene   A gene that codes for a protein or an RNA; distinguished from regions of the DNA that are involved in regulating gene expression but are noncoding.

synapse   A neural communication junction between an axon and a dendrite. Signal transmission occurs when neurotransmitters, released into the junction by the axon of one neuron, stimulate receptors on the dendrite of a second neuron.

syncytium   A large multinucleated cell. Skeletal muscle cells are syncytiums produced by the fusion of many myoblasts.

syngeneic transplants   A patient receives tissue or an organ from an identical twin.

tamoxifen   A drug that is used to treat breast cancer. Tamoxifen blocks the effects of the hormone estrogen in the body. It belongs to the family of drugs called antiestrogens.

T cell (T lymphocyte)   A white blood cell involved in activating and coordinating the immune response.

telomere   The end of a chromosome; replaced by the enzyme telomerase with each round of cell division to prevent shortening of the chromosomes.

telophase   The final stage of mitosis in which the chromosomes decondense and the nuclear envelope reforms.

template   A single strand of DNA or RNA whose sequence serves as a guide for the synthesis of a complementary, or daughter, strand.

therapeutic cloning   The cloning of a human embryo for the purpose of harvesting the inner cell mass (embryonic stem cells).

topoisomerase   An enzyme that makes reversible cuts in DNA to relieve strain or to undo knots.

totipotency   The property by which an undifferentiated animal cell can give rise to all of the body's cell types. The fertilized egg and blastomeres from an early embryo are the only cells possessing this ability.

transcription   The copying of a DNA sequence into RNA, catalyzed by RNA polymerase.

transcription factor   A general term referring to a wide assortment of proteins needed to initiate or regulate transcription.

transfection   Introduction of a foreign gene into a eukaryote or prokaryote cell.

transfer RNA (tRNA)   A collection of small RNA molecules that transfer an amino acid to a growing polypeptide chain on a ribosome. There is a separate tRNA for amino acid.

transgenic organism   A plant or animal that has been transfected with a foreign gene.

trans Golgi network   The membrane surfaces where glycoproteins and glycolipids exit the Golgi complex in transport vesicles.

translation   A ribosome-catalyzed process whereby the nucleotide sequence of a mRNA is used as a template to direct the synthesis of a protein.

transposable element (transposon)   A segment of DNA that can move from one region of a genome to another.

ultrasound (ultrasonography)   A procedure in which high-energy sound waves (ultrasound) are bounced off internal tissues or organs producing echoes that are used to form a picture of body tissues (a sonogram).

umbilical cord blood stem cells   Stem cells, produced by a human fetus and the placenta, that are found in the blood that passes from the placenta to the fetus.

vector   A virus or plasmid used to carry a DNA fragment into a bacterial cell (for cloning) or into a eukaryote to produce a transgenic organism.

vesicle   A membrane-bounded bubble found in eukaryote cells. Vesicles carry material from the ER to the Golgi and from the Golgi to the cell membrane.

virus   A particle containing an RNA or DNA genome surrounded by a protein coat. Viruses are cellular parasites that cause many diseases.

western blotting   The transfer of protein from a polyacrylamide gel to a piece of nylon filter paper. Specific proteins are detected with labeled antibodies. The name was inspired by the original blotting technique invented by the Scottish scientist E. M. Southern in 1975; also known as protein blotting.

xenogeneic transplants (xenograft)   A patient receives tissue or an organ from an animal of a different species.

yeast   Common term for unicellular eukaryotes that are used to brew beer and make bread. *Saccharomyces cerevisiae* (baker's yeast) are also widely used in studies on cell biology.

zygote   A diploid cell produced by the fusion of a sperm and egg.

Further Resources

BOOKS

Alberts, Bruce, Dennis Bray, Karen Hopkins, and Alexander Johnson. *Essential Cell Biology.* 2d ed. New York: Garland, 2003. A basic introduction to cellular structure and function that is suitable for high school students.

Alberts, Bruce, Alexander Johnson, Julian Lewis, Martin Raff, Keith Roberts, and Peter Walter. *Molecular Biology of the Cell.* 5th ed. New York: Garland, 2008. Advanced coverage of cell biology that is suitable for senior high school students and undergraduates.

Arking, Robert. *Biology of Aging: Observations and Principles.* 3rd ed. New York: Oxford University Press, 2006. A general introduction to gerontology.

Beers, Mark H., and Robert Berkow, eds. *The Merck Manual of Geriatrics.* 3rd ed. Whitehouse Station, N.J.: Merck Research Laboratories, 2000. Updates available online. URL: http://www. merck.com/mkgr/mmg/home.jsp. Accessed December 15, 2008. A very handy reference text covering all aspects of health care for the elderly.

de Grey, Aubrey, and Michael Rae. *Ending Aging: The Rejuvenation Breakthroughs That Could Reverse Human Aging in Our Lifetime.* New York: St. Martin's Griffin, 2008. A comprehensive coverage of human aging aimed at the general public, high school students, and undergraduates.

Ganong, William. *Review of Medical Physiology.* 22nd ed. New York: McGraw-Hill, 2005. A well-written overview of human physiology, beginning with basic properties of cells and tissues.

Guarente, Leonard, Linda Partridge, and Charles Douglas. *Molecular Biology of Aging.* Cold Spring Harbor, N.Y.: Cold Spring Harbor Laboratory Press, 2007. A useful reference text for those who wish to delve deeper into the mysteries of cellular aging.

Kane, Robert L., Joseph G. Ouslander, Itamar B. Abrass, and Barbara Resnick. *Essentials of Clinical Geriatrics.* 6th ed. New York: McGraw-Hill, 2008. A comprehensive coverage of the many problems associated with providing care for the elderly.

Krause, W. J. *Krause's Essential Human Histology for Medical Students.* Boca Raton, Fla.: Universal Publishers, 2005. This book goes well with histology videos provided free on Google video.

Mader, Sylvia S. *Biology.* 9th ed. Boston: McGraw-Hill, 2007. A basic high school biology textbook.

Panno, Joseph. *Animal Cloning: The Science of Nuclear Transfer.* Rev. ed. New York: Facts On File, 2010. Medical applications of cloning technology are discussed including therapeutic cloning.

———. *The Cell: Exploring Nature's First Life-form.* Rev. ed. New York: Facts On File, 2010. Everything you need to know about the cell without having to read a 1,000-page textbook.

———. *Cancer: The Role of Genes, Lifestyle, and Environment.* Rev. ed. New York: Facts On File, 2010. The basic nature of cancer written for the general public and young students.

———. *Gene Therapy: Treatments and Cures for Genetic Diseases.* Rev. ed. New York: Facts On File, 2010. Discusses not only the great potential of this therapy, but also its dangers and its many failures.

———. *Stem Cell Research: Medical Applications & Ethical Controversies.* Rev. ed. New York: Facts On File, 2010. All about a special type of cell, the stem cell, and its use in medical therapies.

JOURNALS AND MAGAZINES

Aisen, Paul, et al. "High-dose B Vitamin Supplementation and Cognitive Decline in Alzheimer Disease: a Randomized Controlled Trial." *Journal of the American Medical Association* 300 (2008): 1,774–1,783. This study found that Vitamin B does not slow cognitive decline in subjects with mild to moderate AD.

Brunet, Anne, and Thomas A. Rando. "Ageing: From Stem to Stern." *Nature* 449 (2007): 288–289. This article discusses the topic of immortality and suggests that important insights may be obtained by studying aging in stem cells.

Church, George. "Genomes for All." *Scientific American* 294 (January 2006): 46–54. This article discusses fast and cheap DNA sequencers that could make it possible for everyone to have their genome sequenced, giving new meaning to personalized medicine.

Collins, Francis, Michael Morgan, and Aristides Patrinos. "The Human Genome Project: Lessons from Large-Scale Biology." *Science* 300 (2003): 286–290. Provides an overview of the many organizational problems that had to be overcome in order to complete the project.

Colman, Ricki, et al. "Caloric Restriction Delays Disease Onset and Mortality in Rhesus Monkeys." *Science* 325 (July 10, 2009): 201–204. Colman and his group have shown that caloric restriction works in monkeys much as it does in rats and mice, and should be able to extend the human life span as well.

DeKosky, S. T., et al. "Ginkgo Biloba for Prevention of Dementia." *Journal of the American Medical Association.* 300 (2008): 2,253–2,262. The results of a clinical trial, which showed that Ginkgo biloba does not prevent dementia.

Deretic, Vojo, and Daniel J. Klionsky. "How Cells Clean House." *Scientific American* 298 (May 2008): 74–81. The mechanism for cellular house cleaning, called autophagy, may influence the rate at which humans age.

Doonan, Ryan, et al. "Against the Oxidative Damage Theory of Aging: Superoxide Dismutases Protect Against Oxidative Stress but Have Little or No Effect on Life Span in *Caenorhabditis elegans*." *Genes and Development* 22 (2008): 3,236–3,324. This paper suggests that the oxygen free radical does influence the life span in *C. elegans*.

Downs, Jodi, and Phyllis Wise. "The Role of the Brain in Female Reproductive Aging." *Molecular and Cellular Endocrinology* 299 (February 5, 2009): 32–38. Based on an examination of neural activity and neurotransmitter release, these authors conclude that the hypothalamus plays a crucial role in the age-related decline of the female reproductive system.

Evatt, Marian, et al. "Prevalence of Vitamin D Insufficiency in Patients with Parkinson Disease and Alzheimer Disease." *The Archives of Neurology* 65 (2008): 1,348–1,352. Patients suffering from Parkinson disease appear to have lower levels of vitamin D than healthy controls or patients with AD. These results suggest that a lack of vitamin D may play a role in the development of PD.

Klunk, William, and Chester Mathis. "The Future of Amyloid-beta Imaging: A Tale of Radionuclides and Tracer Proliferation." *Current Opinion in Neurology* 21, no. 6 (December 2008): 683–687. The authors review the development of various methods for detecting beta-amyloid in the human brain.

McGrath, James, and Davor Solter. "Inability of Mouse Blastomere Nuclei Transferred to Enucleated Zygotes to Support Development in Vitro." *Science* 226 (December 14, 1984): 1,317–1,319. The authors conclude from their research that the cloning of mammals is biologically impossible. Relevant here because many scientists today have concluded from their research that human rejuvenation is impossible.

Mizoguchi, K., et al. "Aging Attenuates Glucocorticoid Negative Feedback in Rat Brain." *Neuroscience* 159 (March 3, 2009):

259–270. Japanese researchers describe their work, which shows that aging in rats is associated with a reduction in the brain's ability to respond to hormonal feedback inhibition.

Olshansky, S. J., Leonard Hayflick, and B. A. Carnes. "No Truth to the Fountain of Youth." *Scientific American* 286 (June 2002): 92–95. This article was written to warn the public about the many anti-aging remedies, none of which seem to work.

Perls, Thomas. "The Oldest Old" *Scientific American* 14 (2004): 6–11. Discusses some of the physical attributes of people who live to be 90 or older. This is a special edition dedicated to the science of staying young.

———. "The Different Paths to 100" *American Journal of Clinical Nutrition* 83 (2006): 484S–487S. Perls discusses additional characteristics of centenarians, updating his discussion of 2004, cited above.

Sinclair, David, and Lenny Guarente. "Unlocking the Secrets of Longevity Genes." *Scientific American* 294 (March 2006): 48–57. Discusses longevity genes and the possibility that they hold the key to extending the human life span.

Tavera-Mendoza, Luz, and John White. "Cell Defenses and the Sunshine Vitamin" *Scientific American* 257 (November 2007): 62–72. A comprehensive overview of vitamin D and its role in human physiology and susceptibility to disease.

Warner, H., et al. "Science Fact and the SENS Agenda." *EMBO* 6 (2005): 1,006–1,008. A group of mainstream biogerontologists attack the SENS agenda, a rejuvenation strategy proposed by the British scientist Aubrey de Grey.

Wolfe, Michael. "Shutting Down Alzheimer's." *Scientific American* 294 (May 2006): 73–79. A well-illustrated article that describes the role of beta-amyloid and the protein Tau in the progression of AD.

Wong, Dean, et al. "In Vivo Imaging of Amyloid Deposition in Alzheimer Disease Using the Radioligand 18F-AV-45 (Flobetapir

F 18)." *Journal of Nuclear Medicine* 51, no. 6913-920 (June 2010): 913–920. Daniel Skovronsky and his collaborators describe their method for detecting beta-amyloid in the human brain.

Wu, Di, Grace Lin, and Andrea Gore. "Age-related Changes in Hypothalamic Androgen Receptor and Estrogen Receptor α in Male Rats." *Journal of Comparative Neurology* 512 (February 10, 2009): 688–701. These authors examined the dysregulation of the hypothalamis-pituitary axis by examining androgen receptors in the brains of male rats.

ARTICLES ON THE INTERNET

Alzheimer's Association. "2009 Alzheimer's Disease Facts and Figures." Available online. URL: http://www.alz.org/national/documents/report_alzfactsfigures2009.pdf. Accessed July 31, 2009. A detailed report covering basic symptoms, prevalence, mortality, caregiving, and the overall costs of treating AD. A 12-page executive summary is also available at the association's Web site.

American Institute of Physics. "Madam Curie and the Science of Radioactivity." Available online. URL: http://www.aip.org/history/curie/radinst3.htm. Accessed September 4, 2009. This article discusses the life of Marie Curie and the dangers of working with radioactive materials.

Bakalar, Nicholas. "Gentlemen, 5 Easy Steps to Living Long and Well." *New York Times.* Available online. URL: http://www.nytimes.com/2008/02/19/health/19agin.html?scp=1&sq=Gentlemen,%205 %20Easy%20Steps%20to%20Living%20Long%20and%20Well&st=cse. Accessed September 4, 2009. Describes a study which showed that not smoking, watching one's weight, keeping the blood pressure low, exercising, and avoiding diabetes can have a dramatic effect on prolonging the human life span.

BBC News. "Antioxidants Cannot Slow Ageing." Available online. URL: http://news.bbc.co.uk/2/hi/health/7754644.stm. Accessed

November 4, 2009. A recent study on nematodes suggests that antioxidant vitamins, such as vitamins C and E, may not slow the aging process.

———. "HRT Cancer Connection Confirmed." Available online. URL: http://news.bbc.co.uk/2/hi/health/7869679.stm. Accessed February 5, 2009. A recent American study has shown that hormone replacement therapy does increase a woman's risk of developing breast cancer.

Boston University School of Medicine. "The New England Centenarian Study." Available online. URL: http://www.bumc. bu.edu/centenarian/overview. Accessed July 29, 2009. This study provides many insights into the health of men and women who are 100 years of age or older.

Choi, Charles. "Single Gene Could Lead to Long Life, Better Mental Function." *Scientific American.* Available online. URL: http://www.sciam.com/article.cfm?id=single-gene-could-lead-to. Accessed September 4, 2009. Profiles the *CETP* gene, a variant of which produces a novel form of cholesterol that seems to be associated with longevity and mental acuity in the aged.

Dreifus, Claudia. "Deep in the Sea, Imagining the Cradle of Life on Earth." *New York Times.* Available online. URL: http://www. nytimes.com/2007/10/16/science/16conv.html?scp=1&sq=Deep% 20in%2 0the%20Sea,%20Imagining%20the%20Cradle%20of% 20Life%20on%20Earth&st=cse. Accessed September 4, 2009. An article profiling the work of Dr. Cindy Lee Van Dover, a marine biologist who studies the ecology of the ocean floor.

———. "Finding Clues to Aging in the Fraying Tips of Chromosomes." *New York Times.* Available online. URL: http://www. nytimes.com/2007/07/03/science/03conv.html?scp=1&sq= Finding%20Clu es%20to%20Aging%20in%20the%20Fraying% 20Tips%20of%20Chromosomes&st=cse. Accessed September 4, 2009. This is an interview with Dr. Elizabeth Blackburn, an

American scientist who studies telomeres and their role in the aging process.

Fishing in BC, British Columbia, Canada. "The White Sturgeon." Available online. URL: http://www.bcadventure.com/adventure/angling/game_fish/sturgeon.phtml. Accessed November 4, 2009. An interesting essay on the description, distribution, biology, and relation to man of the white sturgeon.

Genetic Science Learning Center at the Eccles Institute of Human Genetics. "DNA Microarray Virtual Lab." Available online. URL: http://learn.genetics.utah.edu/content/labs/microarray. Accessed September 4, 2009. From the Center at the University of Utah, an experiment to investigate the differences between a healthy cell and a cancer cell using a DNA microarray.

Kinsella, Kevin, and Wan He. "An Aging World: 2008." Available online. URL: http://www.census.gov/prod/2009pubs/p95-09-1.pdf. Accessed July 29, 2009. An exhaustive report on aging trends in the United States and around the world.

Kolata, Gina. "Promise Seen for Detection of Alzheimer's." *New York Times*. Available online. URL: http://www.nytimes.com/2010/06/24/health/research/24scans.html?ref=science. Accessed June 24, 2010. A news article on the possibility of a dye that can identify and track the plaque in the brains of people with Alzheimer's disease.

Maugh, Thomas. "Researchers Prolong Life of Yeast." *Los Angeles Times*. Available online. URL: http://articles.latimes.com/2008/jan/19/science/sci-yeast19. Accessed September 4, 2009. Caloric restriction was used to extend the life span of yeast 10-fold, the most dramatic life span extension ever recorded.

National Institute of Arthritis and Musculoskeletal and Skin Disease. "Osteoporosis: Progress and Promise." Available online. URL: http://www.niams.nih.gov/Health_Info/Bone/Osteoporosis/default.asp. Accessed September 4, 2009. One of many primers dealing with the aging process that is provided by NIH. Other primers, covering topics such as arthritis and Alzheimer's disease, are readily accessible.

National Institute on Aging. "Ginkgo Evaluation of Memory (GEM) Study Fails to Show Benefit in Preventing Dementia in the Elderly." Available online. URL: http://www.nia.nih. gov/NewsAndEvents/PressReleases/PR20081119ginkgo.htm. Accessed September 4, 2009. A news article concerning the use of Ginko as a therapy for dementia.

———. "Findings Show Exceptional Longevity Runs in Families." Available online. URL: http://www.nia.nih.gov/NewsAnd Events/PressReleases/PR20020610Findings.htm. Accessed September 4, 2009. Profiles the work of Thomas Perls and his associates who have shown that brothers and sisters of centenarians also tend to live a very long time.

———. "Dramatic Changes in U.S. Aging Highlighted in New Census, NIH Report." Available online. URL: http://www.nia. nih.gov/NewsAndEvents/PressReleases/PR2006030965Plus Report.htm. Accessed September 4, 2009. A detailed report on the aging population in America.

National Institutes of Health. "Stem Cell Information." Available online. URL: http://stemcells.nih.gov/index.asp. Accessed September 4, 2009. Several articles that cover the promise of stem cells and U.S. policy regarding stem cell research.

Nature Publishing Group. "Double Helix: 50 Years of DNA." Available online. URL: http://www.nature.com/nature/dna50/ index.html. Accessed September 4, 2009. A special issue of many articles assembled by the journal *Nature* to commemorate the 50th anniversary of James Watson and Francis Crick's classic paper describing the structure of DNA.

Pear, Robert. "Serious Deficiencies in Nursing Homes Are Often Missed, Report Says." *New York Times*. Available online. URL: http://www.nytimes.com/2008/05/15/washington/15health. html?scp=1&sq=Serious%2 0Deficiencies%20in%20Nursing%20

Homes%20Are%20Often%20Missed,%20Report%20Says&st=
cse. Accessed September 4, 2009. Congressional investigators
have discovered that nursing home inspectors are overlooking
or minimizing serious problems, such as malnutrition and
severe bed sores, that pose a threat to elderly patients.

Schaffer, Amanda. "In Diabetes, a Complex of Causes." *New
York Times.* Available online. URL: http://www.nytimes.
com/2007/10/16/health/16diab.html. Accessed July 18, 2009.
This article profiles the work of Dr. Gerard Karsenty of Columbia University, who has made some important discoveries
regarding the onset of type II diabetes.

Stein, Lisa. "Is Human Growth Hormone the Key to Eternal
Youth?" *Scientific American.* Available online. URL: http://www.
sciam.com/article.cfm?id=is-human-growth-hormone-t. Accessed September 4, 2009. According to recent research, there is
no proof to support the belief that growth hormone can reverse
the aging process.

U.S. Census Bureau News. "Older Americans Month: May 2009."
Available online. URL: http://www.census.gov/Press-Release/
www/releases/archives/cb09ff-07.pdf. Accessed July 29, 2009.
Facts and figures regarding centenarians and people over 65.

Wade, Nicholas. "Atlas Squeaked: A Complete Map of the Brain of
a Mouse." *New York Times.* Available online. URL: http://www.
nytimes.com/2006/09/26/science/26brain.html?scp=1&sq=Atlas
%20Squeaked:%20A%20Complete%20Map%20of%20the%20
Brain%20of%20a%20Mouse&st=cse. Accessed September 4,
2009. This articles profiles a $41 million project to map gene
expression in specific neurons throughout the brain of a mouse.

———. "How Human Cells Get Their Marching Orders." *New
York Times.* Available online. URL: http://www.nytimes.
com/2006/08/15/science/15skin.html?scp=1&sq=How%20
Human%20Cells%20Get%20Their%20Marching%20Orders&st
=cse. Accessed September 4, 2009. When old cells in the human

body die, new ones form to take their place. This article describes research that is attempting to explain how the new cells
know where to go.

WEB SITES

Department of Energy Human Genome Project (United States).
Available online. URL: http://genomics.energy.gov. Accessed
September 4, 2009. Covers every aspect of the human genome
project with extensive color illustrations.

Dr. Bob's All Creature Site. "The Life Span of Animals." Available online. URL: http://www.sonic.net/~petdoc/life span.htm.
Accessed September 4, 2009. This site is maintained by a veteri-
nary hospital in California.

Genetic Science Learning Center at the Eccles Institute of Human Genetics, University of Utah. Available online. URL:
http://learn.genetics.utah.edu/. Accessed September 4, 2009.
An excellent resource for beginning students. This site contains
information and illustrations covering basic cell biology, animal
cloning, gene therapy, and stem cells.

Google Video. Available online. URL: http://video.google.com/
videosearch?q=histology+tissue&emb=0&aq=3&oq=histology#.
Accessed September 4, 2009. This site contains many videos
covering human histology and cell biology.

Institute of Medicine, Washington, D.C. Available online. URL:
http://www.iom.edu/CMS/3710.aspx. Accessed September 4,
2009. This page of the institute's Web site provides many reports
dealing with the aging American population.

Institute of Molecular Biotechnology, Jena / Germany. Available
online. URL: http://www.imb-jena.de/IMAGE.html. Accessed
September 4, 2009. Image library of biological macromolecules.

National Center for Biotechnology Information (NCBI). Available
online. URL: http://www.ncbi.nlm.nih.gov. Accessed September
4, 2009. This site, established by the National Institutes of Health,

is an excellent resource for anyone interested in biology. The NCBI provides access to GenBank (DNA sequences), literature databases (Medline and others), molecular databases, and topics dealing with genomic biology. With the literature database, for example, anyone can access Medline's 11,000,000 biomedical journal citations to research biomedical questions. Many of these links provide free access to full-length research papers.

National Health Museum Resource Center. Washington, D.C. Available online. URL: http://www.accessexcellence.org/RC/. Accessed September 4, 2009. Covers many areas of biological research, supplemented with extensive graphics and animations.

National Human Genome Research Institute. Available online. URL: http://www.genome.gov/. Accessed September 4, 2009. The institute supports genetic and genomic research, including the ethical, legal and social implications of genetics research.

National Institute on Aging. Available online. URL: http://www.nia.nih.gov. Accessed September 4, 2009. A good source for research papers and news articles dealing with geriatrics, gerontology, and Alzheimer's disease.

National Institutes of Health (NIH). Available online. URL: http://www.nih.gov. Accessed September 4, 2009. The NIH posts information on their Web site that covers a broad range of topics, including general health information, cell biology, aging, cancer research, and much more.

Nature Publishing Group. Available online. URL: http://www.nature.com/nature/supplements/collections/humangenome/commentaries/. Accessed September 4, 2009. The journal *Nature* has provided a comprehensive guide to the human genome. This site provides links to the definitive historical record for the sequences and analyses of human chromosomes. All papers, which are free for downloading, are based on the final draft produced by the Human Genome Project.

Sanger Institute (United Kingdom). Available online. URL: http://www.sanger.ac.uk. Accessed September 4, 2009. DNA sequencing center, named after Fred Sanger, inventor of the most commonly used method for sequencing DNA. The institute is also involved in projects that apply human DNA sequence data to find cures for cancer and other medical disorders.

U.S. Census Bureau. Available online. URL: http://www.census. gov/. Accessed July 29, 2009. The site to visit for population statistics, such as the number of centenarians in the U.S. today and expected number by 2050.

U.S. Food and Drug Administration. Available online. URL: http://www.fda.gov. Accessed September 4, 2009. Provides extensive coverage of general health issues and regulations.

World Health Organization. Available online. URL: http://www. who.int/en. Accessed September 4, 2009. Extensive coverage of age-related issues throughout the world.

Index